PRAISE FOR JACQUES PAUW'S p[...]

In the Heart of the Whore:
The Story of Apartheid's Death Squads

'This book promises to become one of the most important documents in our history'
— former President Nelson Mandela at the book launch

'A book of astonishing investigative journalism'
— Ken Owen, former editor: *Sunday Times*

Into the Heart of Darkness:
Confessions of Apartheid's Assassins

'It's because of journalists like Jacques that we know so much about apartheid's atrocities ... There's not many like him'
— Nobel Laureate Desmond Tutu at the book launch

'Extraordinary in many respects. His book has inestimable value for anyone seeking to find out more about Apartheid's dark heart'
— *Mail & Guardian*

Dances with Devils: A Journalist's Search for Truth

'This is an astonishing book ... this is a must-not-miss read'
— Clive Simpkins, communications strategist

'A testimony of our time. Pauw is a polished story teller'
— *Mail & Guardian*

Little Ice Cream Boy

'A cracking good read ... enthralling'   — *Sunday Independent*

'A book so forceful that it went on to my annual list as one of the novels of the year'   — *The Star*

'One of my top ten books of the year'   — *Sunday Times*

'Well written and well constructed, this is a book that shocks and disturbs on a variety of levels'   — *Natal Witness*

'This is his first novel and one wants to say "More! More", because where this one comes from, there must be many more'
— *Rapport*

RAT ROADS

Jacques Pauw

RAT ROADS

One man's incredible journey

Published by Zebra Press
an imprint of Random House Struik (Pty) Ltd
Reg. No. 1966/003153/07
Wembley Square, First Floor, Solan Road, Gardens, Cape Town, 8001
PO Box 1144, Cape Town, 8000, South Africa

www.zebrapress.co.za

First published 2012

1 3 5 7 9 10 8 6 4 2

Publication © Zebra Press 2012
Text © Jacques Pauw 2012

Cover photographs © Gallo Images/Getty Images

PUBLISHER: Marlene Fryer
MANAGING EDITOR: Robert Plummer
EDITOR: Bronwen Leak
PROOFREADER: Lisa Compton
COVER DESIGNER: Michiel Botha
TEXT DESIGNER: Jacques Kaiser
TYPESETTER: Monique van den Berg/
Monique Oberholzer
INDEXER: Sanet le Roux

Set in 10.5 pt on 14 pt Minion

ISBN 978 1 77022 337 0 (print)
ISBN 978 1 77022 338 7 (ePub)
ISBN 978 1 77022 339 4 (PDF)

Printed and bound by Ultra-Litho, Johannesburg

Contents

Acknowledgements ix
Maps xi

Prologue. 1
1 Going back. 5
2 *Barabara ya panya* (The roads of the rat) 11
3 A royal beginning 17
4 Trouble in Francis's paradise 21
5 Outcasts. 27
6 Idi and Milton 32
7 Dominique. 39
8 Joffrey, Dick, Teddy, Mugara, John and Peter . . 45
9 Braintank. 49
10 Birth of a rebel army. 53
11 Nyinawumuntu. 59
12 The *Inkotanyi* 64
13 Aunt Getruida 70
14 Xavier 74
15 Juvénal and Agathe 80
16 Kajelijeli and Boniface. 86
17 Beatrice 90
18 Rebels with a cause 95
19 Silent killers. 100
20 Kagame's fighting machine. 104
21 An ordinary Rwandan. 110
22 Apocalypse coming 115
23 Genocide. 121
24 A mother and her baby 129
25 Madness. 133
26 The living dead 139
27 The trenches 144
28 Nyarubuye. 149

29 The road to Gisenyi 155
30 The survivors 160
31 The new Rwanda 165
32 Doing evil 170
33 Rwanda's Alcatraz 174
34 Getting out 180
35 Seven million steps 185
36 Towards the Promised Land 190
37 Slumdog 195
38 Homeboys 201
39 Goodbye, Rwanda 206
40 Student no. 22026208 212
41 Esperance 220
42 Parkdog 228
43 Kennedy Gihana, LLB 233
44 Jennifer and Goreth 238
45 'My father's bones' 246
46 The groom and the general 252
47 The birth of a revolution 259
48 The darling dictator 265
49 The sounds of war 271
50 My brave friend 278

References 283
Acronyms and abbreviations 289
Glossary 291
Index 293

Acknowledgements

Since witnessing the genocide in Rwanda in 1994, I've been somewhat obsessed with the events and people in that country. I went back again and again and wolfed down book after book about the once godforsaken place that was elevated to screaming headlines courtesy of the massacre of 800 000 people in the autumn of 1994. Most of these books focused on the horrible demise of the victims, the torment of the survivors and the cruelty of the genocidaires. I always felt that there was another story to tell; the chronicle of just one person, not necessarily a perpetrator who had wielded a machete or a survivor who had no family left or a journalist on a voyeuristic quest, but just someone with a personal story to tell.

Then Kennedy Gihana drifted into my life, seventeen years after the slaughter. I listened to him for a few hours at the beginning of 2011 and, before the summer sun had sunk into Pretoria's skyline, I knew I wanted to write this book. It was in many ways the story I'd been waiting for. Not only did his spell-binding narrative encompass Rwanda, Burundi, Uganda and South Africa, but it was a story of hope, survival and perseverance, speckled with the weakness, malice and goodness of mankind.

What followed was one of the most inspiring but also challenging endeavours of my professional life. It was not, however, a quest I would have forgone for anything. It has left me much wiser and more insightful about the human psyche.

I dedicate this book to Kennedy, for his honesty and bravery and for baring his soul to me, however difficult it was at times. For the many out there who are trapped in cycles of poverty, powerlessness, violence, hardship and repression, I hope you find courage and inspiration in his story.

I also owe gratitude to the countless people who gave me their time and imparted their knowledge and experiences. Some are mentioned and quoted; others preferred to remain anonymous. Many were Rwandan and they came with wide smiles and warm hearts.

This book has taken more out of me than any I have written before – among others because I had to write it while working full-time – and the person who had to cope with my writer's moods (i.e. erratic behaviour) was my partner Sam Rogers. This is the third book I've written during our decade-long relationship and every time she swears: Never again; next time I might just leave you. Thank God she hasn't yet, which is why I dedicate this book also to her. She once again had to endure countless research trips, compromised weekends and the bedside light flickering to life every morning at four or five.

There were many others who encouraged, inspired, understood and advised. I owe all of you so much, especially friend Sue de Groot who read and author Mike Nicol who advised.

The research for this book and its writing were partly funded by a grant from the Taco Kuiper Fund for Investigative Journalism at the Department of Journalism at Wits University. A special word of thanks to Anton Harber.

I've published four books with four different publishers. With this one, I went back to the best one I've had. Thank you to everyone at Zebra Press, especially to managing editor Robert Plummer for pulling this book together and holding me to deadlines, and editor Bronwen Leak for her attentive editing and words of encouragement.

Towards the finishing of this book, I was informed that my friend and compatriot of many decades, who has shared so much of my treasured and scariest moments in God-forgotten places, has been diagnosed with a dreadful illness. I know he is going to fight it with courage and resolve, and therefore I also dedicate this book to Jan de Klerk.

JACQUES PAUW
SEPTEMBER 2012

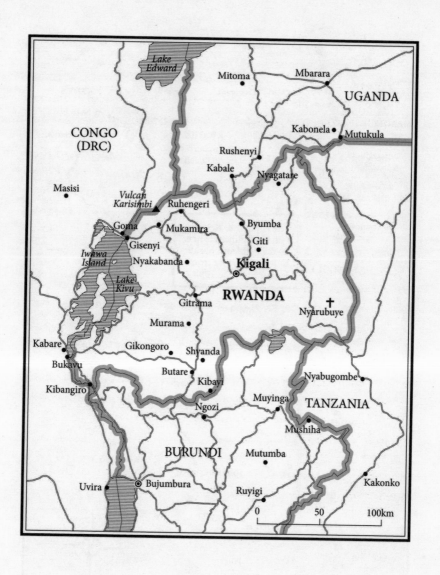

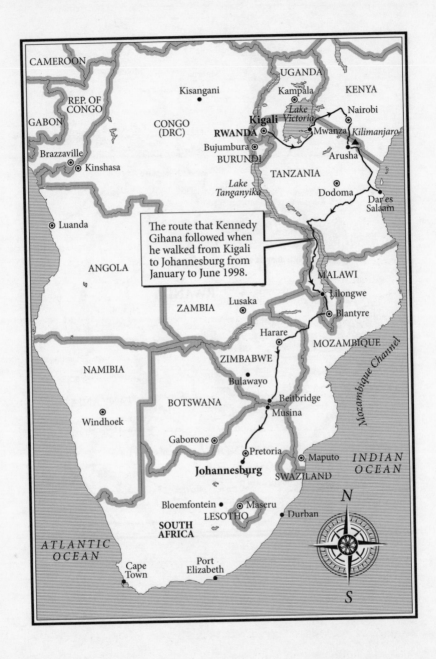

The route that Kennedy Gihana followed when he walked from Kigali to Johannesburg from January to June 1998.

Prologue

The day starts like any other, with Kennedy Gihana rising before the crack of dawn. He wraps himself in his cloth, grabs his stick and darts off to milk the cows. He then walks a kilometre down into the valley to fetch water. On his return, he gulps down a chunk of cassava with milk and washes himself. When Grandma is satisfied that her boy is squeaky clean, she gives him a white shirt and shorts to put on. Kennedy has waited until his eleventh birthday to wear, as he puts it, 'proper clothes' for the first time. And it is only because this day is special. Today he is going to school. Grandpa has told him he can only attend school two days a week. The other three days he has to look after the cows. Shortly after six, Kennedy sets off barefoot and runs the seven kilometres to school. Across the waves of mounts, cavities and rivulets, people resemble ants as they engage in their daily chores. The boy is like a hare, meandering the well-worn *panya* roads – a Swahili word meaning 'rat roads' – past clean-swept villages, through banana groves and up grassy slopes before he bursts from the eucalyptus woodlands and scampers into the grounds of Bigada Primary School in Kabonela, Uganda. Before long, he will acquire the nickname 'Braintank'.

* * *

Among the troops slogging through the mud and mire is Corporal Gihana, gangly and lean-bodied with gaunt features. In his hands he clutches a light machine gun, and bands of bullets are flung around his neck. Villages have been emptied by the killers or abandoned by their terror-stricken inhabitants. Even the fields and hills, exploding this time of year with colourful eruptions of daisies and amaryllis, are lying fallow. The rebel troop reaches Kabuye, a suburb on the outskirts of Kigali, Rwanda. Kennedy and his compatriots slog up a hill and move from house to house, rummaging the area for the *interahamwe* with their bloodied machetes. He enters a compound and swings his gun from one side to the other, his finger curled around the trigger. In the backyard is a longish stick with a sharpened point with seven bodies skewered like a *brochette* – a kebab. The father is on the one end; the mother on the other. Speared between them are their children, the youngest a tot of a few months. He's spiked next to his mother, the eldest next to her father. Kennedy stares rapt and abhorred, incensed and irate at the malevolence and madness engulfing the tiny east African country in the autumn of 1994. When he emerges from the compound, his callous eyes scour the village, his finger taut around the trigger and his heart filled with hatred and a lust for blood.

* * *

It is four years after the genocide, and the lone figure, dressed in jeans, a T-shirt and a pair of sneakers leaves the mangroves and palms of Tanzania's biggest city, Dar es Salaam, and walks down the T1 national road towards Malawi. The T1 is a lingering and dreary artery that stretches for 800 kilometres like a sheeny black snake in front of him. The road climbs up to the African savannah, with its vast rolling plains of acacia and scrub. It is the beginning of March and heat waves whirl and twirl off the searing black asphalt. The horizon at the end of the road is blotched and smudged. It is during sweltering times like this that Africa descends into silence and drowsiness. People turn motionless, animals freeze and activity grinds to a halt. The only relief is a downpour every second day or so when the clouds split apart and quench the thirst of man, beast and land. Kennedy rests during the day and walks at night. Behind him lies a journey on foot that has taken him from his native Rwanda through Kenya to Tanzania. In front of him stretches another few thousand kilometres that will hopefully lead him to an education and a new life. He has nothing except for his matric certificate, which is bound in a plastic bag to his body.

* * *

A decade on, and in a small apartment in Sunnyside, Pretoria, a Rwandan immigrant is getting dressed in a brand new black suit, a red tie and shiny, pointy black shoes. A few hours later, in the Palace of Justice, a judge remarks that nobody has had any objection to the applicant standing in front of him becoming an attorney of the High Court of South Africa. He orders Kennedy Alfred Nurudin Gihana to lift his right hand and swear allegiance to the Constitution of the Republic of South Africa. Minutes later, Kennedy is affirmed as an attorney. If he could wish for anyone to be present to witness his remarkable achievement, it would be Grandpa and Grandma who so many years earlier raised him on the acacia-speckled savannahs of south-eastern Uganda and afforded him his first taste of knowledge. He still doesn't know what happened to them.

I

Going back

It is early morning on the day of our flight when Kennedy calls me. 'How much weight do we have?' he wants to know. I have an inkling of what awaits me. At least part of our voyage will be dedicated to deliveries to friends and family in Uganda. His wife's sister lives in Kampala, his sister-in-law's son studies in Mbarara, his half-sister is somewhere in the south, and so on and so on.

Anybody that has crossed the continent from east to west and from north to south will know that many African airlines operate according to completely different rules from anywhere else. The custom is to stuff elephantine-sized suitcases to capacity and to take whatever you can't fit in as hand luggage on board.

I've been on airlines such as the Congo's Hewa Bora (its fleet was recently declared un-airworthy and relegated to scrap metal). I have seen passengers try to squeeze television sets and hi-fis into the overhead compartments and if they don't fit, simply deposit them in the aisles, causing a human traffic jam and bawling at one another as they wait for cabin staff to resolve the problem. I have creaked and hissed into the air in small propeller-driven aircraft with pungent dried fish and bleating goats, flown by Ukrainian and Russian pilots whose doddering hands and blotchy noses blurt out their perturbing boozing habits.

But this is South African Airways. I tell Kennedy my bag only weighs eight kilos so he's welcome to use the rest of the weight. When I fetch him from his two-bedroom apartment in Pretoria, a ballooning brown bag, as big and heavy as a man, awaits me. It is jam-packed with boxes of red wine, groceries, clothes, oil and toys.

Kennedy's wife, Goreth, greets me. She is holding their newborn in her arms. The tot is tightly wrapped on this chilly Highveld morning. Goreth's complexion is the colour of charcoal and Kennedy is dark skinned as well, yet an olive-skinned face peeks at me through the layers of white wool. He has told me how after her birth the nurses teased him that he couldn't be the father of such a brown baby. He proudly told them that the baby was a Tutsi; a pedigreed Tutsi girl.

When she was born, he said to me: 'A family is like a tree. My tree has been cut down. Only I, a leaf and a seed, remain. I fell to the ground. I want a new tree to grow out of me again. I want to be the stem. That's why the child is so important. I want four children – two boys and two girls.'

Kennedy and Goreth have christened her Lisa Gihana. Lisa is a Hebrew name that means 'God is my oath'. You might think it's logical for Lisa to carry Kennedy and Goreth's surname. But not in Rwandan culture. They have a peculiar tradition in which children are rarely named after their parents and seldom carry their surnames. Wives don't take their husbands' names either. It's a bit like Jimmy Jones and Sandy Smith calling their children Mary Miller and Tommy Taylor. Kennedy's father was Alex Bayingana and his mother Teddy Uwamaria. His grandfather was Francis Semandwa. This custom caused havoc after the genocide, when authorities and organisations attempted to reunite parents and children and orphans and families.

Goreth, a Tutsi from the eastern savannahs of Rwanda, is Kennedy's first and only love. During our interviews, I asked him several times about girlfriends, which rendered him flustered and almost embarrassed. 'I was afraid of girls because it is against our culture. You don't have girlfriends when you grow up as a Tutsi,' he once said. 'If you do it, you have to do it secretly.'

Another time, he concluded: 'I've never had a girlfriend. It was a sin to have sex. I had a lot of things to think about – to study, what to eat, where to sleep, lots of things but sex. What are you going to tell a woman? How are you going to propose and what are you going to tell her? You see, those things are luxuries. It is not a necessity. I didn't even have clothes, where would I get a girlfriend?'

Kennedy met Goreth in Rwanda in 2006 when he went back to the country for a holiday. He proposed, and after several years of long-distance romance, he went back to Rwanda in December 2010 to marry his sweetheart. It was an elaborate traditional wedding that he says he will continue to pay off for years to come. Goreth is fifteen years younger than Kennedy and did her matric in South Africa in 2011.

Kennedy's mother-in-law is also in South Africa. She jetted in from Rwanda a day or two after Lisa's birth, with a bag full of herbs for the newborn and to assist Goreth with the first months of motherhood. She is sending us off to Uganda with an excruciatingly long prayer in

Kinyarwanda, the official language of Rwanda. I'm not religious so I don't close my eyes and instead scrutinise the three earnest faces bowed in utter devotion. Kennedy clutches his rosary in one hand; the other clasps that of Goreth.

'What did she pray about?' I ask Kennedy on our way to the airport.

'She didn't leave anyone or anything out,' he says. 'She prayed for every little thing that can go wrong. So I think we'll be fine, we'll be okay.'

After more than twenty years, Kennedy is going back to the village of Kabonela in the Rakai district in southern Uganda where he grew up. He vividly remembers the day he took up his stick, clutched his bag and waved goodbye to his grandparents, the people who had brought him up and whom he called Mama and Papa; the day he left behind two frail, grey-haired people to attend his last two years of boarding school. He never saw them again.

Days after writing his matric exam, he joined the ranks of the Rwandan Patriotic Army (RPA), the Tutsi rebel force that was waging war against the extremist Hutu dictatorship in Rwanda across the border. It was this regime that had sent his grandparents many years earlier into exile and condemned them as outcasts in a foreign land. Once in the army, Kennedy was instructed to break all contact with the outside world.

Kennedy has no photographs, letters or any other mementoes to remember his grandparents by. He was told many years later that they had both died around 1993. He has been haunted ever since by the knowledge that he couldn't bury them. In turn, they probably thought their only grandson had perished in battle and heartbreak may have hastened their demise. Kennedy wants to find final closure around their last days.

* * *

Few places in Africa embody the beauty and the mystery of the continent quite to the extent that Uganda does. The sight of the boiling waters of the Nile cascading over the Murchison Falls, the soaring and mystical Rwenzori Mountains on its western border and the big apes loitering in its rainforests have seduced poets and writers into painting it with lyrical brushes. Africa's lushest garden is above all the continent's friendliest destination and after a tumultuous start at independence followed by calamitous dictatorships, it now exudes a whiff of promise.

My worst expectations are realised when we spend much of our first day navigating the potholed, congested and frenzied streets of hilly Kampala in search of new housing developments where in-laws reside. It is one of those jumbo African cities – think Nairobi, Accra, Lagos, Khartoum and Addis – that has reproduced itself many times over and is now in a state of permanent asphyxiation, gasping for air. All day long, life on the street resembles a palpitating heart that propels cars and buses and taxis through its clogged arteries. The sidewalks are choked with people that mill around with seemingly nowhere to go. Ugandans refer to them as *bayaye*, people who have abandoned their villages in the country-side and journeyed to the city in the hope of scoring a job or something meaningful to do. Few do, and the majority idle around on the sidewalk where they compete for space or the few cents of parking money from charitable motorists. Many live on the streets, while others find their way to slums that are immersed in a shroud of smoke. Nobody cares, certainly not the shiny-faced and roly-poly politicians and officials who glide past the unfortunate populace in sleek German technology.

It is later that afternoon and our driver, James Serunjogi, takes the two-lane highway to the south. The road winds through banana and coffee plantations and crosses the equator before flattening into the marshes that fringe Lake Victoria. Next to the road, fishmongers wave glistening tilapia fish in the late afternoon sun.

During my previous visits to Uganda, all during the nineties, the high-way was littered with the hulks of armoured personnel carriers and corroded tanks that told of the wars and invasions of the seventies and eighties. Since then, they've been removed, either to be used as scrap metal or to erode painful memories.

James is a walking encyclopaedia and points to one of Idi Amin's secret prisons, where, upon liberation, they found cells strewn with corpses and walls sprayed with blood and greyish brain matter. Political prisoners were ordered to bludgeon their fellow prisoners to death, after which they themselves were executed. The dictator decentralised his reign of terror, and virtually every village and town had its own detention and torture centre where ordinary folk could hear the howls of the tormented before they were liquidated. I suppose it reminded everyone who was in charge. We drive alongside a swamp where his tanks and troops got bogged down in his war against the Tanzanians, and pass a bridge that Yoweri Museveni blew up when he overthrew Milton Obote.

We leave the papyrus-choked swamps around Lake Victoria and the land flattens out into grassland, gentle hills and sloping valleys. The next morning, we turn south at the town of Masaka and head towards the Tanzanian border.

Every ten kilometres or so, we drive through villages that are nothing more than trading posts with half-finished storefronts, chaotic taxi stands sheltering beaten-up minibuses and billboards advertising Nile Special, Colgate and Omo. These outposts haven't changed in decades, except that the arrival of technology has added bursts of colour to otherwise sombre façades. Uganda's three major mobile-phone companies – the one yellow, the other orange and another red – have doused their agents in their colours. More substantial villages have markets offering cascading bunches of green bananas – which Ugandans steam to make a starchy mush called *matoke* – and hum with the sounds of an African town: taxi vendors touting for business, women haggling over prices of cassava and loudspeakers spitting out rap or the empty promises of loud-mouthed Pentecostal evangelists.

In the back seat, Kennedy has fallen silent and is staring at the euca-lyptus groves and grassland rolling by. He has always been hesitant about going back to Uganda. He is scared of what he will find – or not find. He doesn't know if any of the children he grew up with are still here or what has happened to the family he left behind when he went to war. I had asked him the previous night what he was most looking forward to. He thought for a while, took a sip of Nile and said: 'I want to find my best friend Dominique with whom I grew up, I want to know what happened to Mama and Papa, and I want to see cows, many cows.'

His eyes are scouring the land when we round a bend and there next to the road is a herd of sinewy Ankole lolling underneath an acacia tree. We stop and, without saying a word, he gets out of the car and walks into the assembly of bobbing white horns.

Few people understand the value of *inkas* – cows – to Tutsis, and Kennedy is no exception. While in Uganda, he sees the world around him in terms of cows. Every hill is potentially a place where cows can graze, every valley where they can rest, and every small river or lake makes him feel thirsty for the cows.

The perfect Ankole has a reddish coat and gleaming horns that curve out and then inward. The beautiful tongue of Kinyarwanda contains a vast catalogue of cattle names. A cow with white patches across its face might be called *Kiroko*, a reddish-brown one *Ibihogó* and a brown beast with white spots *Umusengo*. A black cow with white spots is usually named *Ikibamba*. The cow is the quintessential paradigm of beauty, elegance and grace. In Rwandan culture it is thus a great compliment to tell a woman that she has *amaso y'inyana* – calf eyes – or reminds you of *inka nzízá* – a beautiful cow.

Every cow has a personality, a name and a character. Many Rwandan names are related to cows, expressions of greeting are about cows and many metaphors originate from cow vocabulary. If, for example, you tell someone to meet you tomorrow morning around seven or eight, you'll say he or she must meet you *inka zahutse* – when the cows go out to graze.

Kennedy is chattering incessantly about his love for these beasts when quite suddenly he points at the acacia-dotted horizon.

'Just over there,' he says excitedly, 'is Kabonela. We are almost home.'

2

Barabara ya panya
(The roads of the rat)

Rwanda and Burundi are so small that on a map of Africa their names are usually printed in neighbouring Congo or Tanzania with arrows indicating the speckles to the right or left. Their northern neighbour, Uganda, is much bigger, although together the trio occupies only a tiny percentage of the African land mass.

All three evoke images of cultivated honeycombed hills painted in shades of green, volcanic slopes blanketed in impenetrable rainforests and silvery-shiny lakes that are the source of the continent's greatest river, the Nile. But enveloping all this natural splendour is human tumult as vicious as the geological rupture that spawned it thousands of millennia ago.

Let us travel back to a time long before humans roamed the planet. Two tectonic plates – one African, the other Arabian – pull apart. Formations shift and heave. The land on top stretches and the middle collapses. The Arabian Peninsula snaps off to give birth to the Red Sea. Africa is re-fashioned by a ravine, more than five thousand kilometres long. The turbulence that ignites this fissure creates lava-spewing volcanoes, shimmering lakes, forest-clad mountains, lush valleys and rolling grasslands. This is today known as the Rift Valley: the cradle of mankind and according to astronauts the most significant feature of the planet visible from space.

In East Africa, the Rift separates into two branches: the Eastern Rift and the Western Rift. The eastern leg runs from the Red Sea through Ethiopia and Kenya to Lake Malawi, and is dotted with the snow-capped peaks of Mounts Kenya and Kilimanjaro. These give way to the plains of the Serengeti that hold the largest concentration of wild animals on the planet.

The Western Rift runs from Lake Malawi north-west along the eastern border of what is today the Democratic Republic of Congo (DRC). This is the roof of Africa: a land cloaked in folklore and presided over by spirits and demigods. Some of Africa's highest mountain ranges – the Rwenzori and the Virunga – edge the Rift, and chiselled into the lava rock and fertile soil is a cascade of freshwater bodies known as the Great Lakes. Nestled in the middle of them are Burundi, Uganda and Rwanda.

Between them, their peoples have endured the continent's bloodiest dictators and hellish political turmoil. Once engulfed in a genocide in which the machetes of the butchers worked faster than Nazi Germany's gas chambers, they seem to be trapped in perpetual cycles of tribal hatred, division, greed and mistrust.

* * *

Kennedy Gihana was born in the one, grew up in the other and fought in another. His refugee papers say he's Burundian, although he has no memory of the refugee camp where he first saw the light of day, and has no desire to ever go back to his country of birth.

He spent his childhood in Uganda and yearns to stock a few hectares of land with longhorn Ankole that he'll christen and graze on the stretches of sunburnt savannah and gentle, rolling hills.

His heart, however, longs for Rwanda, where his forefathers roamed with their beasts and where he wants to be buried. But he cannot go back, yet. As the recently elected leader of a resistance movement intent on overthrowing the current Rwandan regime, in whose name he spilt so much blood, Kennedy believes that if he dares to cross its borders, he might not live to see it. For now, he is banished to his adopted motherland, South Africa.

Kennedy is a Tutsi, or Abatutsi or Watutsi, however you want to refer to this ethnic group. The Tutsis were once the rulers of the great Kingdom of Banyarwanda of the Great Lakes, but are today scattered across the borders of several countries or sprinkled as self-imposed exiles, refugees or simply immigrants around the globe.

Kennedy swears that he is the epitome of what a Tutsi should be: proud, upright, warrior-like, ingenious and dignified. A member of the royal clan, he is a tall man. Although Europeans often depict Tutsis as spindly, stick-like people with 'finer' features like straight noses, thin lips and brown skins, Kennedy is solid, dark skinned and fleshy lipped. Yet he insists that you can spot his 'Tutsi-ness' a mile away. He says Tutsis are 'handsome and beautiful'.

For many decades, Tutsis were virtually unheard of outside of the Great Lakes or the confines of the Belgian colonial empire that spanned the

Congo, Rwanda and Burundi. A Wednesday night in April 1994 changed all that when assassins fired surface-to-air missiles at a plane carrying the presidents of Rwanda and Burundi.

It triggered a killing frenzy that redefined barbarism in the late twentieth century. The Rwandan genocide not only left up to a million dead to rot in mass graves, bloat in rivers, putrefy in pits or decompose next to roads and in churches, but profoundly affected the life of every Rwandan, whether perpetrator, survivor or victim. There's an element of all three in Kennedy.

* * *

I met Kennedy for the first time in September 2001, after I returned from a journey trekking up the volcanic slopes of the Virungas in Rwanda and the Congo in search of mountain gorillas. I was producing a television documentary and, back in Johannesburg, I needed a Rwandan to translate Kinyarwanda into English. The embassy in Pretoria recommended Kennedy and a few days later I picked him up and brought him to Johannesburg. I don't remember much of him – our venture was briefly interrupted by the al-Qaeda attack on New York's Twin Towers and the broadcast of my documentary was postponed for two weeks – except that he was a refugee and was studying at the University of Pretoria. We spent two or three days together and his existence then drifted out of my mind.

I remember listening to John Robbie on Radio 702 a few years later. He was interviewing a refugee who related how his family in Rwanda had been massacred in the genocide and how he had walked to South Africa. John was talking to him because in the face of incredible adversity he had just obtained a degree from the University of Pretoria. I remember thinking: my God, that's a book! I didn't realise that John's guest was none other than Kennedy. But I was busy finishing my third book and 702's guest faded into obscurity.

In early 2011, my cellphone rang. I looked at the 'unknown number' and contemplated whether or not to answer. I seldom do if I don't know who the caller is. I somehow pushed the answer button.

'Hi Pauw, how are you?' bawled a voice on the other end. 'Can you guess who this is?'

I hate it when people play hide-and-seek over the phone, but there was something distinctive about the accent. I knew I had heard it before.

'No, sorry,' I replied, 'but who are you?'

'Kennedy! Kennedy Gihana!'

It still didn't dawn on me. 'Kennedy from where?'

'Kennedy from Rwanda! Don't you remember? I translated for you a long time ago.'

The next afternoon at noon, he was waiting for me in Pretorius Street in downtown Pretoria. Nattily dressed in a brown suit and yellow tie and with a broad smile spanning his affable face, he waved me down, got into the car, threw his arms around me and said: 'Pauw, what happened? You were so thin when I last saw you! Look at you now!'

'It's those bloody volcanoes I had to walk up and down,' I responded. 'And you're the last one to talk. You look like a politician!'

'I'm now an attorney of the High Court in South Africa,' he announced proudly. 'I have my own law firm.'

We went to a bar in Sunnypark where we drank beer, ate schwarmas and talked until a late summer sun paled behind the city's jacarandas and Kennedy's wife called to find out where he was.

* * *

Kennedy's story captivates me, not just because I find him an awe-inspiring human being who exhibits the finest human qualities of resilience and kindness, but also because the destiny of Rwanda and its people occupies a special place in my heart. A month after the shooting down of the presidential plane triggered genocide, I found myself as a journalist slap bang in the bosom of Armageddon. Words to describe what happens when depravity conquers decency still escape me; suffice to say that Rwanda in the autumn of 1994 will prey on my mind for a long time to come. Since then, I have visited the land of a thousand hills several times to produce television documentaries.

Two weeks after my seeing Kennedy, we agreed to write this book. Another week or three on, we started a series of interviews. When I sat down with Kennedy in my lounge in Melville, Johannesburg, switched on my digital recorder and got him talking, I knew that this was one of the most heart-rending human dramas I would ever encounter. I had, however, no inkling of what he was about to lay bare.

What came pouring out during many days of probing and examination was a man tortured not just by the calamitous evil of mass killing, but by his own depravity in attempting to stop it. Even when the killers dropped their bloodied machetes on Rwanda's frayed edges, scampered across her borders and dissipated into chaos, Kennedy continued to dispatch victor's justice on sometimes blameless bystanders.

'I think of it every day, the bodies, the piles of bodies. All these bodies, killed in a different way,' he told me at one point. 'I fought for what? I have blood on my hands for nothing. I killed for what?'

A few days after he uttered those words, his daughter was born. He said: 'She's a gift from God that I will hold with both hands and protect with my life. I want her to know a world that is different from the one her father knew. She must see every human being as a gift from God. She must fight for the rights of others as she wants others to fight for her rights. Please God protect her from what I had to go through.'

Was I shocked to discover his darker side?

No, although some of his utterances sent bolts through my spine. And believe me, in my journalistic career I've listened to tales of unimaginable depravity.

Was I surprised?

No. I've long realised that most of us have a capacity to commit unim-aginable evil, just as we have a gift for incredible goodness.

Nobel Prize winner and Russian martyr Aleksandr Solzhenitsyn reminds us: 'The line separating good and evil passes not through states, nor between classes, nor between political parties either, but right through every human heart, and through all human hearts.'

Kennedy is a prime example of how human it is for humane people to be inhumane. He's as much a perpetrator as a victim, and has dished out as much suffering as he has himself endured.

* * *

'My whole life I had to travel on *panya* roads,' Kennedy says. 'It's a Swahili word that means "rat roads" and they are those little paths that you take in order not to be seen and to stay alive. That's how I've survived.'

The multitude of villages and settlements scattered across rural East Africa are connected to one another by a maze of *panya* or rat roads that are almost invisible to the untrained eye. You have to live in a village to know where the crossings are because they are as secret as they are plentiful.

When Kennedy was a boy he criss-crossed the rat roads of the Rakai district of south-western Uganda, whether to deliver messages or a calabash of milk, to go to school, to fetch his grandpa a litre of banana beer in town or just to roam the African savannah.

Rat roads are, however, not just part of everyday African life, but are also stealthy passages used by smugglers, traffickers, immigrants, refugees, rebels and infiltrators to slink past the prying eyes of officials, soldiers and police.

When Kennedy was older and found himself in the army, he prowled the *panya* roads of northern Rwanda and the Virunga Mountains in the north-west in order to gain intelligence and outmanoeuvre the enemy.

He plied *barabara ya panya* – the roads of the rat – on his long foot-slog to South Africa, using them to avoid robbers and soldiers and to cross borders without a passport or money in his pocket.

And once encased in the concrete jungle of Hillbrow, he lived like a rat, preferring to use the back alleys and side streets in order to avoid attention and thieves. This continued even when he succeeded in gaining entry into university and had to sidestep the institution's authorities because he couldn't pay his class fees.

Today Kennedy is once again trooping *panya* roads, among other reasons because he believes he's on a Rwandan government hit list – and he may well be. He avoids attention, moves with eyes in the back of his head and walks in circles when he returns home.

No wonder he calls himself a boy and a man of Africa's rat roads.

3

A royal beginning

Kennedy Gihana's story begins in the summer of 1918 with the birth of his grandfather, Francis Semandwa, in the southern Rwandan hill town of Gikongoro. Little is known about Francis's earliest years, except that he was born in a hut made of sticks and mud, and the world he was introduced to must have been green and lush. His earliest olfactory memory was probably one of cooking fires and his first aural sensations the chatter of his people, the mooing of cattle, the muffled barking of dogs and a drumbeat in the far distance. The pastures where the cows grazed would have exploded with kaleidoscopes of butterflies and colourful bursts of daisies, marigolds and amaryllis. Like the rest of Rwanda, Gikongoro is a land painted in tones of green with pot-bellied clouds cuddling the tilled hills and paddle-like banana leaves gently flapping in the soft breeze.

The family had a few rows of sorghum and cassava (a root vegetable), a banana grove and a herd of cows grazing on the grassy meadows. On a clear day, the boy could see from hill to hill and watch neighbours huddled in their fields tending to their crops. As cattle-owners, Francis's family were considered superior to those who only tilled the land or tended crops. At that time and for decades afterwards, Rwanda was a 'cow-centric' society, where wealth, prestige and power depended on the number of beasts in one's kraal.

When he was old enough, every morning after milking the cows, Francis wrapped himself in a calfskin, tied it with a banana rope around his waist, clasped his stick and took the cows to pasture in the valleys and hills. Francis never attended school. It wasn't necessary, because he would one day inherit cattle from his father and thus become the next-generation land and cattle owner.

Francis was a young boy when his father told him he should never forget that he is not just a Tutsi, but a member of the royal clan, the Abanyiginya (its totem is the crested crane). They were therefore descendants of the *mwami* – king – who was ruling the land from his throne in the royal palace in Nyanza many miles away. The family's sub-clan was the

Abenegitori, named after the king's hunting dog. According to legend, the animal sniffed out an abandoned baby girl during a royal hunt. She was taken to the palace and became a child in the king's household. Every child she gave birth to was an Abenegitori.

Sixty years later, under a mango tree with a calabash of traditional *urwagwa* (banana beer) at his feet, Francis would chronicle his childhood in Gikongoro to the young Kennedy. As thin as a stick, with big, black eyes and rubbery, cracked feet, the old man conjured up images of a land so lovely that he was convinced that God slept there at night.

'*Imana yirirwa ahandi igataha mu Rwanda*,' the old man murmured. (God spends the day elsewhere, but sleeps in Rwanda.)

'He said it was between those valleys and lakes and mountains where God puts down his head at night,' Kennedy remembers. 'The cows were fat and big and produced rich and sweet milk. Every day, people danced and laughed and got married and had many children.'

Francis, being a member of the royal clan, was a young man when the *mwami* appointed him as a *shurushefu* – local chief – in Gikongoro. As bearer of royal tradition, he represented the king and collected taxes and gifts for the royal household. One of his most important duties was to settle disputes through Rwanda's *gacaca* system. Loosely translated from Kinyarwanda, *gacaca* means 'on the grass'. If someone had a problem with a neighbour or villager, he didn't take revenge; he brought it to the attention of the elders, who would call for *gacaca*. If you had stolen someone's cow, you wouldn't just give it back; you would hand him another one. If you did not have any cows, you would till his field for the next moon. The aggrieved men usually shared banana beer at the end of the proceedings and returned to their village as friends.

The divide between Tutsi and Hutu was a matter of wealth and affluence in the Rwanda in which Francis Semandwa prospered. Tutsis had cattle and occupied top military and political offices; Hutus were mostly servants or farmed the land, while Rwanda's third population group, the Twa – descendants of the pygmy – subsisted on whatever they could gather in the forests. The Batwa were never more than a per cent of the population, Tutsis around 15 per cent and Hutus the vast majority.

What people don't realise is that many Hutus, as they acquired cattle, were assimilated into the Tutsi population. Conversely, Tutsis who squandered their wealth lost their privileged position and could be considered

Hutu. In pre-colonial Rwanda, Tutsis were the aristocracy, while Hutus were held in bondage.

Kennedy remembers his grandfather as a tall, righteous and noble man who never abandoned his regal demeanour. He was always cloaked in brown robes and his appearance was that of an emperor. In contrast, his grandmother Kamabera, born around the same time as Francis in the southern town of Butare, was short and stubby.

'You wouldn't think she was a Tutsi,' Kennedy says. 'Her fingers were short and she was very black. People teased her that she was a Hutu and wanted to know how it was possible that she had such handsome kids. But her heart was unimaginable, bursting with love.'

The pillars of traditional Rwanda were the king, the cow and the drum. People believed that without the *mwami*, the drums would fall silent and the cows would refuse to give milk or calves. The ancestor of Rwanda, Gihanga, is referred to in Kinyarwanda as *Gihanga cyahanze inka n'ingoma* – Gihanga who created cows and drums.

'Grandpa had many, many cows. Also many servants, who we called the *abagaragu*. If they didn't listen or didn't work hard, he thrashed them. They were Hutus. The Twa were useless; they just danced in the palace to entertain the king. If a Twa danced nicely, he could get a cow. Those who didn't dance made the clay pots. Grandpa said Rwanda was paradise.'

The *mwami* was adulated as almost a celestial being and his power was absolute and unchallenged. According to tribal folklore, the lineage of the *mwami* had a heavenly origin and he was revered as the 'eye of God'. Below him was an administrative hierarchy of military chiefs, cattle chiefs, land chiefs, local chiefs and neighbourhood chiefs.

Francis told Kennedy spellbinding tales about life in the royal palace; about the *intore* dancers, adorned with brilliant, multicoloured headdresses, their feet pounding and their chests heaving, leaping into the air as they moved around the royal *kalinga*, a sacred drum said to be hung with the genitals of the king's conquered enemies.

The *mwami* was regal and statuesque and wrapped flowing white robes around his lean body. He lived in a royal compound of circular straw huts. The *mwami*'s hut was by far the tallest as he had to enter without bending. Some photographs show his headdress as a cascading plumage of white sisal; in others his hair is shaped into two stumpy horns on his head, reminiscent of a young bull.

Francis told his grandson how, day after day, the *mwami*'s subjects bestowed gifts on him: decorated pots of honey, drums, skins of predators, carved wooden chairs and, of course, longhorn Ankole cows with new-born calves. Unsurprisingly, the *mwami* had his own sacred herd of cows called the *Inyambo*. They were the most splendid of beasts, their lyre-shaped horns as long as a man's leg and adorned with beaded necklaces.

Francis despised white people and Hutus. The trouble in Rwanda started, he told Kennedy, when the white man arrived and incited Hutus. Before colonialists set foot over the Virungas or crossed the Akagera, he said, the land was paradise. Hutu and Tutsi lived in peace and even loved one another, marrying, nurturing children and rearing cows.

4

Trouble in Francis's paradise

Understanding Rwandan history is difficult, one reason being that there is no written record. Tradition is oral and therefore manipulative, dictated by those who wield power. Besides local and colonial versions of history, somewhere along the way myths and legends became fact and truth.

The common belief is that the Batwa were the first inhabitants to arrive in Rwanda, followed by successive migrations from the north and east that brought farmers – Hutus – and cattle herders – Tutsis. It is important to remember that virtually every African is an immigrant who arrived from somewhere else before settling down in his current homeland. The continent's peoples have from the earliest times been a moving, shifting and wandering lot.

Tutsi cattle herders eventually dominated the central parts of what is now Rwanda and entrenched their power. Colonists arrived in Rwanda later than in most other African territories. The continent was carved up and dished out to European colonial powers at the 1884 Berlin Conference, but Rwanda's fate was only determined several years later in Brussels, when it was handed to the German empire in exchange for Germany renouncing all claims on Uganda. By then, no white man had ever set foot there.

The explorer Henry Morton Stanley tried to visit the kingdom in the early 1890s, but retreated under a hail of arrows. One of the first white men to enter Rwanda was Count Gustav Adolf von Götzen, who led an expedition in 1894 to claim the hinterlands of the German colony of Tanganyika (today Tanzania). He found a sophisticated warrior-kingdom ruled and governed by the *mwami*. Later, a war that few Rwandans had heard of or had any part in – the First World War – changed them from German to Belgian subjects. Belgium ruled the territory until independence in 1962.

* * *

Europeans were, in the 1800s and the first half of the previous century, obsessed by so-called race science. Bands of colonial intelligentsia were at work all over Africa to try to justify the European enslavement and exploitation of local peoples; to explain why it was okay for Belgians to amputate the hands of 'lazy' natives in the rubber plantations alongside the Congo River or for the French to kill, humiliate and rape in Algeria.

It wasn't long before the colonialists developed the so-called Hamitic hypothesis in Rwanda. They surmised that Tutsis were 'black Aryans' who originated from the Ethiopian highlands near the headwaters of the Blue Nile. It was simply centuries of Africa's harsh sun that had coloured their skins, they reckoned. Hutus and Batwa were 'Negroids' and therefore intellectually and physically inferior. What divided the peoples of Rwanda in the end was an invented history.

If I have learned anything from spending much time in Rwanda, it is that Hutu and Tutsi as a pure ethnic divide is a fallacy. They share a common language, religion and culture. Ask a Tutsi what makes him a Tutsi and he'll probably tell you why a Hutu is not one. Confusing? You bet! For centuries, however, the distinction was used to separate the affluent from the deprived and ultimately to wage genocide.

The English explorer John Hanning Speke, who was the first white man to set eyes on Lake Victoria, remarked that Tutsis were a lost tribe of Christians with 'fine oval faces, large eyes, a bridged instead of a bridge-less nose ... denoting the best blood of Abyssinia [today Ethiopia]'. In contrast, the Hutu was a 'curly head, flat-nosed, pouch-mouthed Negro' who was probably a descendant of the biblical sinner Ham.

In the early thirties, the Belgians shipped scientists to Rwanda and, armed with an array of instruments, they started to measure noses and skulls – and therefore brains. Needless to say, Tutsi skulls were deemed bigger than those of Hutus. According to the nasal guide, a Tutsi nose was almost three millimetres longer and five millimetres narrower than the standard Hutu nose.

All of this spelled superiority and even Tutsi kinship to Europeans. Rwandans were classified into Tutsi, Hutu and Twa, and each and every Rwandan had to carry an identity card stating his or her ethnicity. They were classified according to the race of the father, regardless of that of the mother. People who had ten cows or more were automatically classified as Tutsi – never mind the width of their nose. Hutu and Tutsi identity was based as much on social factors and levels of affluence as it was on race or ethnicity.

Several years before apartheid's architects introduced pass laws or racial classification in South Africa, the Belgians were already ruling their colony along ethnic lines. This practice continued until its abolition by the post-genocide government in 1994. But so deeply entrenched is ethnicity in the Rwandan mentality that it is difficult to find a Rwandan who wouldn't describe him- or herself as either Tutsi or Hutu.

The stereotypes about Hutus and Tutsis persist to this day. Ask anyone what a Tutsi looks like, and he may say: 'Paul Kagame.' This man, whom you'll hear a lot about later, is Rwanda's current president and a besmirched Tutsi war hero. He is the epitome of what race scientists will tell you a Tutsi looks like: a gangly and spindly figure with a birdlike face. During the genocide, if the machete-wielding masses had asked the genocidaires (those who perpetrated genocide) who they must chop up, they would have conjured up a description of Kagame. Many Tutsis, however, are squat and dark with flat noses and fleshy lips and live, like the rest of the Hutu peasantry, off the land. Kennedy may think that they're distinctively handsome and beautiful, but the majority look pretty much like Hutus to me.

The Belgians are generally branded as the worst colonialists that Africa has endured and it was no different in Rwanda. They imposed taxes on cows by forcing owners to donate milk every day to local Belgian administrators. The colonialists were given power to seize cattle for slaughter. (Rwandans very seldom kill cows for meat.) All Rwandan men over the age of eighteen had to pay 'body tax' – called *uburetwa* – by performing hard labour to build roads, churches and buildings.

The colonial Force Publique – the same paramilitary unit that amputated hands and decapitated 'lazy' Bantus in the Congo – ruled Rwanda in a reign of terror. For failure to produce quotas or report for body tax, the *ikiboko* – a whip made of raw, sun-dried hippopotamus hide – was widely used, especially on Hutus. Many died receiving their punishment.

* * *

By the fifties, trouble was looming in Francis's paradise. Hutus were being denied senior positions in government, higher education and land ownership, and the peasantry had grown increasingly resentful of its harsh exploitation by the Tutsi overlords.

An emerging elite of Hutus who had succeeded in gaining access to Catholic divinity schools were now demanding their share of the country's wealth that was being monopolised by Tutsis. The campaign was led by

Grégoire Kayibanda, founder of Paramehutu (Parti du Mouvement de l'Emancipation Hutu; Hutu Emancipation Party) and co-signatory of the 'Hutu Manifesto', who spoke about 'two nations in one state' and the necessity of a democratic election where the winner takes all. The Hutus, after all, had the numbers.

More Hutu political parties sprang up, all arguing for Hutus to unite in their 'Hutu-ness' against Tutsis in their 'Tutsi-ness'. Ironically, many Hutus embraced the notion of Tutsis being 'black Aryans' because that branded them foreign invaders who had many hundreds of years ago taken a detour from Abyssinia and encroached on someone else's land. Their monarchy had lasted centuries, but it was time to send them back and leave Rwanda to the true Rwandans.

The Belgian rulers, under pressure from the Catholic Church, switched allegiance from the *mwami* to the new Hutu gentry. In response to this new threat, Tutsis founded their own political party that propagated for immediate independence with a government based on the existing Tutsi monarchy. Nobody, it seemed, was prepared to share, because the less you share, the more you can keep for yourself. Rwanda was ripe for revolution, for its own Uhuru.

The *mwami* at the time was Mutara Rudahigwa, at six foot nine surely the tallest monarch in the world. He could speak French, toured his king-dom in a Lincoln convertible and lived in a residence with a wide veranda in the manner of a European villa. In July 1959, the *mwami* fell sick while in Burundi en route to New York to present Rwanda's case for independence to the United Nations (UN). It was rumoured that he had a venereal disease and was taken to hospital, where he was treated by a Belgian physician. As he left, he clutched his head and slumped stone dead to the ground. Many Tutsis believed the Belgians had poisoned him.

Later in 1959, some Tutsis tried to assassinate Kayibanda, but were un-successful. Hutus rose up, and across the land Tutsis were killed, their land seized and their cattle pillaged. The style of killing – stabbing, clubbing and slashing – was the same as that used thirty-five years later by the genocidaires. The social revolution was in full swing.

The Belgians were blatantly biased towards their new friends. White-collared fathers blessed the Hutu cause while Belgian officers directed attacks. The administration in Brussels merely looked on – a precursor of what was to happen more than three decades later when the international community, debilitated and paralysed by a mixture of fear, indifference and racism, witnessed the extermination of almost a million Rwandans.

* * *

Francis was at the royal court in Nyanza when the 1959 attacks commenced. The new *mwami*, the twenty-five-year-old Kigeli V, had assembled his chiefs to discuss the political upheaval and to deploy their own royal fighting force against the marauding hordes.

Kennedy's grandmother, Kamabera, was at home in Gikongoro when a mob of Hutus pounced. One of the intruders bashed her over the head with an *ubuhiri* – a stick studded with nails that was also a favoured weapon during the 1994 genocide. She crumpled to the ground in a pool of blood and, satisfied that she was dead, the attackers pillaged the homestead, took the cows and left.

Kamabera regained consciousness, struggled to her feet, assembled the children that were hiding in the bushes and dragged them to the Burundian border. They crossed into foreign land, were loaded onto trucks and dumped in the Tutsi refugee camp at Mushiha in the eastern part of the country on the border with Tanzania. Kennedy says that for the rest of his grandmother's life, she had a bald patch on her head where she was struck.

Ironically, many Hutu servants fled with their Tutsi masters into exile. In the refugee camp, everyone was equal and the Hutus were absorbed into the Tutsi community – another example of how artificial the ethnic division was and still is.

Francis found his way back to Gikongoro and was confronted by his ransacked home. The cattle were looted and even the crops destroyed. Neighbours told him his family had fled to Burundi and so, with little more than his walking stick, he headed south. The family was reunited in Mushiha, by now a camp of shelters strung together by plastic sheeting provided by relief agencies, smouldering fires and hastily dug pit latrines. This is where they would live for the next thirteen years on handouts from the United Nations High Commissioner for Refugees (UNHCR).

The Belgian army in Rwanda allowed its Hutu troops, under command of a colonial officer, to loot and rape for several weeks. Kinyarwanda traditionally did not have a word for rape. After 1959 it had: *gufalinga*, which is derived from the name of a Belgian automatic gun widely carried by troops – the Fusil Automatique Léger, commonly known as a FAL.

After the Belgians had finally restored a semblance of order, they installed a Hutu-led administration. The monarchy was abandoned in 1961 and *mwami* Kigeli V fled into exile. Tutsi superiority was replaced by Hutu domination – the old order now stood on its head.

5

Outcasts

The colonial era in Africa was coming to an end. It started with Sudan in 1956, spread to the Gold Coast – renamed Ghana – and then gained a life and momentum all of its own. By the dawn of the 1960s, the Congo was already sovereign, and the Brits were planning an exit from their 'fairytale kingdom of Uganda' – as Winston Churchill had fondly called it – across the border to the north. In 1960 alone, seventeen African countries unshackled themselves from colonialism.

In September 1961, Rwandans voted overwhelmingly to become a republic, and in July of the following year, Belgium bid farewell to its green patch of empire in Africa's warm heart. As the Belgian flag was lowered and the thirty-eight-year-old Grégoire Kayibanda was sworn in as the new prime minister, people walked with torchlights through the capital city Kigali. Across the land, from hill to hill, bonfires blazed and drums beat in jubilation of a new nation. Its new flag featured vertical bands of red, yellow and green with a big black 'R' in the centre. Red stood for the blood of the martyrs, yellow for the rising sun and green for the harvest and vegetation.

By then, thousands of Tutsis had been killed – it's very difficult to get an accurate figure – and many more had fled to neighbouring states. Even more would cross Rwanda's borders in the following years as Hutu Power became entrenched in every sector of society. The government introduced quotas for Tutsis and suddenly they couldn't get access to higher education or job opportunities in government or the armed forces. Every schoolchild was raised in the doctrine of racial superiority and inferiority. By the mid-sixties, an estimated 300 000 Tutsis – half of the population – lived outside of Rwanda.

Burundi gained independence at the same time as Rwanda, but, unlike its neighbour, a tiny clique of Tutsi officers continued to cling to power. The country has roughly the same ethnic mix as Rwanda, and therefore its Tutsi rulers welcomed the exiles in an effort to boost their numbers. Tutsis pride themselves on being ferocious warriors – theirs was one of the only regions in Africa where Arab and European slave traders were never able to conduct raids – and it wasn't long before the exiles had forged themselves into a haphazard fighting force. Between 1961 and 1967, they invaded Rwanda more than a dozen times but were no match for the government's firepower.

During these attacks, Hutu politicians started branding Tutsis as *inyenzis* – cockroaches – a label that was resurrected with a vengeance during the genocide. Initially it referred to the speed with which the Tutsi exiles struck from their hideouts in Burundi before scuttling back to safety across the border, but later it was used to brand Tutsis in general as vermin.

After an *inyenzi* attack in 1963, the government retaliated by massacring 40 000 Tutsis in Gikongoro. The philosopher Bertrand Russell described it as 'the most horrible and systematic mass killing' since the Holocaust. But nobody paid attention. By then, Rwanda was an almost forgotten enclave somewhere in darkest Africa. No major highway ran through it, there were no big cities, there was nothing that anyone wanted. There were no international observers or foreign correspondents or independent commissions. That's why it's so difficult to determine how many perished during the early years of independence.

In years to come, this cycle of violence would repeat itself in Rwanda – and to a lesser extent in Burundi – with the regularity of an African drumbeat. The upheaval of 1959 was followed by slaughters in 1962, 1963, 1967, 1972, 1988, 1990, 1991, 1993 and eventually full-scale genocide in 1994.

* * *

It is difficult to envisage what life in Mushiha must have been like for Francis Semandwa and his family. Mushiha is located in the middle of nowhere. Life in a refugee camp has been described as one of enforced idleness and dependency. They are human warehouses where lives are on indefinite hold, not unlike prison, except that their occupants have not committed any crimes. Most refugee camps conjure up images of sprawling, smoke-filled tents or blue UNHCR canvasses, bland and resigned faces, figures crouched around smouldering fires, forlorn and snot-nosed children.

'Can you imagine what this did to him? A chief who had lots of cattle and servants but was now a foreigner in a strange land?' Kennedy asks rhetorically. 'He was sad, always sad. He never spoke about it, but I could see the sadness. He longed for his cows and his land and his people. He was nothing but an outcast.'

In time, though, the refugee camp at Mushiha became more like a village. Refugees constructed simple structures of mud, sticks and grass and were given pieces of land to cultivate bananas, maize and cassava. Francis became the cattle herder at the nearby red-bricked Roman Catholic church while Granny Kamabera traded produce for clothes and daily necessities in nearby villages. In time, hope of soon returning to Rwanda faded as more Tutsis arrived in Mushiha with stories of their subjugation and degradation at the hands of the Hutu rulers.

In the winter of 1971, one of Francis's daughters, Teddy Uwamaria, fell pregnant by Alex Bayingana. Both were still in their teens. They never got married and, in February 1972, Kennedy was born. We can only presume that Francis followed all the pomp that is supposed to accompany the birth of a Rwandan baby. On the eighth day of the infant's life, for example, the community gathers to celebrate his or her coming. Banana beer is served and the child is triumphantly held up in the sky and touched by relatives and friends, who also suggest names.

Francis christened his grandson Kennedy Alfred Gihana in the nearby Roman Catholic church. He was named after John Fitzgerald Kennedy, the thirty-fifth president of the United States. Francis never went to school, but was what Kennedy calls a 'peasant historian'. He could read the Bible and write his name, and he listened incessantly to the BBC World Service. That's probably where he heard of JFK. Francis later told his grandson that his American namesake had been a visionary and dynamic leader who had changed the destiny of the world. JFK had also been a Roman Catholic and the year of his assassination – 1963 – marked the year the Tutsi exiles hit back against their Hutu oppressors. Alfred was merely a Christian or European name but his surname, Gihana, occupies a special place in Tutsi annals. Gihana was a lion-hearted warrior prince who sacrificed himself to save the great Kingdom of Banyarwanda. He is known as the *umutabazi* – the liberator – and a flame had burnt in his memory at the royal court until the abolishment of the monarchy.

I only recently discovered that Kennedy has another name: Nurudin. 'You have another name!' I exclaimed, looking at his identity document. 'What's this Nurudin?'

He chortled almost sheepishly and said, 'Oh my God, it's my Muslim name. I don't like it but I'm now sitting with it and cannot get rid of it.' It's a story for later, but Nurudin appears everywhere; not just in his ID book but on his degree certificates, refugee papers and all other documents as well.

Kennedy's father died soon after his son's birth. Kennedy once confided to me, with tears in his eyes: 'I am a bastard child. In ancient Tutsi culture, such children were sometimes killed, although they were later given to grandparents to look after. That's why I call my grandfather and grandmother Papa and Mama. It's them that brought me up. They were everything to me.'

Kennedy's birth coincided with turbulent events in Burundian history. The president, a former army captain, had ordered his forces to crack down and repel a Hutu uprising that had swept through the capital. Two hundred thousand mostly Hutus were massacred and many more fled their homes for the relative safety of the countryside. Burundi was, like its neighbour to the north, in the grip of terror and on the brink of calamity. It was time to leave.

One of Francis's sons found a job in a sugar factory in southern Uganda. He sent a message to his family in Mushiha that the land was spacious and empty and that the new ruler of the republic, Idi Amin Dada, welcomed Rwandan exiles. After being warehoused for thirteen years, the family packed their meagre belongings, Teddy tied Kennedy to her back and they journeyed on foot through western Tanzania alongside the border with Rwanda.

When they crossed into Uganda, Francis cast his eyes over the grassland and rolling hills dotted with flat-top acacia and speckled with Ankole cows. 'This is perfect,' he said. 'This is where we will stay.'

* * *

After crossing the Tanzanian–Ugandan border, Francis and his family moved ten kilometres up the main road, came to the village of Kabonela, turned inland and, about a kilometre further, settled on a gentle slope overlooking a valley sprinkled with banana groves, patches of maize and Ankole. In time to come, the family would buy the land with the income from the sugar factory.

Francis constructed a traditional grass hut, banned the use of English in his house and wouldn't eat any other meat but beef – and that usually only once a year at Christmas or on other special occasions. His grandchildren were not allowed to eat anything given to them by the Baganda, an ethnic group native to Uganda. Kennedy was just a little boy when Francis ordered him to get his stick and accompany him to graze the cows.

Says Kennedy, 'I am what I am because of my grandfather. He taught me to respect. He taught me to be strong whatever the situation. He taught me to work hard. It's the spirit of Grandpa that made me go on. He taught me a Tutsi boy never fails and that I should be proud of myself. He said to me I should never steal, even if it is to eat. Never do a bad thing to better yourself. Never kill, even if you do it in order to survive.'

Teddy Uwamaria fell pregnant again and gave birth to Kennedy's half-sister, Nyinawumuntu. She soon after left both children with Francis and Kamabera and went to live in another southern Ugandan village, where she married and had more children. Kennedy saw her a handful of times after this but she played no further role in his or Nyinawumuntu's life. It was Grandma, he says, who kept them alive and showered them with love.

'She was my mother. She did everything to see that we had something to eat. In summer, there was less milk because it was dry and didn't rain. We even had to move to find water and grass for the cows. But we still had to eat so Mama had to go and work for the Baganda to get *posho* [porridge] and cassava. Without that woman we would have died of hunger. The love she gave us was amazing. The reason why I'm feeling pain is that I never buried her.'

6

Idi and Milton

Francis was determined to raise his grandson in true Tutsi tradition and custom, even though he had few cows of his own and was as such a man of little standing. Kennedy was clothed in brown cloth – it should have been calfskin if the family had enough cows – which he wrapped around his body, draped over his shoulder and tied with banana rope. He was put to work at the age of four or five, fetching water, collecting cow dung and learning how to milk the cows. He was six when he started looking after calves.

'Grandpa had to look for a job with the Baganda people and was again a cattle herder. He was paid with milk that we drank or sold or swapped at the market for other food. We were very poor; I didn't know shoes as a child. The Baganda around us were rich and had many cows. They have a different tradition and culture to ours, but Grandpa befriended them. That's how we again got a few cows,' recalls Kennedy.

Like all Tutsi children, Kennedy was taught from an early age to revere these animals as the givers of all sustenance. Francis showed him how to massage the animals and to tend to them like siblings. When he was older, he was taught the cow praise poems and songs that herders recite when calling their herds to the watering place, when tending to them while they graze and when bringing them home in the evening.

'When we dance, we hold our arms as though they are horns in order to symbolise the biggest bull in the herd. There are many songs about cows and I knew every one of them. When you get married, the father of the bride sends someone to choose cows, usually ten or twelve. When the bride has a child, the family gives one cow back. If you don't have cows you are useless. But in Uganda we didn't have lots of cows so I think Grandpa felt like a nobody.'

In turn, Kamabera took charge of her granddaughter's upbringing. Nyinawumuntu helped her grandmother sweep the homestead with a bundle of twigs bound together to make a broom, till the patch of maize and cassava, and take care of the container of milk that the men brought home.

Although in exile and dirt poor, Francis regained his chieftain status. Members of the exiled Tutsi community queued at their front door to ask for advice on anything from marriage breakdowns to cow problems. Kennedy remembers his grandfather as an incredibly hospitable person, like most Rwandans are. Strangers who turned up on his doorstep were received with open arms and sheltered and accommodated. The family would go hungry in order to feed their guests, and Kennedy was ordered to give up his bed and had to sleep with the cattle in the veld. He often had to scuttle off to the local shebeen in Kabonela to buy a calabash of *urwagwa* for guests. This banana brew is the symbol of both good-heartedness and conviviality in Rwanda. Men got beer, women milk. When Kennedy was slightly older, he got a sip of *urwagwa* as a tip and was allowed to sit closer to the elders. As he grew bigger, the sip got longer.

When he wasn't grazing the cows, counselling his countrymen or reciting stories to his grandson, Francis sat with his transistor radio at his ear listening to the BBC World Service. When his batteries ran flat and money for new ones was scant, the young boy once again had to dash to Kabonela to find someone listening to the radio. Kennedy had to be all ears and report world events back to his grandpa.

Kennedy describes his early childhood as a time of both hardship and happiness. I presume his contentment was partly due to the joy of an unbounded life on the sweeping African savannah. 'I had lots of love and even though we had nothing, Grandma and Grandpa gave us what they could. There was usually only one meal, and that was cassava and a glass of milk. At night, you drank your milk and you went to bed. Sometimes we ate beans or *matoke*, but I was always hungry. Some days there was no food and your stomach just stayed empty until you got a piece of cassava again.'

* * *

The seventies were a tumultuous time in Uganda. A few hundred kilometres from Kabonela, in the capital of Kampala, a homicidal buffoon was conducting a reign of terror against his countrymen. Idi Amin's reign of terror is equated to those of Hitler, Lenin, Stalin, Pol Pot, Bokassa, Pinochet, Hussein and other twentieth-century merchants of death.

In between executing his opponents by firing squad in public squares or torturing them to death, Amin was crowned Uganda's rally-driving champion by racing around in Kampala in his red Maserati. Those who challenged him had to lose, or else. He promoted himself to the rank of field marshal and claimed to be the king of Scotland. In 1977, after Britain broke diplomatic relations with his regime, Amin declared that he had defeated the British and conferred on himself the decoration of CBE, which, he said, stood for 'Conqueror of the British Empire'. Radio Uganda was constantly required to read out his full title: 'His Excellency President for Life, Field Marshal Al Hadji Dr Idi Amin Dada, VC, DSO, MC, CBE.'

In order to demonstrate his military genius, Amin entertained diplomatic guests at his residence on Lake Victoria with an extravagant ball and, once, a mock attack on apartheid South Africa, represented by an offshore island. When his warplanes missed the island and their bombs fell harmlessly into the lake, he fired his air force chief and had him executed a while later. His syphilis-infected brain sent between 300 000 and half a million of his countrymen to a similar fate.

Like most other exiled Tutsis, Kennedy's grandfather supported Amin because he left them in peace and went as far as inviting the *mwami* to settle in Uganda.

By the late seventies, however, there were rumblings of war in Uganda after Amin's troops had crossed into Tanzania in pursuit of dissidents opposing his regime. They had looted and wrecked villages along the Kagera River. Tanzanian president Julius Nyerere, who had always condemned Amin as a dangerous and unbalanced man, retaliated. When an armoured Tanzanian column invaded in 1979, Kabonela was in the path of the rolling tanks and advancing infantry. Francis and his family were on the move once again.

Francis ordered Kennedy to fetch the cows and pack what they could. Amin's soldiers and tanks were on the road pushing towards the border, where Tanzania was amassing troops and hardware. The area was a war zone.

'I can't remember much, except that we had to run for our lives with the two cattle we had,' recalls Kennedy. 'Grandma was too weak for the journey and we had to leave her behind with other old people to hide in the mountains. We walked for many, many days right across Uganda until we were in the south-west of the country. We stayed there for a few months and then went back to rebuild our home.'

Three months after invading Uganda, the Tanzanians captured Kampala and Amin took flight. During his reign he had converted to Islam and was now calling on the brotherhood to look after one of their kin. The Saudi Arabian royal family offered him sanctuary in the holy city of Jeddah in return for him staying clear of politics. The departure of 'Big Dada' paved the way for Milton Obote, Uganda's first post-independence prime minister and president until his deposition by Amin in 1971, to once again seize power.

* * *

Obote's nefarious human rights record is dwarfed by that of Amin, but he was nonetheless an equally profane despot who had scant regard for human dignity. Across the country, the corpses of his adversaries piled up in state mortuaries and decomposed in shallow graves and pits. He furthermore despised the presence of Rwandan refugees in his land and wanted them gone, not least because many had supported Amin.

Kennedy remembers: 'I heard the grown-ups and Grandpa saying that this man's head is not right and that there's big problems coming for us Rwandans. But I didn't know what was going on because I was innocent and just a cattle boy grazing my cows. We were far away from politicians and life went on.'

Kennedy was about ten when he was promoted to cattle herder. It was around this age that Francis decided it was time for the youngster to go to school. 'I never thought then I would ever see the inside of such a place. I just wanted to be with my cows and I thought that's how I would spend the rest of my life,' says Kennedy.

Because he himself had never had any formal education, Francis didn't want his grandson to suffer like he did. 'The majority of Tutsis in Uganda never went to school because they couldn't afford it. Education was not free for foreigners. You had to pay even for primary school. I grew up without money because we only had milk and that we exchanged for soap, oil and things like that. So where would money come from to send your kid to school? My friend Dominique never saw what a classroom looked like. His and many other parents couldn't afford it.'

Before Kennedy could start his education, however, there were again rumblings from the Ugandan government that Rwandans must return home. Obote, a construction worker and university dropout, said the time had come to incarcerate refugees in camps. He incited anti-Rwandan feeling further when he declared that *abagwira* – foreigners – were taking land from locals and should give it back.

Local militia, supported by police, swept through areas where Rwandans were known to live, including the Rakai district around Kabonela, and rounded up the *abalalo* – those who look after cows. Several Rwandans were killed, many were beaten up, and an estimated 16 000 homes were destroyed and 45 000 head of cattle looted.

When the militia arrived at Francis's homestead, they told him and his family to take whatever they could carry and wait to be taken back to Rwanda. Kennedy had to fetch the cows, which were then handed over to a local. They were transported in big trucks to the border post. There was a general belief among the exiles that Tutsis who had already been repatriated had been killed by the regime across the border. Rumours circulated that men were separated from women and children and buried alive.

'Can you imagine how upset Grandpa was?' Kennedy asks. 'He was traumatised. He thought this was the end of us and the Tutsis. We were going to be killed. He said even if they allowed us to live, they would put us in camps and we would never get our land back. The Hutus had long ago taken our land and wouldn't give it back. We were doomed. We were being marched to our graves.'

Forty thousand refugees were forced across the border into Rwanda to face an uncertain future. Francis and his family were still waiting to be repatriated when, in November 1982, the military regime in Kigali closed its borders with Uganda and declared there wasn't space in the country for any more returning Rwandans. The dictator, General Juvénal Habyarimana, likened Rwanda to a glass of water that was not just full, but already overflowing. Ninety-five per cent of Rwanda's land was already cultivated and the average family had no more than a hectare or two to live from. By the mid-eighties, Rwanda had the highest birth rate in the world – 8.2 live births per woman – and 25 000 new families needed land every year, but there wasn't any.

While Obote and Habyarimana squabbled like spoilt brats, Francis and his family were among 4 000 Rwandan refugees trapped inside Uganda with the border post in sight. 'Dominique and his family were with us and we stood like stray animals next to the road for almost a month. There was no food, no clean water, nothing. We were hungry. Kids were crying and people were getting sick. There was no medicine or fresh water. We were waiting for our deaths. Grandpa said when we got to the other side our graves would already have been dug. But if we stayed here, we'd also die.'

The expulsion of Rwandan refugees violated both human rights and international law. Uganda was condemned by the UN and there was enormous pressure on the regime to revoke its earlier decision. Obote denied ever ordering the Rwandans to go back, explaining that it was their 'spontaneous decision' to return home. The refugees at the border post were subsequently ordered to return to where they had come from. Francis and his family returned to Kabonela to find their home looted and their cattle gone.

By then, I presume, they were so tempered by disaster that they were resigned to their fate. Fairness, equality and justice are First World luxuries. However, for people facing such calamity, it doesn't help to sink down in a state of despair or exasperation, because there is no one to help you. You have to rebuild yourself. It is a remarkable and inextinguishable African characteristic that I have admired time and again: picking up the pieces and starting life all over again. This is exactly what Francis and his family did.

Says Kennedy, 'All this hardness prepared me for what happened later in life. It made me strong.'

* * *

Kennedy's schooling was put on hold. He would have to wait until the following year for his formal learning to commence. Until such time, however, every morning he would cloak his weedy body in his brown cloth, wolf down a piece of cassava (if there was any) and a glass of milk, take his stick and wait for his friend Dominique Kashugi before the duo would dart off to milk the cows and then shepherd them onto the savannah to graze. The two were inseparable and their families, who were neighbours, were inter-reliant. In the true African tradition of *ubuntu* (meaning 'human generosity'), they shared, pinned their faith on one another and together endured taxing times. Dominique's family were also Rwandan Tutsis, forced into exile following the 1959 upheaval.

More than thirty years on, and Dominique is foremost in Kennedy's mind when a rusty signpost announces that we have arrived in Kabonela, a hodgepodge settlement ten kilometres from the Tanzanian frontier.

'This is where I grew up,' he says. 'Turn up that muddy road over there. We are home.'

7

Dominique

Minutes after we turn off onto a reddish dirt path, Kennedy tells James to stop at a patch of maize. He walks through the cultivated fields and stops at a ruin. It is their old homestead. Kennedy shakes his head and comes back to the car. 'There's nothing left. The new owners have demolished the house, but under that mango tree, that's where I always sat with Grandpa. Let's go look for Dominique.'

A few hundred metres on, we stop at a eucalyptus grove and walk up the hill towards two small mud huts with tin roofs and a banana plantation at the back. A boy greets us and introduces himself as Geoffrey. He extends his hand and says to me in perfect English: 'Good morning, sir, and how is sir today?' He adds: 'And I'm going to be a teacher one day, sir,' before switching to Kinyarwanda. Kennedy grins from ear to ear. 'We are at the right place. This is Dominique's firstborn.'

Geoffrey says Dominique is in the valley below working somebody's land. He calls a smaller brother and the two trot off to fetch their father. Dominique's wife, Veronica Kirabo, is sitting under an avocado tree. She's a slight, dark woman with intense eyes that are glazed with sadness. She emits a yelp and her face for a moment lights up when Kennedy tells her his name and who his grandparents were. She greets him in the traditional manner, pressing first her one and then her other shoulder against each of his and exchanging formalities in a whining manner, before flinging herself on the ground at his feet. The yard is neat and swept, but there is nothing more than two or three goats tied to a tree and two bunches of green bananas lying on the ground.

Veronica, already surrounded by a rugby team of snot-nosed organ pipes, is thirty-four years old and pregnant with her tenth child. Dominique has two children born out of wedlock who live with them. Dominique's sister has stomach cancer and her husband has abandoned her. She and her three children have also moved in. She is in severe pain but the hospital has run out of painkillers.

'When we go to the clinic in Kakuto for treatment, there is never any medicine,' says Veronica. 'There weren't even pills for me when I was pregnant and sick. You have to pay the sister and the doctor to get treatment. It's worse for us because they say we're Rwandans. In the whole district, there is only one hospital. That's our only hope.'

The children are in rags and Veronica says they cannot afford school fees. Although Dominique and his family have lived in Uganda for almost forty years, they are still regarded as foreigners and have to fork out much higher school fees than locals. Veronica says they have to tell Geoffrey, who is seventeen but doesn't look older than twelve or thirteen, that he won't be going back to school in the new term. Their two cows were recently stolen, which is why Dominique is cultivating other people's lands. There are sixteen people depending on him for their daily bread. Dominique earns 1500 Ugandan shillings – around half a dollar – a day.

'Can you believe this?' Kennedy whispers to me. 'When I grew up, we were poor and some days we went without food, but we were never like this. Dominique's family never lived like this. It is unbelievable. I don't know what happened.'

* * *

The two boys didn't just grow up together; Kennedy regarded Dominique's mother and father as his second parents. The families depended on each other, and when Kennedy left, Dominique looked after his grandparents. It was in fact Francis who helped Dominique find a wife and conducted the negotiations on his behalf. Veronica tells Kennedy that Francis and Kamabera left Kabonela just after she and Dominique got married. She thinks it was just after the genocide.

'I called them my parents, and they were much respected in the community,' she says. 'They gave me love like you give love to your own child. I remember that last Christmas because they sent us a calabash of milk, butter and some meat. We were very sad when they left. But Kennedy's grandfather was old and he wanted to go back before he died. They packed everything and left with their cows. Nobody saw them again.'

Kennedy is dropping by Dominique's sick sister when out of the banana plantation bursts a scrawny and dark-skinned man who struts up to me and pants: 'Gihana? Gihana Kennedy?' (Rwandans always say the surname first.)

I point in the direction of the hut and a few moments later the two men are flinging themselves into each other's arms. It is the kind of embrace reserved for long-lost brothers or a father whose son has returned from war or an extended sojourn.

'I thought you were dead!' exclaims Dominique. 'But others said you had gone to Canada to find your riches.'

Kennedy compliments Dominique, saying that he looks exactly like he did two decades ago when he last saw him. The latter is more forthright and says: 'You were very tall and thin when you left. But now you are big and look like those people in the cities who are rich. So where were you?'

Kennedy clears his throat and shifts his Samsung Galaxy tablet (it doesn't work in Uganda) from one hand to the other. 'I am now an attorney of the High Court of South Africa.'

The two men babble for the next hour or so under a mango tree. Kennedy wants to know what happened to his grandparents. Dominique clears his throat, looks straight ahead and says that he thinks they went back to Rwanda before the genocide. But it could have been afterwards. He cannot remember.

Kennedy now knows their graves are not in Uganda, but it still doesn't bring him closure as to how they met their maker. Did the machetes of the *interahamwe* (the Hutu militia) cut them down during the mass killings, or did Francis die peacefully in his beloved motherland with God resting next to him? Dominique says he has heard that one of Kennedy's aunts went back with Francis and Kamabera to Rwanda, but returned to Uganda shortly afterwards and is still living near Kabonela. He will ask around and locate her.

* * *

Dominique sets up base with us in the border town of Mutukula, which boasts the only 'hotel' in the area. There is, however, no food in this hustling, bustling, dusty, dirty, messy frontier outpost and the madam of the guesthouse has to drive us through narrow, eroded dirt roads over the border to Tanzania to a makeshift restaurant advertising itself as Silver Lights. Except that there are no lights. The electricity is out on both sides of the border. The restaurant is windowless, wrapped in red plastic and as hot as a pizza oven, but from the darkness emerges a hearty banana and vegetable stew with fried chicken that we gobble down with lukewarm beer by candlelight. The chicken is obviously free-range, and its long, lean and tough legs and thighs testify that from birth birds run for dear life in this part of the world.

Dominique speaks in short, nervous bursts, often followed by hysterical sniggers. He looks at Kennedy and says: 'He is like a ghost that woke up over the fields and walked back. Most thought he'd died in the war, but now it turns out that he was in Canada.'

Kennedy explains that although he has told Dominique that he has gone to South Africa, it makes no sense to his friend. When Kennedy left, several Rwandans in Uganda received bursaries to study in Canada. Every far-flung place is therefore Canada and in Dominique's mind that is exactly where Kennedy has been all these years. Dominique also wants to know if I am from Canada. Kennedy says it's a compliment; bad white people are Belgian and good ones Canadian.

Dominique went to school for only a year or two. After the death of his parents and the arrival of his children, he slipped further and further into poverty. It costs him 200 000 shillings a year – around R600 – to keep Geoffrey in school. 'The children don't eat enough,' he says, 'they are malfunctioning. They are not growing. They get sick. We use traditional medicine and we boil leaves that we find in the forest. The hospital in Kakuto is not functioning. You have to pay to see a doctor and there is no medicine. There is a campaign by the government to teach children who have failed in school a skill so that they can help themselves. But our children don't qualify for that programme because they say they are Rwandan. When it suits them, they still see us as foreigners.'

Kennedy wants to know why the couple doesn't do family planning. Dominique explains that they use traditional medicine for birth control, but that it doesn't always work. They used to get pills from the clinic so that Veronica couldn't conceive, but then she fell sick from the medicine and stopped taking it. Now she is pregnant again.

'I can't care for all of them, not even for food,' laments Dominique. 'Clothes are out of the question. It is difficult for all of us to eat one meal every day. Some of them are in primary school, but others don't go to school at all.'

As we drive away, Kennedy says: 'I have a mixture of sadness and happiness. I'm happy that Dominique is alive. But I'm sad because the poverty here is even worse than when I grew up. There's been no improvement;

everybody is still struggling for survival. The misery just never ends. It brought back old memories, some good, some bad, of people like my cousin, Sarah, who got meningitis. She was sick for only two days and then she died because the hospital didn't have medicine. But now it's worse than I imagined. In this place you thank God that a day has passed and you're still alive. There's not much else to say thank you for.'

* * *

Kennedy later observes that Dominique's problem is that he no longer lives like a Tutsi. He has become 'Baganda-ised' and is living like a peasant. The Baganda, he contends, are like Hutus. When he grew up, the exiles regarded the Baganda as inferior, partly because there was a belief they ate everything. Kennedy is even convinced that some eat human flesh. He remembers as a boy how a Baganda had threatened to eat him and had chased him through a forest.

I'm afraid that much of what Francis drilled into Kennedy persists, especially with regards to the superiority of Tutsis. Francis believed they were handsome and smart and so does Kennedy. In Francis's Rwanda, Tutsis were in charge and, according to him, rightfully so because they were a superior race. He believed their ancestors marched from far north and settled around the Great Lakes, making them not just more advanced, but different from other Rwandans.

It's important to remember that Kennedy didn't grow up with Hutus. He says: 'Everyone who spoke Kinyarwanda in Uganda was a Tutsi. Grandpa said that people who didn't speak Kinyarwanda were Hutus. I heard of them, but I never saw them. They were across the border in Rwanda and Grandpa said they killed us and took our cows.'

Kennedy first encountered Hutus when he joined the rebel army and then they were the enemy. Now he's the first to embrace Hutus as his fellow countrymen, but deep inside, an element of Francis's ethnic prejudice endures. An incident on our journey back to Kampala towards the end of our trip illustrates this. Driver James is, like most Ugandans, an affable, likeable and cheery fellow. Short and dark skinned, he's a Muganda. James is telling us about their customs and culture when Kennedy lets loose: 'These people are Bantus, but we Tutsis are not. We're Hamites.'

James and I are for a few seconds taken aback, and then an argument ensues. It's important to clarify that the Bantu we are talking about here are the hundreds of ethnic groups in sub-Saharan Africa that speak inter-related languages, and not the ugly ogres of apartheid ideology.

James is affronted and accuses Kennedy of being racist. Kennedy stands his ground: Tutsis are pastoralists who trekked from far away with their cows. He incites further bad blood when he remarks, 'We only eat cow meat; *they* eat other things.'

'Like what things?' I want to know.

'Insects like *ensenene* – grasshoppers.'

'And therefore you're not a Bantu?'

'No, we're Hamites. We only eat cows, beans and vegetables.'

Exasperated, James and I eventually let it go and we drive on in silence. That night, I do a simple internet search for the genetic origin of Tutsis. Sorry, Kennedy, but modern-day genetic studies of the Y chromosome suggest that Tutsis are of Bantu extraction. Their closest ethnic kinship is to Hutus.

8

Joffrey, Dick, Teddy, Mugara, John and Peter

Dominique takes Kennedy in search of old friends and acquaintances along the dusty row of shops that line Kabonela's main road to the Tanzanian border post. News of Kennedy's homecoming must have spread like veld fire, because they emerge from nowhere and, within seconds, the dreary surroundings are transformed by shrieks of laughter and cries of joy. They embrace one another. On a dusty patch next to a makeshift butchery where slabs of goat and beef are ripening in the midday sun, the band of Tutsi men share childhood memories and stare in awe at the village boy who has made it big, really big, in a faraway land.

Among them are Joffrey Mushabe, Dick Bizimungu, Teddy Rwagitare, Mugara Muyambi, John Rukumba and Peter Mugenyi. They all knew Kennedy as a boy and most were like him, barefooted cattle herders with sticks and dogs and cloth wrapped around their loins, roaming the acacia-speckled plains of south-eastern Uganda in search of the greenest grass and the sweetest water. What tied them together and sustained their love for one another, Kennedy later explains, was their 'Tutsi-ness'.

A group of barefooted boys who are booting around a flat soccer ball in a cloud of dust abandon their play and edge closer to get a better view of Kabonela's long-lost son. After all have expressed amazement at how big and meaty Kennedy is, Dominique announces that their friend is now a learned man of the law and what makes his success even more remarkable is that he has achieved all of this in far-flung South Africa, of all places. Those who went to school with Kennedy nod their heads and say they are not surprised, because he couldn't wait to leave his cows and go to school where he always achieved better marks than any of them.

'Yes,' Kennedy confirms in an authoritative voice, 'I am now an attorney of the High Court in South Africa.'

Some nod their heads; others gape in anticipation of a clearer explanation. There are no attorneys in Uganda, so as far as they are concerned it is a rather useless skill for which no need exists. Kennedy explains that a lawyer is similar to an advocate – there are many of those in Uganda – and the crowd again nod their heads. I'm not sure how many grasp his achievement, but it doesn't really matter. Kennedy is back and he has a story to tell. He switches to Kinyarwanda, points in the direction of Rwanda, waves his hand south and embarks on an explanation that ends with 'master's degree in international law'. Most shake their heads and utter noises of esteem. One wants to know: 'Did you actually get that diploma or did you just buy it next to the road as many do here in Uganda?'

Taken aback, Kennedy assures him that he had to study for many years and that his academic qualification was obtained at the University of Pretoria, which he describes as 'one of the best universities in the world'. Just to rub it in, he turns to me and adds, 'Is that not so, Jacques?'

I nod my head, upon which another wants to know who the *muzungu* (white person) is. It's not meant with any degree of hostility, but is merely descriptive.

'That is my good friend and he is writing my book. I think we will come and launch the book here in Kabonela. You will all be here and there will be a big celebration. Is that not so, Jacques?'

I again nod my head. I'm not sure how the Kinyarwanda translation goes down, but it must be the first time ever that a local has arrived in Kabonela with a white lackey in tow. Both of us look the part. Kennedy, clutching his BlackBerry and Samsung Galaxy, is nattily dressed in a red Manchester United shirt. I, on the other hand, appear sapped after another sleepless night in our scorching and mosquito-infested guesthouse in Mutukula.

Kennedy's appearance and academic achievements reek of financial success. One immediately wants to know how much these attorneys in South Africa earn. Kennedy explains that he has just started his own law firm and has recently tied the knot and become a father. He switches on his Samsung and shows pictures of little Lisa wrapped in a white blanket lying snugly in her cot. The baby's fair complexion evokes the expected reaction.

'Have you married a *muzungu* in that place where you now live?' He shows them a picture of Goreth and explains that she is a Tutsi, and that he went to Rwanda to marry her. This is met with general approval.

I ask them to describe what Kennedy looked like growing up.

'Like a stick! Thin as a reed!' they shriek at once. 'Very tall and thin! As one who never had enough to eat!'

'Not like now,' says another. 'He looks like a man who has lots of food to eat.'

'His body has multiplied many, many times since the last time I saw him. I can see he's leading a very good life,' observes another.

It takes some time before we succeed in derailing the scrutiny of Kennedy's monetary position and redirect the conversation to him as a boy. They are all babbling at the same time when Kennedy just about folds double with delight and waves me closer.

'I have completely forgotten to tell you this story!' he exclaims. 'Rukumba John reminded me of this.'

It is the story of how Kennedy's status skyrocketed among members of the clan. And not surprisingly, its subject is a cow.

Among the herd that Kennedy was charged with looking after was a smallish, reddish bull called Rubarasi, a name acquired as a result of white stripes around his neck.

'He was not big,' Kennedy says, 'but my man, could this animal fight! And he also produced very nice calves!'

On this day, Baganda herders and Tutsi boys were grazing their cattle in the same area and, before long, the one had challenged the other to a bullfight, a cattleman's ultimate show of strength. According to Kennedy, a Baganda boy was boasting about the invincibility of his beast. His bull was much bigger, built like a caterpillar, and flaunted a magnificent pair of horns, the base as thick as a man's leg.

'What this silly boy didn't know,' says Kennedy, 'was that Rubarasi had been in many fights and had never been defeated. He never gave up!' The bull had scars in his neck where opponents had gored him, yet he always emerged victorious. Whenever Kennedy had to sleep with the cattle in the veld, he sharpened Rubarasi's horns with broken glass.

Kennedy and his Baganda opponent urged their herds closer together, isolated the two bulls and prodded them towards each other. As Kennedy tells me the story, those bystanders who witnessed the epic battle grimace from ear to ear. Bullfights can last a long time and have been known to end in one's horn penetrating the other bull and the injured animal bleeding to death.

Rubarasi stamped his hoof on the ground, scratched up a cloud of dust, lowered his head, pointed his sharpened horns and rammed the Baganda bull. And just like that, it was over. Kennedy pushes his finger against his throat. 'This is where the horn went in,' he explains, 'and,' indicating the point at the back of his neck where the spine joins the skull, 'this is where it went out.'

'Really?' I ask, whereupon he waves his hand towards the crowd. 'Ask them!' he says.

Everyone, even those who were not born yet, exclaim confirmation and a sea of heads bob up and down. 'He fell dead. I saw it,' corroborates Dominique. 'You never saw anything like that.' Another adds, 'I was also there. I saw it with my own eyes.'

'That Baganda boy cried because he knew he was in shit,' says Kennedy. 'His father was going to kill him. His family came to see Grandfather and demanded compensation, but we just chased them away.'

'Rubarasi and you were just the same, Gihana,' says one. 'Small but dangerous!'

Talk shifts to someone's dog that was renowned for hunting impala, which the boys skinned and barbecued in the veld. Kennedy explains that they never took any meat home because the elders didn't allow them to eat such strange things. Only cow meat was permitted. One of the men stretches his arms in front of him and recounts the day a monster cobra hoisted itself in front of Kennedy, spat its venom over him and lunged at the ducking and diving boy. The fangs missed Kennedy, but he was in agony for days as the poison temporarily blinded him. Another man recalled that Kennedy was the champion stick fighter. Sticks were chosen and cut to a V-shape at the end to resemble a bull's horns. Kennedy shows a mark on his arm where a sharpened stick once penetrated his flesh.

'Even with stick-fighting,' Kennedy says, 'we hammered them. I hit them hard. We sharpened them and put stripes on them by burning them in the fire. These Baganda boys soon realised: don't mess with a Tutsi boy.'

The conversation wanders to primary school days – Kennedy is the only one among them who made it to secondary school – and again he shrieks with merriment when one of the men evokes a memory of yester-year. He points to me and says to them: 'Tell my friend what my nickname was at school!'

'Braintank!' they holler. 'Braintank!'

9

Braintank

To this day Kennedy is not sure where the money came from, but shortly before his eleventh birthday and after calm had returned to the areas where Rwandans lived, Francis decided it was time for Kennedy to learn. Although Tutsi boys belonged in the pastures, Francis wanted his boy to read the Bible, understand road signs in towns and write a letter if the need arose.

Kennedy remembers the day well. It started like any other. He rose before the crack of dawn, wrapped himself in his cloth, grabbed his stick and darted off to milk the cows. He then walked a kilometre down into the valley to fetch water. By the time he returned, the sun was already blazing over the African savannah. On the equator, night comes quickly and seems to envelop you like black satin, while at dawn the sun bursts forth from the night sky and within minutes ascends the stratosphere above the horizon.

Kennedy gulped down a chunk of cassava with milk and then washed himself. After Grandma was satisfied that her boy was squeaky clean, she gave him a white shirt and short pants to put on. Kennedy had waited eleven years to wear, as he puts it, proper clothes. And it was only because this was a special day: he was going to school.

Francis gave him a big hug, and shortly after six, Kennedy set off barefoot and ran the seven kilometres to school. He was like a hare, scampering along the well-worn *panya* roads, past clean-swept villages, through banana groves and up grassy slopes before bursting from the eucalyptus woodlands into the grounds of Bigada Primary School.

Kennedy remembers the loneliness of this first day, not just because his friends were far away roaming the savannah, but also because the other children were accompanied by their parents, who entrusted them to the teacher before saying goodbye. It was simply too far for Francis to walk, and he was unable to attend parent meetings too, which caused his grandson great distress.

There were several snags to Kennedy's education. Not only should he have started school long before then, but Francis also ruled that Kennedy would only attend classes two days a week. He was too old to look after the cows himself, which meant that Kennedy would have to be cattle herder for the other three days. As a result, the boy was often pelted at school for missing so many days. To complicate matters, education was in English, a language that Francis had outlawed in his home.

'That's how it was and that's how I accepted it. Mama and Papa sacrificed a lot to send me to school. Sometimes they couldn't afford to pay the fees and I would be sent home. Or I even had to skip a year because there was no money. Grandpa warned me that I had to be first in my class. He wouldn't tolerate any Muganda getting higher marks than me. Grandpa beat me if I didn't perform well at school. Grandma tried to intervene and said if it wasn't for me looking after the cows, we would have nothing to eat. Yet Grandpa was furious when any other boy outperformed me. He wanted to know why this other boy had better marks than me. He said I was a Tutsi from Rwanda, how could anyone beat me?'

There were only five Rwandans in the school and Kennedy says they were like a family, united against the onslaught of the Baganda pupils. It was still the reign of Milton Obote and although Bigada was a Catholic school, and discrimination therefore prohibited, the presence of Rwandans in schools was discouraged and frowned upon. The Rwandans brought sticks to school, which they hid in the eucalyptus woods during the day and took out again after school as they often had to fight their way back home.

'The Baganda came with food to school but even if they gave me and I had an empty stomach, I could not eat it,' recalls Kennedy. 'We were not allowed to eat outside of the house. Grandpa was too proud and said these natives shouldn't undermine us. I got beaten a lot those days. We were always running to school and raced other boys to see who's first. They locked the gate at eight. There was a teacher with a cane waiting for us. We had to lie down and they thrashed us. Sometimes you bled.'

It was Mr Rwabuduri Kahira – the only Rwandan teacher at Bigada Primary – who gave Kennedy the name Braintank. Rwabuduri was a Tutsi himself and became a father figure to the Rwandans in the school. Kennedy's appetite for learning was so profound that he leapfrogged from Primary 1 to 3, and a year or two later jumped another grade. Kahira understood why the boy couldn't be in school every day, and instead of beating him he ordered Kennedy to cultivate the gardens.

On the days that Kennedy had to bunk school, he took the cattle down the valley behind their homestead and drove them towards Gakoma Hill that in summer resembled a velvety green carpet, but during the dry seasons looked more like a parched and stubby doormat.

* * *

Rwabuduri Kahira is a stocky man with a weather-beaten face and the knobby, craggy hands of a seasoned cattle farmer. One of his eight children, a spindly girl of about twelve, pushes a glass of milk into my hands. Everywhere we go, however poor or rich people are, we are always offered milk, rich and sweet and deliciously spiced by the pastures of the south-east.

When the former Bigada Primary School teacher sees Kennedy, he shakes his head, opens his arms and clasps his old pupil in a tight hug before exclaiming, 'I can see I have done a good job, a very good job! I always knew this Braintank was going to excel!'

Rwabuduri, who has only a Secondary 6 certificate, left the teaching profession many years ago and now farms with 200 Ankole on 400 hectares of land. He immediately offers Kennedy a few cows should he decide to return to Uganda, the only condition being that he has to promise to continue farming with Ankole. More and more Ugandan farmers are switching to plump and hornless American Holsteins with their dappled white and black coats that can give up to twenty times more milk but are far more susceptible to disease. Traditionalists like Rwabuduri cling to their hardy longhorns.

He accompanies us to Bigada Primary, which is nothing more than a single row of classrooms built around an overgrown square. Both men agree that the school ground is unkempt and the buildings derelict and in desperate need of a coat of paint. The school is still run and funded by the Catholic Church, and head teacher Sister Alirwa Prisca welcomes Kennedy as a celebrity and promptly installs him as the guest of honour at a choir competition being held on the soccer field.

The sister laments conditions at her school: 'We have 550 pupils so there are up to ninety in one class. Sometimes they can't all fit into one room and they have to sit under that tree. And we have lots of orphans. AIDS is causing havoc and this is one of the most affected areas. The disease is consuming us.'

In the early 1990s, Ugandan president Yoweri Museveni was regarded as a new breed of African leader who aggressively confronted the AIDS epidemic sweeping the continent. He introduced wide-reaching and candid health education programmes, and HIV/AIDS cases among adult Ugandans dropped from an estimated 15 per cent in 1992 to roughly 6 per cent by 2004. But in that same year he made a U-turn, declaring war on condom use and promoting abstinence. Billboards advertising condoms were replaced by messages celebrating virginity, and condom ads disappeared from radio. Bigada Primary is a living example of that failed campaign, and two signs on the playground warn pupils: 'Say no to sex' and 'Stay a virgin'.

After Kennedy has recited his long walk to education, Sister Alirwa asks him, 'So Kennedy, don't you think you can help us to fund a solar system for the school? It will mean so much to the children.'

When he asks her how much it will cost, she mentions an amount of a few hundred thousand Ugandan shillings, probably a few thousand rand. He looks at me and says, 'That would be absolutely no problem. I'm sure we can raise that, can't we Jacques?'

I shake my head. For months afterwards, the sister incessantly phones Kennedy in South Africa to find out what has happened to her solar system. Every time he sees me, he wants to know: 'Can't you make a plan? That nun is a Catholic and I've made a promise.'

Eventually, a year after returning from Uganda, Kennedy sends a few thousand rand via Western Union to Sister Alirwa. His legacy at Bigada Primary School lives on.

10

Birth of a rebel army

The mid-eighties saw Uganda once again in turmoil. A former army general and minister of defence, Yoweri Museveni, took up arms against the dictatorship of Milton Obote. This conflict would ultimately not just change the destiny of Uganda but would alter the fate of every Rwandan in the Great Lakes.

Museveni belongs to the Bahima ethnic group. When he was a baby, his parents placed him on the back of an Ankole cow with a mock bow and arrow in a baptism ritual showing him in defence of the clan's herd. The Bahima are as 'cow-centric' as the Tutsis and the two show a close kinship. The Bahima were subjected to the same Hamitic myth as the Tutsis – tall, lithe, light skinned and more advanced – and were therefore regarded as superior to other 'Negroids' in Uganda. Like the Tutsis, they started believing in their own superiority.

Rwandans supported Museveni in their thousands. Obote in fact referred to his opponent as Rwandan. At the height of the conflict, nearly a quarter of Museveni's National Resistance Army (NRA) was Rwandan and several of his most trusted allies and officers were Tutsis. They utilised their *inyenzi* experiences from Burundi in the sixties to launch lightning-fast attacks against Obote's military installations from their hideouts and strongholds in south-west and northern Uganda.

In turn, the dictator reacted with counteroffensives against Museveni. In one such reprisal in 1983, 30 000 Ugandans were killed and more than a million new refugees created. Many of the orphans became *kadogos*, the child soldiers who swelled the ranks of the NRA. Across the continent, brutal crusades have spawned thousands upon thousands of little boys who have found shelter and food in the barracks and camps of armies and rebels.

At first, they act as scouts, cleaners, porters and runners – boys of the regiment – but as the adults die and platoon numbers dwindle, in order to repel attacks or embark on offensives the children are armed and pushed into a baptism of fire. Modern technology has made it easy for a ten- or twelve-year-old to handle a semi-automatic gun and children are generally fearless, don't comprehend death and don't yet value life. They are, in short, perfect soldiers.

In the early eighties, however, Museveni's militia had only 400 guns shared among 4000 troops. It was only after some ingenious raids on Obote's armouries that the NRA started making serious advances towards the capital.

Kennedy recalls: 'We all supported Museveni because he was the same as us Tutsis. I wanted to join myself, but it was very far to walk to the north to get to his bases. Other boys, even younger than me, became Resistance Army soldiers. I remember sitting with Grandpa with his transistor listening to BBC's Swahili service about Museveni's advances and Obote's defeats. When the batteries went flat, I had to run very fast to get the news in town and run back again to tell Grandpa. He would then tell everyone around us. It was very important because many Rwandans fought in that war.'

By the time the NRA captured Kampala in January 1986, Museveni commanded a motley army of 14 000 peasants and children, 4 000 of whom were Rwandan. Museveni took charge of a destroyed and almost desolate capital, carrying the scars of a country that had turned on itself since independence in 1962.

The shops in the old Indian merchant quarters had been laid to waste, their owners branded as aliens and expelled by Idi Amin. Kampala's churches, banks and business district had been gutted. Amin had killed the head of the central bank, the university's vice-chancellor and other 'anti-revolutionary' academics, as well as the Anglican archbishop and some of his 'liberal' clerics. Obote's rise to power had merely signified a change of guard as he continued on Amin's path of destruction. When Museveni took the oath of office in the pockmarked Parliament building, there were still corpses on Kampala's streets.

Many Rwandans were taken up in the new Ugandan defence force. Among them were the head of military intelligence, Paul Kagame, and the NRA's chief of staff, General Fred Rwigyema. Rwandan exiles were suddenly not *abagwira* – foreigners – any longer and they felt their future in Uganda was secure under Museveni. The Rwandan Tutsi cause, however, continued to burn in their hearts and in the next year the NRA spawned a rebel offshoot called the Rwandan Patriotic Front (RPF).

Thousands of Rwandan exiles had cut their military teeth in the NRA and, having defeated one dictator, they now peered across the border at Juvénal Habyarimana and his Forces Armées Rwandaises (FAR, or Rwandan Armed Forces) and started plotting their overthrow.

The formation of the RPF had been a secret and Kennedy says neither he nor his grandfather knew about the movement. However, not long after Museveni's rise to power, he invited Habyarimana in a gesture of good neighbourliness to attend a military parade in Uganda. Rwigyema was present, and Kennedy remembers Francis, who had his ear glued to the radio, saying to those around him: 'Can you believe it? Habyarimana is a general but Rwigyema is also a general! We now have a son who is their equal. I'm telling you now, we are going home. I don't know when, but we are going home! May I live to see it.'

* * *

Kennedy was almost sixteen when he wrapped up his primary school education at the end of 1987. By then, he was dreaming of 'becoming someone or a something someday'. Like most boys of his age, he wanted to be a doctor or a politician or a lawyer. Youngsters in Uganda generally don't aspire to become policemen (who are scoffed at and regarded as lowly), soldiers (there are far too many wars in this part of the world) or firemen or nurses (who are grossly underpaid and work in dire conditions).

Kennedy had passed his subjects with flying colours and yearned to know more about the earth's geography, the continent's history and those minuscule particles that make up every piece of matter on the planet. Although Francis was in favour of his grandson pursuing higher education, there was no money for school fees. Unless Kennedy could raise the money himself, he was destined to roam the plains with his cattle for the rest of his life.

At the beginning of 1988, Kennedy hit the bright lights of the big city for the first time. There was a Rwandan in Kabonela who sold cows to the abattoir in Kampala. He suggested that Kennedy accompany him to the capital to find an odd job that could pay for his school fees. Francis detested the thought of his grandson being exposed to Sodom and Gomorrah, but realised that it was his only chance of furthering his education. He gave Kennedy bus fare and, one morning, the boy boarded a bus.

'Was this your first bus trip?' I ask him.

'The very first. And I couldn't believe how we were flying through the countryside.'

'And what were you wearing?'

'My shorts and sandals. But not real sandals. Those ones they make of car tyre. I got real shoes only much later.'

'And what was the big city like?'

'Oh my God, it was unbelievable. I had never seen so many people and so many cars. I remember walking past the Parliament building and saw these guys with black suits getting out of black cars and walking into this very smart building. I realised they made the laws of the country and were very important people. I also wanted to be a someone one day. But to be that, I had to study.'

'Had you seen a television set by then?'

'Where? I saw one for the first time in Kampala in a shop. I never knew such things existed. When I saw a computer many years later, I thought it was a new kind of television set.'

'And what other things did you see for the first time?'

'Like electricity. I knew about it, but to think you push a button and the whole room lights up! Amazing!'

'And what about a girlfriend?'

'You must be joking. I was afraid of girls and it was against our culture as Tutsis to have such things. If you do it, you have to be secret. When you want to get married, you tell your parents and they arrange everything. I was too scared to approach girls. My first real girlfriend was the woman I married, and then I was thirty-something. But even then we didn't sleep together until after the wedding. Running after women is not in our culture. Having sex with a woman when you are not married is not done.'

I'm not sure how true that is and Kennedy may be an exception. Rwandans – both Tutsis and Hutus – don't have a rite of passage or initiation and so males often celebrate their coming of manhood by fathering a child, a contributing factor to the country bursting out of its seams and the high birth rate.

Kennedy stayed in Kampala for two months without finding a job. He waited for days at the ministry of education to see an official, only to be told that there were no bursaries available and that they couldn't assist him. He walked the few hundred kilometres back to Kabonela, sleeping on the way with various Rwandan families.

He grazed his cows for another month or two, but then realised that he was sixteen years old and unless a miracle happened he was going to die on the savannah. He told his grandfather that he was going to try again to get into a school. Before he left, he visited his mother, who was living in a village across the furthest mountains. It was the last time he would ever see her. Not long afterwards, she and her family packed up their belongings and returned to their ancestral village in southern Rwanda.

* * *

Kennedy left the cattle in Dominique's care and started walking, this time to the administrative centre of Rakai, where the district education authority was based. The 150-kilometre or so walk took him three days to complete.

Despite their new status under Museveni, Rwandans still found it almost impossible to gain access to secondary education. The locals' general resentment of their southern neighbours had also increased. During the military campaign, Museveni had promised citizenship to Rwandans who fought alongside him. Once he entrenched his power, however, he went back on his undertaking and there was a strong government lobby to bar Rwandans from land ownership and remove them from the armed forces.

When he arrived in Rakai, Kennedy set up camp in front of the office of the district education officer, a former NRA captain by the name of Karusigarira. 'I slept in front of his office and told his secretary that I'm not leaving until I've seen the big man. I don't think I ate, maybe a piece of cassava but nothing more. I wasn't hungry because I was thinking too much of this meeting. This was my last chance.'

After three days, Karusigarira called in the knobbly-kneed boy, offered him something to eat and engaged his story. Kennedy told him everything: about the upheavals in his life, his hard upbringing and life of poverty, and his incredible quest and thirst for knowledge. Karusigarira said he didn't have money to pay Kennedy's school fees but he had a big banana farm with many goats. Kennedy could work on the farm over holidays and weekends and, instead of paying him a wage, Karusigarira would fund his schooling and enlist him in boarding school. I'm not sure what the district education officer's motivation was for offering Kennedy this arrangement, because he could have simply ordered the boy's attendance at school. He was probably seeking nothing less than cheap labour for his banana farm.

'I wanted to jump through the roof,' recalls Kennedy. 'I was going to school! It was the middle of the year but I said to Mr Karusigarira that I'm ready to start tomorrow and I promised him that I'll pass at the end of the year. I sent a message to Grandma and Grandpa that I'm back in school and that they must not worry. Karusigarira gave me a black-and-white uniform and the next day, I was a pupil at Kabale Senior Secondary School. It was a school on a hill, surrounded by banana plantations and many, many goats.'

He was one of a handful of Rwandans in the school and, once again, was a victim of teasing and bullying. An older Rwandan boy protected him in the boarding house. Every Friday afternoon, a truck picked up Kennedy and other boys and took them to the farm where they cultivated the land. 'I worked from six in the morning until six at night,' he says. 'I wasn't used to cultivating and had sores on my hands. I felt lonely. I had no love and no care. I was another man's slave.' His daily diet, on both the farm and at school, consisted of porridge and sweet potatoes.

II

Nyinawumuntu

It was the start of the new school term at Kabale Senior Secondary School when one of Kennedy's Rwandan compatriots passed him a message. The boy had gone home for the holiday but Kennedy had stayed behind to work on the farm. The boy told him that his sister, Nyinawumuntu, had been kidnapped and forced into marriage. A chill ran down Kennedy's spine. 'Bride-kidnapping' or *guterura*, which means 'lifting', is an ancient, barbarous and sadistic custom among Banyankole and Bahima pastoralists that, although outdated in many areas, still happens to this day in Uganda.

By the time Kennedy heard of Nyinawumuntu's snatching, it was several months after the fact. He then had to wait another month or three before he was granted a weekend off. He borrowed bus fare and travelled to the village where Nyinawumuntu was condemned into bridal servitude. When he arrived she had just given birth to a baby. She was fourteen years old.

Guterura is a shrouded, unspoken practice whereby girls anywhere between the ages of twelve and eighteen are snatched by prospective husbands, kept in captivity in kraals, raped and forced into marriage. Once the 'damage' is done, the new husband sends representatives to the bride's parents to negotiate compensation, usually of a cow or two.

Guterura often causes bitter feuds and fights, especially when families try to rescue their daughters before they are violated. Once the girl has been raped and therefore 'used', there is little that the aggrieved family can do but to accept compensation. Ugandan police, as badly trained, under-paid and corrupt as anywhere else on the continent, claim they find it impossible to persuade kidnapped girls to testify against their husbands, and perpetrators are seldom prosecuted for kidnapping and rape.

The architect of Nyinawumuntu's kidnapping was a relation of the paedophile and a close friend of Kennedy's grandmother, Kamabera. The children had grown up in front of her and had often been to her kraal. It was therefore not strange when she invited Nyinawumuntu to visit her. The unsuspecting girl walked into an ambush. Men grabbed her, tied her up and delivered her to the 'groom', who lived many kilometres away.

Two days after Nyinawumuntu's disappearance, the man's family visited Francis and Kamabera to inform them that their granddaughter was happily married and to negotiate damages. Kennedy says he was too disgusted to even ask his grandparents what his half-sister's innocence and life had been worth.

'My grandparents were too old to protect Nyinawumuntu against such evil things and it was easy to snatch her. There was nobody to look after her,' he says. 'The husband was a very old man and I wanted to kill him. But there was nothing I could do because they were married and he had paid damages to Grandfather. I think it was two cows or something like that. I left her and didn't see her again for many, many years.'

Nyinawumuntu was twenty when her kidnapper husband died, leaving her with two children. Shortly afterwards she married a Muslim by the name of Yassim Matsiko.

* * *

It is early morning and the sun is blazing. The day unfolds with Kennedy emerging from his hotel room decked out in a natty grey suit with a red tie and shiny, pointy black shoes that he later tells me he bought when he was admitted as an attorney in the High Court.

'Why are you dressed as though you're about to address a judge?' I want to know. 'We're only visiting your sister, and she lives in a rural area way off the main road where we'll have to negotiate washed-away and rutted dirt roads.'

His BlackBerry and Samsung Galaxy in hand, Kennedy mutters something about it being a Monday morning and he feels like wearing 'something different'. His jacket stays on for the entire day.

Kennedy resembled a London male model on a photo shoot throughout our Uganda junket. I warned him when we departed from O.R. Tambo International Airport that his dress sense was going to evoke images of prosperity and lead to endless pleas for financial aid. And so it does. This one has to keep a child in school, that one wants another cow and another needs a few hundred thousand shillings to add a hectare to his plot.

'My sister asked me last year at my wedding for 550 000 shillings to help their firstborn to study, but I just ignored the question because I cannot help them. She has two kids from her kidnapped marriage and many more from her second marriage. The husband has always refused to look after the first two,' he tells me.

The season is changing and the southern countryside where Nyinawumuntu lives is turning from shades of green to tones of bronze and tan. The hillsides are littered with cream- and carrot-coloured brick homesteads, topped with shiny tin roofs – an indication of the newfound wealth that is popping up around the country. Driver James is convinced that the majority were illegally grabbed, acquired or dished out to Museveni's cronies and allies. Many of the farms are adorned with herds of American Holsteins, which causes Kennedy to snigger in disgust as he mutters time and again: 'Look at them. These are not real cows.'

I have never got the sense that Nyinawumuntu and Kennedy are close or that she played any significant role in his life despite their being no more than two years apart. When I ask him about her, he explains that she was always in the kitchen helping their grandmother to tend to the milk, cook food and clean, although every Saturday they walked fifteen kilometres together to a forest and back to collect firewood. Kennedy remembers this because the wood was far heavier than he was.

For some reason, Nyinawumuntu was never baptised and therefore had just the one name until she got married. It is odd that someone as religious as Francis never christened his granddaughter. It may have been because she was illegitimate, but then so was Kennedy. She attended primary school for two or three years, but then dropped out to help Kamabera full-time in the kitchen. Throughout our many hours and days of interviews, Kennedy mentioned her only a handful of times, and then mostly in connection with the kidnapping incident.

* * *

Nyinawumuntu is a comely woman with high cheekbones, glowing café-au-lait skin and a full mouth. She and Yassim farm a few hectares of land against a hill near the southern town of Masaka. They have four Ankole, a banana plantation and half a hectare of maize. The sole adornments against the yellowing wall of their two-roomed house are two election posters of Museveni that read 'Peace, Unity and Transformation for Prosperity'.

Minutes after we arrive, milk and fried calf's liver are served. Kennedy shows them pictures of his newborn, upon which Nyinawumuntu shrieks with delight, observing that the child's pouting mouth proves that only Kennedy can be the father and she the aunt.

Yassim – who has six fingers on one hand – has not worked for nine months and walks with a stick after his leg was smashed in a motorcycle accident. He claims the local hospital hardly functions, forcing him to turn to a traditional healer on whom he has spent a fortune. He is planning to build a new home for the family – the bricks are already piled up at a site he has cleared further up the hill – but because of the accident he has had to postpone the new venture.

Besides the two from Nyinawumuntu's forced marriage, the couple have eight children of their own. Yassim has an additional three from his previous marriage. Nyinawumuntu's first two children have left home, but the couple still has eleven hungry mouths to feed. The oldest is twenty and the youngest two.

'So why don't you guys do family planning?' Kennedy asks.

'I see many people in hospital that took those pills they give you not to have babies,' replies Yassim. 'They get sick and some are even operated on. So you can't take them, it's too dangerous. The hospitals here give us fake pills or those that have an old date. So now we reproduce, so God helps us.'

They say the standard of the state primary school in town is so poor that they removed the children and enlisted them in a private school down the road. In Uganda, all primary school children write the same national exam, and year after year those in the state school fail. The couple has four children in the private school and tuition is costing them a fortune.

Unsurprisingly, Yassim observes that Kennedy looks like a very important person who sits in a big office. One of their children, Feisal, who is in Secondary 2, chips in and says he wants to be a big man one day too.

'And like whom?' I ask him.

'The president. I want to be president one day.' He points at Museveni's poster against the wall. The president is wearing a black suit with a white shirt, similar to Kennedy's.

'So can't you take over the education of my firstborn and pay for him to finish his mechanic training? He needs another two years of training and then he can start his own business and look after us,' Yassim adds.

Kennedy explains that he has just become a father and started his own business where he has yet to establish himself, but Yassim perseveres:

'Can't you just give us one million shillings to help us put Farook through his training?'

'That is only a few hundred dollars,' says Kennedy and looks at me. 'I'm sure that's not a problem. I am sure that between me and Jacques we can raise it.'

I don't say anything.

'Hey, Jacques? Don't you think?'

Kennedy tells Nyinawumuntu he is trying to establish how their grandparents died. She turns sombre, shakes her head and says, 'The love we got from them was unbelievable, so I hope they died peacefully in Rwanda. I think they lived just for us and when both of us were gone, they packed up and went back to die.'

We will know soon, says Kennedy. Dominique phoned earlier this morning to say that he has traced Kennedy's surviving aunt, who lives not far from Kabonela. She holds the key to the riddle that has preyed on his mind for most of his life.

12

The *Inkotanyi*

The image I have of Kennedy at school is one of a reserved, introverted and conscientious boy who had few friends, studied far too hard and didn't socialise or participate in sport. 'To go back to Rwanda was driving me in everything I did,' he says. 'I never thought about women or cars or money. I finished high school without even knowing what a woman was. It wasn't my priority. Anyway, without education, how could you get that? I was just thinking of going home and studying. After that I would make money and then think about women. There was no girl I was in love with and no girl that I found pretty. Those things were for mature people ready for marriage. The Rwandese girls I saw as my sisters. We regarded the Baganda as inferior so I didn't even look at those girls. I didn't drink beer and I didn't smoke. The Baganda boys would escape from the dormitory and go to the pub in town. I never had a childhood. I grew up with the problems of an adult. I missed out on my childhood because I was too busy surviving.'

Kennedy passed his year-end exam in 1988 with flying colours, despite having been in school for only a few months. He skipped Secondary 2 and advanced to Secondary 3. When he went home for a brief visit over Christmas, he found Francis – then seventy-one years old – exhilarated and talking non-stop about going home.

'He said we were all members of the Patriotic Front and we were going back to paradise. I believed him. I was awake at night and thinking of how I was going to take my grandparents home and that we would all be happy together. Rwanda would be a place with many cows where it would be easy to study. I wasn't happy then because I was a slave and far away from home. But at least I had hope.'

In 1989, a new teacher who had just completed his studies at Makerere University in Kampala arrived at Kabale Senior Secondary. He was secretly an RPF office bearer and it wasn't long before he was having meetings with Kennedy and the other Rwandan boys. Although the military offshoot of the RPF, the RPA, had not yet officially been formed, there was much talk of returning to the motherland through the barrel of a gun. The RPF was already known as the *Inkotanyi*, a name taken from the conquering nineteenth-century *mwami* Kigeli IV, whose 'sword-name' was *Inkotanyi-cyane* – the tireless combatant.

'I said I'm ready to fight but the teacher said it's not time yet. We must in the meantime recruit members and mobilise the Rwandan community. From that day on, the RPF became the parents I never had. I thought they would look after me and help me to fulfil my dreams. How wrong I was.'

Kennedy was appointed youth leader of the RPF cell in his area. He had to spread information about the RPF and Rwanda to the youth and enlist as many as he could. 'I was sleeping in the dormitory, but I didn't really attend school. I was mostly in the forest and on the hills mobilising young Rwandans. I promised them the RPF was taking us back home and that they had to be ready to sacrifice, because force would have to be used and the organisation needed all the support it could get. I told them about 1959 and how our parents and grandparents were driven out of the country. We shouldn't allow them to die in a foreign land. I bunked school more and more and pretended to be sick. My marks suffered, although I still passed. There was little time to study because I also had to work on that farm to pay my school fees. Liberation first, then education,' Kennedy tells me.

There's a proverb in Kinyarwanda that was extensively used during the recruitment drive: '*Wima igihugu amaraso, imbwa zikayanywera ubusa*' – if you deny the homeland your blood, the dogs will take it for free. The RPF had an alluring eight-point programme to guide the struggle home, which Kennedy learnt by heart and passed on to others. It promised to establish genuine democracy, eradicate corruption and promote social welfare, among other things. Around the world, tyrants, despots and führers have ascended their thrones with equally flowery vows that are soon washed away by the rivers of blood besmirching their reigns. Rwanda was and is no different. Nearly two decades after coming to power, the RPF's eight-point programme isn't worth the paper it was written on.

By this time, the blood pact between Museveni and his Rwandan compatriots was in tatters. The Ugandan president had broken his promise of naturalisation. He blocked the promotion of Rwandans in his armed forces and forbade refugees from owning land. For the exiled Rwandans, going home had become the only permanent solution to their plight.

Museveni surreptitiously supported their cause because he had had enough of Rwandan refugees in his country.

By 1990, military preparations for an RPA invasion were in full swing. Nobody spoke openly about it, but everyone knew that a blitz was being contrived in hushed voices behind closed doors in the officers' quarters at defence HQ in Kampala. Museveni was in an awkward position. On the one hand, he could not be seen to allow his territory to be used as a staging ground for the planned overthrow of a legitimate neighbouring government. But on the other hand, it allowed him to export his refugee problem back whence it came. He therefore observed developments with a blinkered eye. Museveni removed Rwigyema as his deputy minister of defence in November 1989, allowing the Rwandan to spend all his energy fine-tuning when and where to pounce.

Across the border, the dictator Habyarimana was cognisant of the imminent threat to his regime. He boosted his armed forces with new weapons and asked the international community to deter the potential aggressors. He further attempted to defuse the situation by announcing in July 1990 that Rwanda would return to a multiparty system and by appointing a committee to discuss the return of refugees to their homeland. The RPF scoffed at his overtures of conciliation.

* * *

On 1 October 1990, 4000 *Inkotanyi*, under the guise of the RPA and commanded by the charismatic Rwigyema, invaded Rwanda. The date was planned to coincide with a UN conference in New York that both Museveni and Habyarimana would be attending. All the RPF combatants were NRA troopers who had slipped out of their barracks the night before the invasion, exchanged their official uniforms for bush fatigues and assembled close to the Rwandan border with their weapons. With initial surprise on their side, they pushed into northern Rwanda.

On the second day, calamity struck when Rwigyema was fatally wounded – seemingly by his own men. Rumours circulated that he had been executed following a power struggle, although the RPF ascribed his demise to crossfire or sniper fire. Controversy rages to this day over Rwigyema's fate, although evidence emerged fifteen years after the incident that he was slain by two of his own lieutenants. They in turn were hauled in front of a firing squad and executed. This was a precursor of what was to come in later years when the RPF broke apart, turned on itself and devoured its own.

Paul Kagame, at the time Museveni's head of military intelligence, was on a course in the United States, but rushed back home to take command of the RPF. Their initial military success was short-lived, however, as Habyarimana appealed to his friends, French president François Mitterrand and Zairian president Mobutu Sese Seko, to come to his rescue. Within a day or two, France dropped French paratroopers at the airport, a warning that Paris was not going to allow this piece of Francophonie to be upset by Anglo-speaking marauders from the north. Habyarimana's FAR repelled the RPA offensive and the rebels regrouped in the Virungas in the north-west of Rwanda, where they changed their tactics and embarked on a guerrilla war.

'When we heard of the invasion on the BBC World Service, we celebrated. Can you imagine how proud we were of our boys who were fighting and killing the enemy?' asks Kennedy. 'It didn't matter that we had to fall back, because we now had an army that was taking us home. I wanted to join to help to liberate my country, but they said no, stay where you are and organise and recruit.'

The RPF/RPA was now a brazen rebel army. It established a training base called Juru Camp in Nyakivara, south-western Uganda, only a stone's throw from the Rwandan border.

Inside the homeland, the invasion had calamitous consequences for Tutsis. Days after the offensive, Habyarimana staged a mock attack on Kigali and blamed the gun- and cannon fire on the *inyenzis*. He seized the opportunity to round up, imprison and kill Tutsis. In the north of the country, the civil war displaced hundreds of thousands of Hutus, who were dumped in refugee camps. The dictator initially had little fear of the Tutsi cockroaches hiding out in the forests in the north-west of his country. His army was disciplined and well trained, and he could rely on the support of his allies in Brussels and Paris. (Having said that, the supposedly elite Zairian presidential guard was given its marching orders back to Kinshasa because its members were drunk and unruly and got involved in incidents of raping and looting.)

'I attended one class and then ran off to mobilise the youth,' remembers Kennedy. 'Thousands joined the RPA because we convinced them that paradise was waiting for them across the mountains. By then I had made up my mind to stay in school and pass matric so that I could go to university in Rwanda. I wanted to be someone so that I could contribute to my country and look after my grandparents. How could I have known that the RPF, who was my father and my mother, would kill me in the end? We believed them!'

In the year to come, Kennedy was groomed for his future role in the rebel army: that of an intelligence soldier, formally known in the RPA as intelligence staff or IS. They were among the elite: highly respected and feared, often better educated and trained than ordinary infantry troops. Few soldiers in the RPA had progressed beyond primary school education. IS members had to be able to at least read, write and speak Kinyarwanda and Swahili – the latter being the lingua franca of the RPA.

Kennedy was dispatched on several probing missions to collect intelligence. One such assignment, which caused him to miss a week of schooling, took him back to his country of birth, Burundi. Because Rwanda's northern border was a war zone, RPA recruits inside Rwanda had to cross surreptitiously through the southern border and into Burundi. From there they had to make their way through Tanzania to the Ugandan border town of Mutukula, where trucks picked them up and drove them to the training camp at Nyakivara. Habyarimana had dispatched his own intelligence units to Burundi to counter the RPA's recruitment drive and several conscripts were poisoned in that country. Kennedy's task was to alert them to be careful and then embark on a recruitment drive through Tutsi refugee camps. He made a brief stop in Mushiha, where he was born – by now nothing more than a collection of huts where dirt-poor peasants scrounged the earth in search of something to eat. It was nonetheless fertile recruitment ground.

* * *

Kennedy saw his grandparents for the last time at the end of 1990 when he went home for Christmas. By the next year's festive season he would be finished with matric and on his way to war. He remembers his last visit for two things: Grandpa babbling like a stuck gramophone about their boys in the bush liberating paradise, and how old they had become. Both Francis and Kamabera were grey and sickly.

'They had a hard life and it was showing. They had old-age diseases but they didn't go to hospital or get pills. How were they supposed to get there? They used traditional medicine that others found for them in the forests. Grandpa wanted to die in Rwanda, but I wasn't sure that he was going to make it.'

Francis swelled with pride when his grandson told him he was working for the RPF. Before Kennedy left, they went to church and prayed together. Kennedy was about to embark on his final year of secondary school, and both men must have known that unless a miracle happened and the tyrant Habyarimana embraced the rebels and invited them back to their country of birth, the young man was heading for war. Francis embraced his grandson and waved him goodbye with his stick.

For more than twenty years, Kennedy has been haunted by the unknown fate of the people he called Mama and Papa, and probably riddled with guilt for not making more of an effort to see them before going to war. Throughout his life, and even now as we journey through Uganda, they have been foremost in his thoughts.

It is June 2011 and we are turning up a two-track, red dirt road near Kabonela in search of his aunt Getruida Mukayuhi and, hopefully, some answers.

13

Aunt Getruida

The old woman is sitting under an avocado tree in front of her two-roomed brick house cutting banana leaves when we stop. The hum of village life freezes and people fall silent when we get out of the car. A man pushing a bicycle with aluminium milk pots strapped to the back stops in his tracks and gazes. Children who a second before were scattering up and down the dirt road turn and for a few seconds stand motionless before they cautiously edge closer to our car.

Getruida looks me up and down as I get out. It is unusual for a *muzungu* to be paying her a visit. Her eyes shift to Kennedy on the other side of the vehicle. The banana leaf spills out of her hand and flutters to the ground, her mouth falls open and an expression of stupefaction sweeps her face. She stumbles to her feet, squeals as though she has seen a phantom and scampers around the back of the house, disappearing for a moment or two before peeking around the corner.

'O Jesus, O Jesus, God is great! God is great! This is Gihana! Gihana Kennedy!' she screeches before throwing herself into his arms. Their eyes are moist when they pull away, look at each other and embrace again. Finally she says, 'You are a big, big man. You look just like your grandfather!'

Getruida, named after a wife of a *mwami*, is one of Kamabera's nieces and used to live a stone's throw from Kennedy's grandparents. In line with custom, Kennedy called her Mama as well. He assumed that she had returned to Rwanda after 1994 and perhaps died. She is already over seventy years old. The mother of thirteen children, she has outlived ten of them.

A throng of children – and some adults – accompany us into the house. Some are Getruida's grandchildren, while others are determined not to miss any of the action. It has all the elements of a village thriller: a *muzungu*, the homecoming of a smartly dressed war hero and a wailing woman. There are only two chairs in the living room and they are designated to Kennedy and me. Getruida plonks herself down at our feet and looks at me warily. 'And who is this *umunyamahanga* [foreigner]? Is he *Umutalyiani* [Italian]?'

Kennedy bursts out laughing. Above my head is a Roman Catholic calendar – dating from 2008 – with a photograph of a hoary and grizzled Pope Benedict XVI on the cover. 'This *muzungu* looks just like him,' Getruida remarks.

One of her neighbours, a stick-thin old woman with a creased face and crooked teeth, seizes her opportunity and says to Kennedy: 'Thank you for bringing the white man here.' Through Kennedy, she tells me that she's in dire need of help. A few years ago a crippled young woman, who was also mentally disturbed, pitched up at her door. The woman was Rwandan and living in a refugee camp in Tanzania. She fled after being raped and was now pregnant. The woman gave birth to twins, but died shortly afterwards. Getruida's neighbour points to two tots in rags, about four years old. 'These are the children,' she says, 'and I can't look after them any longer. Because they are Rwandan, they don't qualify for any benefits. Can you help?'

It takes some time and more pleas for help before Getruida asks Kennedy, 'And so, did you come about your grandparents?' He nods his head, takes off his glasses and, for the next few minutes, he listens while she speaks. He utters '*yego, yego*' (yes, yes) from time to time. He then gets to his feet and, with tears rolling from his eyes, embraces her. It takes a while before he regains his composure.

After the 1994 genocide, he tells me, Francis and Kamabera announced that they were returning to Rwanda. They sold their land, packed what they could and started walking back to paradise. Getruida and some of her children accompanied them. Once they crossed the border, they settled in the north-eastern town of Matunguru.

Francis died peacefully less than a year later and Kamabera perished shortly afterwards. 'I buried both of them,' Getruida tells Kennedy. 'They were at peace. It was only you that they wanted to see again. But then old age overcame them and they passed on.'

Getruida returned to Uganda when some of the cows died of a strange disease. By then, most people accepted that Kennedy had perished in the war. She, however, maintained that the boy was far too clever to get himself killed. She was convinced he had gone to Canada to find his treasure and would return one day.

When we leave a while later, Kennedy says: 'Today this *mgogo* [grandmother] who I love so much has soothed my soul. God bless her.'

* * *

We spend our last days in Uganda on an island in the middle of a crystal-clear lake in the south-western corner of the country with the hazy outcrop of the Virungas beckoning in the distance. We sleep in safari tents on the edge of the water and eat fresh-caught tilapia and freshly slaughtered chicken. Kennedy admits after the first night that he hasn't closed an eye and that he's scared of the menacing dark and the proximity of the Rwandan border. He asks management for a padlock to lock his tent at night.

Kennedy leaves Uganda disillusioned, despite having found closure around the passing of his grandparents. He feels overwhelmed by the desperation of people like Dominique and Nyinawumuntu and his inability to help them.

I realised while in Uganda just how remarkable Kennedy's achievements are. He so easily could have continued to graze Ankoles on the African savannah, multiplied carelessly and condemned his offspring to empty stomachs. Or tried his luck as a *bayaye* on the streets of Kampala, Nairobi or Kigali, scrounging for handouts from do-gooders. Or turned to petty crime, scraping an existence from bag snatching or car break-ins. Others with his experience and skills have become hired guns and expert hijackers or house burglars. He could have stretched himself out with a bottle of glue on a park bench or capitulated to cheap Nigerian imports on the streets of an African metropolis. But he didn't. He knew the only way out of his plight was an education, and so he enlightened himself.

I had underestimated how difficult it was for someone like Kennedy to 'catch up'; to make up for time lost and wasted. He boarded an aeroplane for the first time only a few years ago and has hardly ever stayed in a hotel. When we go to a restaurant, he shoves the menu across the table and says, 'You order for me.'

Although an astute individual, as a result of his earlier life his worldly grounding is limited and even debilitating. When we drive through the glorious Queen Elizabeth National Park in western Uganda, the tanned pastures are filled with elephant, giraffe and buffalo. Kennedy wants to know why there are no cows grazing alongside them. They will eat very nicely here, he contends, and it's unfair that only wild animals are allowed to nourish themselves on the sweet grass. 'When we come to power in Rwanda,' he adds (he regards himself as a future justice or foreign minister), 'we'll cut down the forests so that cows can graze there.'

I am horrified but realise that Kennedy, despite having grown up with wild animals, has no grasp of nature conservation. Look at those elephants, I counter, aren't they magnificent? Yes, but why can't cows graze there as well? And what happens to the elephants, I want to know? They will graze with the cows. But herders and people will move into the park and eventually the wild animals will disappear and the tourists will leave with them, I say. By the time we track chimpanzees a day or two later, Kennedy is an avid conservationist; the forests in Rwanda are safe.

And yet, he can hold his own in any company. A few days after we return to South Africa, I meet him at a luxury hotel in Pretoria, where there is a UN conference on the expansion of the number of permanent seats on the Security Council. I call Kennedy – decked out in a black suit and red tie, tablet in hand – out of the conference and we settle in the bar with a glass of wine. Minutes later, a blubbery guy waddles up to us, shakes Kennedy's hand and heaps praise on him for the insightful questions he asked during the debate. Kennedy introduces him as his friend, the ambassador. I leave the two a while later in deep conversation about the failures and oversights of the council. Kennedy is on home turf, razor sharp and insightful.

Once we grasp where he comes from, it is much easier to understand why in the next chapter of his life he acted as he did.

And the miracle that he managed to escape from it.

14

Xavier

A quick detour to the land of a thousand hills. Rwanda is blanketed by waves of soft, emerald hills bathed in a balmy, sunny haze. Every steep slope has been tamed right to the top by man's patient toil; homesteads cling to the muddy slopes. The map size of the country is deceiving because it's much bigger than it looks in an atlas. Think of Rwanda as a crumpled piece of paper. If you uncrumple the paper and iron it out on a flat surface, it increases two- or threefold in size.

On Rwanda's north-western border with Uganda and the Congo stands one of Africa's most stirring sights: the volcano-studded Virunga mountain range that straddles all three countries and houses a national park in each. The reserve on the Rwandan side was founded in 1925 and is the oldest national park in Africa. This chain of six extinct and two active volcanoes is linked by fertile saddles that were formed by solidified lava flows. The crown jewel in all of Africa's national parks, its interrelated and intertwined natural habitats contain the largest number of mammals (its most revered dweller is the mountain gorilla), birds and reptiles and have more endemic species than any other place on the continent. The two-million-hectare strip of dazzling geography holds alpine forest, moorland, tropical forest and savannah. The first white man to encounter mountain gorillas was a German officer, Captain Robert von Beringe, in 1902. He promptly shot two.

For all its beauty, the Virunga range is also the bloodiest spot on the planet. It lies at the epicentre of man's greatest beastliness to man: the 1994 Rwandan genocide in which 800 000 were butchered, and the Congo civil wars of 1996–1997 and 1998–2003 in which millions – figures range from three to seven million – perished. It is a miracle that the 650-odd (that is, if you include the 300 in the Bwindi Impenetrable National Park in Uganda) mountain gorillas with their piano-shaped backs that roam its slopes and loll around in its coiled and twirled undergrowth have survived the human ring of fire that fences them in. It's a credit to authorities and conservation organisations in Uganda and Rwanda that this critically endangered population has, over the past two decades, not just stayed stable but increased.

On the Congolese side, they remain at the mercy of AK-wielding renegades who continue to plunder the area for its riches. The pressing question is whether there is enough leg-, elbow- and headroom for both man and beast.

The areas around the volcanoes are among the most densely populated on the continent, with around 450 people per square kilometre. People crowd in because of the fertile soil, generous rainfall and a high altitude that keeps mosquitoes and tsetse flies at bay. Fields of cassava, beans and bananas are cultivated right up to the park's edge. Rwanda's pressing population and socio-economic problems are nowhere more visible than at the roof of Africa's unruly rift.

When genocide occurred in 1994, Rwanda had a population of between seven and eight million. In 2012, it had risen to twelve million. At the current rate of increase, the population will double every twenty-five years. The African average is thirty people per square kilometre. In Rwanda, the average is 230.

The most dominant and highest volcano in the Virungas is Mount Karisimbi, perched at a height of 4507 metres on the western edge of the park. One of the towns loitering in the shadow of the volcano and halfway between the north-western provincial capital of Ruhengeri and the resort town of Gisenyi is Mukamira.

It's a rather nondescript and drab settlement with a medley of stores, a church, a school and a few prefecture buildings. About a kilometre from Mukamira on a black-soiled dirt road strewn with boulders and lubricated with mud is a tiny settlement. This is where Xavier Mushatsi Niyonzima Ngabo (his surname means 'God is everything'), son of Edward Mushatsi and Beatrice Ndebereho, was born in 1973. They are Tutsis from the Banyiginya clan.

You might wonder why the birth of Xavier is important. While interviewing Kennedy, I asked him what it was like for Tutsi children growing up in Rwanda. 'I don't really know,' he said. 'We heard a lot about how bad it was, but we didn't really know.' I asked him who I could speak to in order to find out more.

'You must speak to Xavier. He would know. He was right there.'

Xavier is an old friend of Kennedy. They are around the same age, joined the rebel army at the same time and fought side by side in one of the civil war's most ferocious battles. They lost contact in the mid-nineties. Almost a decade later, Kennedy was at Johannesburg's international airport with a friend when he bumped into Xavier. He had come to South Africa a few years after Kennedy. The two resumed their friendship but then lost contact again; I'm not sure why. By the time I spoke to Kennedy, he had heard that Xavier was in Australia. We started searching for him, and a few months later discovered that he was still in South Africa.

When I called him, he asked me to send him an email. I told him who I was and that I was writing a biography on Kennedy. He still wanted me to email him, which I did. Nothing. I called again. He wanted me to email him questions. I told him that wasn't going to work; I needed to see him in person. After that, he didn't answer his phone for about two weeks, but eventually agreed to see me. I was given an address in Brakpan where I was to pick him up.

* * *

It's a winter's morning in July 2011 when I venture to Brakpan, a scruffy mining town about forty kilometres east of Johannesburg. I take the highway to Springs, passing an industrial area before a stretch of black-burnt veld announces the turn-off to Brakpan. To Johannesburgers, Springs is generally known as the sticks. Brakpan, however, is the sticks' sticks.

Many years ago, gold mines thrived and Brakpan was a booming community. Since then, shafts have closed down and many townspeople are impoverished. The town is trapped in a time warp with fading art deco buildings, a host of loan sharks, a ramshackle hotel, cheap furniture shops and 'No jobs' signs pasted in windows. Drug dealers, human traffickers and illegal immigrants have moved into downmarket suburbs where houses are cheap to rent. They use Brakpan as a base to sell their narcotics, girls or labour to Johannesburg. This is where Xavier shares a house with other Rwandan immigrants.

He's a tall, athletic man with a square chin, high cheekbones and a coal-black complexion who speaks English with a distinct French accent. When I ask him where we shall talk, he suggests Carnival City.

'Why on earth do you want to go there?'

'Because I see that place every day but I have never been inside.'

It requires a vast vocabulary and agile writing skills to do justice to the depravity of this gambling complex perched on the outskirts of Brakpan next to the highway and adjacent to worked-out mine dumps. An architect who could only have been on an acid trip gone wrong – his licence should be revoked – conjured up a circus theme and the exterior is a mishmash of cone shapes and vivid obelisks that soar into the sky. It's intended to mimic a fête that promises much ebullience in the form of money-spewing gambling contraptions. The walkway to the entrance is paved with tiles that flaunt an engraved array of jackpot winnings over the past few years.

The inside is no different from similar gambling dens dotted around the country. Devoid of natural light, the lasting impression is one of forlorn and hapless souls perched in front of twinkling machines. They are aunties from the East Rand, *magogo* (grandmothers) from the township, miners just off night shift, redundant workers and worn housewives. Almost in a state of stupefaction, they shove coins into the ravenous beast's belly with one hand while the other yanks its shaft. They recap this movement over and over till they've glutted the swine and have to plod back through the revolving exit doors to confront their broken dreams. The sniggering face of a clown waves them goodbye. I loathe casinos. My godfather shot his wife and then turned the gun on himself after losing everything on Sol Kerzner's roulette and blackjack tables.

'And what do you think?' I ask him after we've shuffled into a phoney Italian trattoria that serves Xavier a meaty *bosveld* breakfast and me rubbery scrambled eggs.

'It's an amazing place. Really amazing.'

I give him a previous book I've written that contains three chapters about the Rwandan genocide. He starts reading, and after a silence of fifteen or twenty minutes he nods his head and says: 'I can see you know about my country.'

I ask him where he grew up. He says his village is a stone's throw from Karisimbi. I ask him the question that probably everyone who meets him does: So did you see lots of gorillas when you grew up? (As though it is a Sunday-afternoon walk in the park to spot them.) He laughs and says he has never seen any of those animals. They knew they were somewhere in the forests but were told to stay away and leave them for Europeans who paid lots of money to see them. But have *you* seen the gorillas, he wants to know?

I tell him I've been up the volcanoes three times. The first was in the late nineties, but halfway up our armed escort received a message that it was dangerous and we had to turn around. A few years on, I spent a birthday with the gorillas and two days later went up again.

And how was it, he asks with unmistakable pride in his voice. Fantastic, I say. The air was heavy and humid and we were plodding along a muddy footway that snaked through tangled vines and creepers where things skulked that bit, nibbled, gnawed, stung, spat, scratched, pierced, gashed and attacked. By the time a warden announced with a '*shht*' that we'd made it to one of the world's most revered sights, my knees were quivering and I was hanging on to my walking stick that I'd embedded in the mud in front of me.

We heard their soft, contented grumbles before we saw them. In a temporary clearing in the bush, a silverback stared at me in a semi-upright position, his sinewy arms held like Ankole horns in front of him. I gawked back in a state of bewilderment. Two apes eyeballing one another. No one who looks into a gorilla's eyes – gentle and intelligent – can remain unmoved. What a shame that not more Rwandans can visit their fellow primates in the forest.

* * *

Xavier is the eldest of four children, but his deceased uncle's six kids lived with them, which in effect meant he had nine brothers and sisters. His father was once a cattle farmer, but he sold most of his cows and became a dressmaker in town.

Edward Mushatsi and his family had fled to neighbouring Congo during the 1959 Hutu uprising. His brother was killed in the revolt, but after a few years the family returned to the north-west and was, according to Xavier, leading a 'cautious' life, mindful and wary to avoid unnecessary attention.

'The situation was not too bad,' says Xavier. 'There was enough to eat and drink, but there was not money for anything else. Papa had to work very hard to support us. Mama also had to try to sell things to get money for food and clothes. She had some education, he had very little.'

Virtually all their neighbours were Hutus and for the first few years of his life, Xavier was unaware of who was what. That was until he went to school to register, where teachers asked him if he was Hutu or Tutsi.

'They said the Hutus must stand in one line, the Tutsis in another. I got confused. Where am I going to stand? My friends also got confused. Some Tutsis joined the line of the Hutus because that was where their friends or neighbours were. When you are kids, you don't know about these things. We were just neighbours and our parents didn't teach us about Hutu and Tutsi. The teacher said we must go and ask our parents what we are. I asked my father and he got angry and he wanted to know what kind of teaching this was. He said, "Tell them you're a Tutsi".'

That, says Xavier, is how the hatred started.

15

Juvénal and Agathe

Many Friday afternoons, Xavier watched a sleek, black motorcade as it slithered past Mukamira. It was whisking President Juvénal Habyarimana and his wife, Agathe, to their weekend farm in the district. The president was a native of the area and the north-west was his refuge and stronghold. Many of Rwanda's most fanatical Hutu ideologues and extremists were born in the areas around the volcanoes and rose with Habyarimana to positions of influence. It was from here that they spewed their racial lava and plotted the extermination of the Tutsis.

Habyarimana, Rwanda's former army chief and minister of defence, had overthrown Grégoire Kayibanda in a *coup d'état* in 1973 – the year in which Xavier was born – and declared himself president of the Second Republic. Kayibanda was later starved to death while under house arrest. Many of his closest confidants and high-ranking supporters were imprisoned or deposited in shallow graves.

For the next twenty-one years, Habyarimana ruled Rwanda with iron-clad oppression. He declared his Mouvement Révolutionnaire National pour le Développement (MRND; National Revolutionary Movement for Development) the only legal political party. Dedicated to the enrichment of the northern Hutu, it blamed Tutsis for the impoverishment of the remaining populace.

With each passing year, Rwanda increasingly became the dictator and his family's private domain. Habyarimana had evolved into Rwanda's new *mwami*. Most of his cabinet ministers and the top echelons of the police, the army and the elite presidential guard were Hutus from the north-west. His relations and cronies acquired huge properties and businesses, and a percentage of the aid money that the West poured into Rwanda was skimmed into the ruler's coffers. Ethnic quotas and ethnic identity cards were maintained and there wasn't a single Tutsi *bourgmestre* (mayor) in the whole country. Only two Tutsis sat in a Parliament of seventy members.

Habyarimana had created a bureaucracy that controlled even the remotest corners of the country. Rwanda was divided into ten prefectures run by government-appointed prefects, then into 145 communes, and finally into cells or *collines*. Identity cards included place of residence and citizens had to get formal permission to change address. Each commune had to submit reports to the state security agencies about births, deaths, the movements of its inhabitants and newcomers. Every name on every list was accompanied by the person's ethnicity. Residents were encouraged to keep an eye on one another and report suspicious people and events.

The international community, seduced by their opulent living quarters in Kigali, the year-round balmy weather and the lukewarm water of Lake Kivu lapping at their colonial villas, turned a blind eye. Instead they praised Habyarimana's tribal rule for bringing stability and plonked more aid money into his coffers. Switzerland sent more development aid to Rwanda than to any other country. France, Belgium, Japan, Canada and a host of others counted Kigali as a preferred charity. The hills were alive with pale aid workers and Western do-gooders who flocked to this dark but stable spot to lend a hand to the sons and daughters of the soil.

Xavier went to the same primary school that Habyarimana had attended and, when he was in Primary 4, the dictator paid a surprise visit to the institution. He joked with the children about how he had been beaten by the maths teacher and reminded the Hutus among them what a good career the military was. Xavier says it was as though this spurred on the teachers and they started teaching the children Hutu liberation songs composed in honour of the 1959 uprising.

'One of my Tutsi friends said to me: "Do you understand what we are singing? It is how they drove the Tutsis out of the country and killed our grandfathers. Listen to the words: *We are killing them, we are killing them. The king is gone, the king is gone*",' recalls Xavier. 'The teacher was happy and telling us to sing even louder. That was how I came to know that in 1959 something very big happened, and that it was about Hutus against Tutsis. The teachers in the end played a very important role in preparing for genocide.'

When he was twelve years old, Xavier learnt the official history of the 1959 uprising. The teacher pointed at him and said: 'Stand up!' After the boy had risen to his feet, the teacher continued: 'That is what a Tutsi looks like! Look at his nose! Their king and queen killed Hutus, took our land and treated us as slaves.' Xavier says after that his relationships with Hutu children deteriorated, and during break the Hutus were in one group, the Tutsis in another.

'We were taunted at school: "Ha-ha, look at your nose! It is ugly! You look like a Belgian!" Even my friends started changing because the teachers were brainwashing their minds. That is how they prepared them for genocide. They taught them that we were the enemy. They would say to us: "Hey Tutsi, you are the minority, your grandparents have killed our grandparents!" It was nothing but hatred. Even back home, we were not playing together that much any longer. We prayed together in church every Sunday but that was about it. The poison was changing their minds.'

* * *

Rwandan children had to write a national exam in Primary 8 that they needed to pass in order to gain access to secondary school. They were required to state their ethnicity next to their name on the exam papers. Tutsis generally failed and were barred from acquiring a secondary education. In line with this, Xavier flunked his exam, as did his cousin who was first in his class and today holds a doctorate in chemistry. In fact, not a single Tutsi in the school passed. Those with middle-income or wealthy parents resorted to private schooling, while poorer Tutsis cultivated the land – much like Hutus used to do in colonial times – or became unskilled labourers.

Xavier was destined to toil the black, loamy soil or barter his body as a lowly hired hand until his father one day announced: 'You're going to school. I'm sending you to Zaire [now the DRC] to further your education.' Edward Mushatsi had a sister in the North Kivu province and she was prepared to take his firstborn in and put him through secondary school. Xavier was fourteen when he made his way to the town of Massissi in Zaire. He was armed with a new school uniform, pens and pencils, and school fees buried deep in his pocket.

He travelled by bus from Mukamira to Gisenyi on the shore of Lake Kivu, Rwanda's biggest lake. The result of ancient volcanic spewing, its surface sheens in the equatorial sun with a metallic, silvery hardness. The lake, virtually without fish life, is lodged on a methane gas bed and some scientists have warned that the town could be annihilated in the event of a gaseous eruption. A lane lined with colour-bursting bougainvillea and fading colonial villas brought Xavier to the border post and the Zairian provincial city of Goma on the opposite side.

I'm not sure what Goma was like in the summer of 1986 when Xavier passed through. Magnificently located on the shore of Lake Kivu, its climate warm and generous, one can only imagine a city sprinkled with once-grandiose colonial edifices that have long lost their lustre. So desirable was it once that the kleptocrat Mobutu Sese Seko kept a palace (long since destroyed) on the lake shore for occasional visits.

That was then. The Goma I visited in the wake of the 1994 genocide and in the early twenty-first century to search for mountain gorillas was a dire shanty town, its main boulevards annexed by AK-toting men in camouflage uniforms who answered to no one. Goma is one of the most dangerous cities in the world, and not just because it is at the mercy of mutineers that loot, rape and kill in the name of the FDLR, the MLC, the AFDL, the RCD or the CNDP (I'm not joking, they all exist in the eastern Congo), but also because it is positioned in the shadow of seething Mount Nyiragongo, one of the world's most active volcanoes. The volcano spewed molten rock towards the city in 1977 and 2002, killing hundreds and forcing thousands out of the city. Seismologists are anxiously awaiting the next mortal emission.

When Xavier passed through in 1986, the city still paraded a semblance of order and Mobutu's presidential guard was holding the reins – and pocketing the bribes. Xavier's father instructed him to keep his school fees in one pocket, his palm-greasing offerings in the other.

In Mobutu's Zaire, corruption went all the way to the top of the ladder and down again. Trapped at the bottom were the peasants – the farmers in the fields, the hunters in the forests and the traders on the streets. For their right to get assistance from a public servant, have their children enrolled in school, obtain medical care or get a policeman to investigate a crime, they had to pay *matabiches* – bribes. State officials were seldom paid and, in order to maintain some semblance of a middle-class lifestyle, they were forced to recoup lost earnings from peasants and foreigners. Most of the elite not only remunerated themselves generously, but were entitled to 'commissions' from government contracts and demanded gifts from investors. Their roly-poly physiques filled the first-class seats on the Air France flights to Paris, where they gorged on pâté de foie gras while Madame indulged at the haute couture salons on Avenue Montaigne.

The leeches started sucking at Xavier the moment he crossed the border. 'I got arrested the first time I entered Congo and had to pay a bribe. Nobody got paid, not the teachers, the police, the civil servants or the soldiers. Everybody wanted money. Mobutu told them to look after themselves and to see to their own survival. Even the teachers wanted something. My aunt had cattle, so every day I took the teachers a can of milk. Others paid cash. That was how it worked, everywhere. When I went to register, my aunt had to pay a little something before they accepted me in school. It was a way of life. If you want something, you pay. If you want a service, you pay.'

Xavier loved life in Massissi. It was peaceful, his aunt and her Rwandan Tutsi husband had a big farm and he excelled in school, even skipping a year. He went home for holidays, soliciting lifts on trucks and paying sweeteners to the soldiers, policemen and immigration officials on the way.

In July 1990, Xavier went home for the main holiday (Rwanda was then following the European school calendar). He read an exposé in a government newspaper which reported that Tutsis across the border in Uganda were plotting to return by force to Rwanda the *mwami* who would again enslave Hutus. He knew this meant trouble. Xavier asked his father what was going to happen. He responded by saying that they'd be okay, but he wanted Xavier to continue his schooling in Goma because it was much closer to home.

The new school year was hardly under way when the RPA invaded Rwanda from its hideout in Uganda.

Habyarimana used the RPA invasion and the fake attack on the capital to evoke the spectre of a common enemy: the Tutsi. If any Hutu was in any doubt about the murderous intention of their long-nosed countrymen, the first few days of October 1990 saw to that. Every Tutsi was considered an RPA *ibyitso* – an accomplice – and therefore a potential rebel. In the days that followed the mock assault, 8 000 Tutsis were rounded up. The invasion gave the extremists who had been disgorging their ethnic emissions for more than a decade a perfect excuse to give life to their fantasy of a Tutsi-free Rwanda.

Many say that by then Habyarimana was no longer in charge. That dubious honour belonged to his spouse, Agathe, a member of a distinguished and noble Hutu family. In contrast, the president was regarded as a peasant. There were even rumours that he wasn't a true Rwandan but had been born in the Congo. Agathe, some family members and a mob of fanatical and despotic Hutu ideologues became known as the *Akazu* (literally 'little hut'). They infested every labyrinth of economic and political power, from where they promulgated the seeds of hatred and division, calling Tutsis foreigners who had to be sent back to their Nilotic homeland.

* * *

Over watery cappuccinos on which floated blobs of cream, and with one-arm bandits clanging in the background, Xavier says to me: 'I'm now going to tell you a story which I have spoken about only once before. This is now the second time I am telling it.'

'And why don't you talk about it?' I ask.

'It is too painful.'

16

Kajelijeli and Boniface

Carnival City is hardly the venue for a testimony of murder, mass slaughter and depravity. The image of Xavier sobbing as he recounts the slaying of his family against the background of mankind engaging in one of its most odious exploits will forever be etched in my mind. I interview Xavier for two days at Carnival City and then insist that we find an alternative venue.

We land up in a sports bar, adorned with false rocks. It isn't a good idea either – it is Saturday and South Africa is battling Australia in a Tri Nations rugby Test match. By lunchtime, the bar is a bawling jumble of probably the best and the worst that Brakpan has to offer. They are in their green-and-gold jerseys, knocking back Klippies and Coke and Springbokkie shooters – layers of Amarula cream and peppermint liqueur. Among the patrons are a midget couple with a lanky teenage daughter, a guy without legs in a wheelchair doing wheelies down the aisle and a pissed bloke who smashes into a glass door. A waitress wants to know if Xavier is okay. Tears are trickling down his cheeks.

* * *

Soon after the failed October 1990 rebel foray, Xavier received a letter from his father advising that he should no longer go home. The area around Mukamira was swarming with soldiers and every Tutsi was being interrogated about their suspected links with the rebels. Edward had been picked up and, along with a truckload of Tutsis, taken to a nearby military camp where they were detained, interrogated and tortured for a month. Xavier's uncle, Manzi, who was a teacher in a private school, had also been arrested and driven away. A few weeks later, a policeman visited the family and informed them that he was dead. They never received the body or any explanation for his death. The FAR threw a ring of steel around Rwanda to prevent youngsters from leaving the country and joining the rebels. Tutsi men in the north-west were put under house arrest and had to get police permission to move from one commune to another. Edward had to give up his job in Mukamira, depriving the family of his vital income. Xavier didn't join his family for Christmas that year. He maintained contact with them through his cousin, Charlotte Nyirashene, who was slightly younger than him and also in school in Goma. Tutsi women and children had more freedom to move around and Charlotte travelled from Mukamira to Goma every day, not just to attend school, but to keep Xavier up to date about events in his home village.

After the failed offensive, the battered RPA regrouped and exchanged the open savannah of north-eastern Rwanda for the swirling grey fog and rain-drenched slopes of the Virungas in the north-west. Despite being cold, wet and poorly equipped, the rebels launched a night blitzkrieg in January 1991 on Ruhengeri and seized the city for a day or two until government troops and French paratroopers repelled them back to their hideouts in the forest.

The rebel attack was again ill-advised. The rebels inflicted heavy casualties on civilians and opened the gates of Ruhengeri prison, freeing many prisoners and enrolling them as fighters. They then embarked on a looting spree and, according to human rights organisations, 400 people were forced out of their homes to help carry the loot. As the rebels retreated back into the Virungas, many of these civilians were killed. Another 150 Hutus were fatally wounded along the way.

To this day it remains unclear what Kagame's military strategy behind the blitzkrieg was, other than to loot, kill Hutus and swell his ranks with criminals. Can you blame ordinary Rwandans for regarding the rebels as marauding thugs who had no regard for human life and who wanted to reinstate Tutsi supremacy and subjugate Hutus? Kagame and his top command regarded Hutus with the same mistrust and disdain with which Habyarimana and his extremists regarded Tutsis. The outcome of all this political conniving and misgiving could only have been calamitous.

By the beginning of 1991, the seeds for genocide had already been sown and were ready to germinate. Although the training of the Hutu militia, known as the *interahamwe* – those who stand/fight together – had not yet commenced, the *Akazu* had decided to probe the readiness of the Hutu populace to kill their Tutsi countrymen. The *bourgmestre* of the Mukingo commune in Ruhengeri, Juvénal Kajelijeli, was a member of the *Akazu* and a maniacal bigot who openly called for 'real' Rwandans to send the long-nosed, plundering looters back to where they came from. He commanded and trained one of the first militia killing squads in Rwanda. After the genocide, he was hauled before the International Criminal Tribunal for

Rwanda (ICTR) in Arusha, Tanzania, convicted of genocide and sentenced to forty-five years imprisonment.

Within hours of the rebel attack, Kajelijeli had mobilised his militia and embarked on a killing spree against the Bagogwe, a quasi-nomadic Tutsi subgroup that lived in the area. Nobody is sure how many were killed because the victims were earthed up in mass graves, but the body count ran into the hundreds. Throughout the commune, militia swept through villages looking for Tutsi men.

Kajelijeli, bolstered by police and the army, personally led his band of killers. Some of the captured men were taken to the military camp for interrogation and torture; others were summarily executed and buried in mass graves in the bamboo forests at the foot of the volcano. Most Tutsi men and older boys took cover in the forests and in the mountains. At night, they sneaked from their hideaways and went home to fetch food and to see if their families were still alive.

The *Akazu*'s stronghold in the north-west was the ideal theatre to test genocide. It was an area at war; a militarised zone in which every citizen was expected to contribute to safeguarding the country. Hutus nervously scoured the volcanoes in fear of rebels pouncing from their hideouts to seize their land and subjugate them into bondage. Mukamira specifically was shrouded from probing eyes and surrounded by an ocean of Hutu zeal. The *Akazu* had a simple recipe for genocide: on the hills, in the villages, in the tilled fields, in the town squares, on the savannah and in the markets, Hutus had to kill their Tutsi neighbours, friends and relatives. The regime was too poor to build Auschwitzes and gas chambers; it was up to the rabble to do the dirty work.

* * *

A day or two after the attack, army officers arrived in Mukamira and organised the males into paramilitary units to guard roadblocks and patrol. Edward, one of his brothers William Karahamuheto, and their Hutu neighbours Boniface, Fati, Jean-Paul, Bandora and two others were assigned to roadblock duty. Edward had grown up with these men. Together they had toiled the land, shared calabashes of beer and prayed every Sunday. When Boniface got married, Edward's father had paid his *lobola*.

'These were our brothers and sisters and we never discussed politics,' says Xavier. 'Boniface's land and our land bordered one another and I saw him and his family every day. I ate in his house and he drank beer in ours. He was father's friend and brother. We depended on one another.'

'Did you notice anything different when you went home during previous holidays?' I want to know. 'Did he change?'

'I afterwards realised that Boniface and my father didn't see each other that much any longer. The children were also not playing with us. Maybe the poison had got to their heads. But my father said nothing. The last time I saw him he said we must stay out of politics and we will be fine. I said, "Dad, but in Congo the Tutsis say all of you here are going to be killed." He said, "Don't listen to that nonsense."'

We don't know if any of Edward's neighbours were among Kajelijeli's execution apprentices, but what we do know is that when Edward and William reported for roadblock duty at the end of January 1991 their neighbours were ominously hushed and drunk. Their eyes were rolling up in their sockets and their legs were wobbly. They stood with machetes and *ubuhiris* – sticks studded with nails – in their hands. There was usually an armed policeman or soldier present at the roadblock, but that night there was nobody. It was dark and gloomy; mist tossed and tumbled from the volcanoes and swept through the lowlands.

'Hi guys!' Edward greeted.

They didn't answer.

'What's going on with you tonight?'

They didn't answer.

'Is anything wrong?'

Boniface stood half a metre in front of the others. He turned his head towards them and uttered the words 'Let's go to work'.

17

Beatrice

Charlotte Nyirashene failed to attend school for more than two weeks and Xavier didn't know if his family was okay and had survived the turmoil in the north-west. When Charlotte eventually showed up in Goma, she was unusually quiet and reserved. When Xavier saw her he wanted to know: 'Is everything okay?' She nodded her head. 'Is my family okay?' She nodded her head. 'Are you sure?' She nodded her head.

That afternoon, he walked with her to the border post. She stopped and turned to him. 'Xavier, I came to give you a message. There's something I have to tell you. I was afraid to tell you this morning but now I have to. Your father is dead. They killed him. I know it's difficult but you have to accept it. Please be strong.'

Xavier and I are sitting in the bar in downtown Brakpan with a horde of bawling locals in the background spurring on their green and gold. He holds his head in his hands and sobs uncontrollably. It takes some time before he looks up at me and says, 'I am crying now, but back then I was strong. I didn't weep, I didn't do anything. I just stood there.'

Xavier eventually asked Charlotte who had killed his father.

'It was the neighbours who killed him,' she said. 'They cut him with a machete at the roadblock.'

'It was Boniface?'

'Yes, and Jean-Paul and Fati and Bandora and the others.'

'So how did he die?'

'It was very terrible. They cut him and left him next to the road. He cried and screamed, but we couldn't help him. He only died on the second day. I'm sorry, Ngabo, but you must be strong.'

'And where is my father now?'

'We don't know. After he died, they took his body away. They buried him somewhere. We don't know where.'

'So Papa was just lying on the street?'

'Yes, but we couldn't do anything. Tutsis were getting killed and we had to stay inside our houses.'

Before Charlotte left, she handed Xavier a letter from his mother, Beatrice. *Your father is dead*, she confirmed. *But please, son, I want you to stay where you are. Don't come home. There are no Tutsi men moving around. If you come now, they will think you're a rebel soldier. They will kill not just you, but all of us.*

'I sat next to the road with the letter in my hand,' remembers Xavier. 'I don't know what I was thinking. My head and my heart were empty. There was nothing left, nothing to do, nowhere to go. It was as though my life had ended.'

Beatrice also asked Xavier to promise her that he wouldn't join the RPA. *You are our firstborn and we want you to live. So stay where you are. Go to school so that you can be a somebody one day.*

'So what did you do?' I ask.

'At that moment,' Xavier replies, 'I knew I was going to war. I was going to the RPA. If you die in the war, at least you die as a patriot. In Rwanda, you die for nothing. Like my father you die like a dog. Our lives were worth nothing.'

* * *

In the days that followed, Xavier was consumed by the mental picture of his father lying screaming next to the road. He had to know what had happened. He waited for two weeks for calm to return to the north-west. One night, he slipped across the border into the Virungas, crossed the saddle of the volcanoes and took the *panya* roads back to Mukamira.

'I saw soldiers on these little roads. They were everywhere. But I had grown up there and knew exactly where to walk. I could walk them with my eyes closed in the middle of the night.'

He knocked softly on the door and his mother opened. She pulled him inside and threw her arms around him. While she lit a candle and prepared a meal of potatoes, Xavier went to greet each and every brother and sister.

'My brother was five years old and his name was Jean de Dieu. It means "John of God". When I woke him up, the first thing he said was: "Xavier, do you know who killed Papa? It was Boniface! You must be careful, Xavier, because he was going to kill you as well. Please don't let Boniface kill you." That's what the boy said. Can you believe it? He was five years old and even he knew who had killed our papa! Everybody knew who had killed my father. But nobody could do anything. There were six killers and they all grew up with us. Boniface's house was a few hundred metres away and he was there, sleeping in his bed. I knew they were devils, but what could I do?'

'Didn't you feel like killing them?' I ask.

'No, I didn't think about it. It was anyway impossible. I couldn't kill all of them. If I killed them and ran away, they would kill my family. And we couldn't escape. Even the *panya* roads were blocked.'

'What were you going to do?'

'I didn't know. I didn't even hate them. It just gave me lots of pain. I was wondering how it was possible for this to have happened. My father had helped them for a long time, how could they do this? We were a community, we were religious. We believed that Jesus would save us and the Bible told us to love another. That was the way we lived. I was very confused.'

Beatrice told Xavier exactly what had happened on that fateful night. When Boniface gave the order to attack, three men pounced on Edward and three on William. Edward got an *ubuhiri* blow to his head and fell down. William – who recounted the full story to Xavier many months later – managed to get away with two neighbours in hot pursuit. The other four – including Fati and Boniface – pounced on Edward, slashing him with machetes and bashing him with *ubuhiris*. He was screaming for help and the killers dragged him from the road to a small eucalyptus grove where they continued to cut, slash and bash. When he stopped moving, they were convinced they had finished him and went home. The next morning, however, Edward regained consciousness and pleaded for help and howled in pain and agony. His cries for help cut like a sharp knife through the village the whole day.

'And why didn't anybody help him?' Xavier asked Beatrice.

'There were soldiers and militia everywhere. I tried to leave the house to go to him but they chased me back and said, "Woman, if we see you again, we'll kill you and your children." I even offered them money. They took it, but still wouldn't let me go to him.'

'Why not?'

'It was the orders of the *bourgmestre*. Nobody should help him.'

'So Papa was just lying there crying?'

'Yes, the soldiers and militia walked past and laughed at him.'

'And Boniface and Fati and the others?'

'I heard they were drinking and were happy.'

The next morning, Edward was still alive and conscious, but weak and dying. His screams had given way to whimpers and whines. His very best friend in the village was a Hutu man by the name of Muhire. At around nine, Muhire emerged from his house and walked past the militia and policemen, whom he greeted politely. He walked up to Edward, kneeled at his side, put his hands around his throat and strangled him. When he was sure Edward had stopped breathing, he slowly got up and walked home.

Many years later, Xavier visited Muhire to thank him for his incredible act of mercy. Muhire, then an old man, shook his head and told Xavier he couldn't remember anything. He didn't want to get involved. Tutsis were then again in charge and it was dangerous for a Hutu to admit that he had killed a Tutsi.

'Where is Papa buried?' Xavier asked his mother.

'I don't know. They took him away.'

'We must find his body and bury him properly.'

'Yes, we must, but I don't know how.'

'Boniface must know. Do you see him?'

'I see them but there is nothing I can do. They pretend there is nothing wrong.'

At five that morning, Beatrice asked Xavier to leave. 'Please go now,' she said, 'before anyone discovers you.' He said goodbye to her and left. It was the last time he would see his mother, brothers and sisters. Xavier again followed the *panya* roads and, by the time the sun had broken through the foggy haze and shone on the pearls of morning dew, he had safely crossed the border and was back in Zaire.

* * *

Many years after the genocide, I'm still dumbfounded by the fact that many victims awaited their fate so submissively. The Hutu ideologues, extremist politicians and hardliners in the armed forces openly spewed their ethnic hatred. Tutsis knew that lists with their names had been drawn up, that militia had trained to exterminate them and that their neighbours had been incited to lend a hand in their demise. Why did they stay, I ask Xavier?

'I asked my mother exactly that. She said the neighbours would see them leaving and call the militia or soldiers to cut them off before they got to the border post. There were nine children. How do you leave quietly? She thought if they just stayed without making a noise, they would survive.

There were no men of fighting age left in the house, so maybe they would be left in peace.'

Perhaps the victims had been mentally prepared for death long before the genocide started. They had lost the will to fight. There were instances where the killers told their victims to sit down so that they could be killed. They sat down. Victims would often plead not for their lives, but for the grace from their killers to be allowed to pray before dying or to be chopped up in the privacy of their homes rather than on the street.

Back in Goma, Xavier wrote a letter to his mother that Charlotte delivered. *Please accept that I am going to the front line,* he wrote. *I have no choice to join because my father has died for nothing and I don't want you and my brothers and sisters to die innocently as well. I am nineteen years old and I know I still have three years to do at school. But for now I have to go and fight. Enough is enough. Don't worry because God will protect me and God will protect you and He will guide me to finish school and be someone some day. Don't send any more money because I won't need it. God bless you and I love you very much.*

A few days later, Charlotte handed him a letter from Beatrice. It was short and to the point: *I cannot stop you. Please go, but come back. We need you. You are the man in the house. God protects you and my heart is with you.*

In late 1991, Xavier boarded a bus that took him north alongside the Virungas to the Zaire/Uganda border to join the rebels. He wasn't scared or even apprehensive. His only thought was for his mother.

'Can you imagine the life that this woman had led?' asks Xavier. 'The suffering she'd been through? For years after the killing of my father, she had to pretend that nothing was wrong. She had to live side by side with the killers and she saw them every day. The children went to the same school and everybody went to the same church where they prayed together and asked God for forgiveness.'

Beatrice was the first Tutsi genocide widow in Mukamira. More than two years later, when the country descended into hell, she was also the last Tutsi in the village to die. After all her children had been massacred and every Tutsi in Mukamira annihilated, gangly *interahamwe* with darting bloodshot eyes dragged her from her hiding place.

By then, she begged them to kill her.

18

Rebels with a cause

'Welcome to the place where children cry but mothers can't hear.'

These were the words that ushered Kennedy Gihana and a host of other recruits into the ranks of the RPA upon arrival at its Juru Camp in Nyaki-vara in south-western Uganda in early 1992. The instructor who spat them out was a veteran of Yoweri Museveni's military campaign against Milton Obote and probably understood what it would entail to mould a haphazard bunch of cattle herders and school leavers into a rebel army capable of routing a seasoned and well-equipped professional army that was boosted and supported by a European superpower. And he only had a month in which to do it.

A few days after Kennedy received his matric results at the end of 1991, he and three Rwandan Tutsi school friends made their way to Nyakivara to join the RPA. Before embarking on his military venture, he waited for his matric certificate, which he carefully wrapped in plastic and kept on his person. Not only had he passed all his subjects, but he had earned distinctions in several. He was convinced that the certificate was his passport to a better life and higher education once they had liberated Rwanda from the Hutu extremists.

Kennedy left for the army still dressed in his school uniform and carrying his sole possessions: a bag of books and a set of bed sheets. It was a year since he had last seen his grandparents and there was no way to say goodbye or send a message. He knew that once in the army he would be forced to break all contact with any family and friends.

'That guy in uniform asked me what was in the bag. I said my sheets and my books. He shook his head. He said in Swahili: "So do you think you came to sleep here? If you want to sleep go back to your mother and sleep there." Then he kicked my bag! They took it and I lost everything. I had only my matric certificate. Then I said to myself: What is going on here? This is like a slave camp!'

The same day the new recruits arrived, they were each given a bag and told to fill it with stones. Then they were ordered to start running with their bags. Some collapsed. Thirsty and exhausted, those still on their feet were told to run two or three kilometres down the hill to a dam to fetch water. They were instructed not to drink the water. Some couldn't resist and indulged, and minutes later collapsed with excruciating stomach cramps and diarrhoea.

'The water in that lake was green! Green like a leaf!' recalls Kennedy. 'You drank it and you died the same day. It was like poison. But it was hot and we were thirsty but we couldn't drink any water. I started getting scared. There were soldiers around us with guns guarding us. We were like prisoners. Some guys tried to run away but were caught, brought back and beaten severely. There was no way out. This was another world I had entered, a world I wish on no one else.'

Everyone who set foot in Juru seems to recall the toxic brew in the only dam within walking distance of the base. When I ask Xavier Ngabo if he remembers it, he bursts out laughing and says, 'I nearly died! I got there and fell on my knees and started drinking. Then I got cramps all over and I thought I was going to die. But God was with me. I survived. Others didn't.'

Xavier had arrived at Juru a month or two before Kennedy. Soon after his training commenced, someone shouted his name. When he swung around, he looked into the welcoming face of his uncle, William Karahamuheto, the man who had been with his father that fateful night. William had managed to escape to Uganda and eventually made his way to Nyakivara.

'His one ear was cut off by the machetes of the killers,' Xavier tells me. 'When I saw him I said, "Uncle, do you think you will be able to deal with these army things?" He was already an old man, in his forties, but he was still very, very strong. We were both motivated by what had happened to my father. The others were told about the coming of genocide, but we had already tasted it. That was why I wasn't scared of the army. My mind was too strong.'

That night, after another day of running, drilling and political lectures, Xavier and William sat down in a quiet spot where the older man told him in detail what had happened at the roadblock that night.

'I wanted to know from my uncle why he didn't help my father. He said there were too many and all he could do was to run. I asked him what could have changed the minds of the neighbours. He said there was a rich businessman in Mukamira by the name of Rukabo who was an extremist and paid the neighbours to kill my father. He told them if they killed the rest of the family as well, they could keep our land. By then, I had already accepted that my family was going to die. They were not going to survive the hatred. My mother was going to die. My brothers and sisters were going to die. My uncle said his family was going to die too. But we must survive so that we can bring justice for all of them. I said, "Uncle, but we are going to war and we might die too." He said no, we must be strong and we must live. We made an oath to one another that after we had liberated our country, the killers of my father would pay. We knew who they were and my uncle was a witness. We were going to take them to prison. That was when the RPA became my father and my mother. I gave them my body and my energy.'

* * *

By the middle of 1992, the rebels occupied an extensive enclave of northern Rwandan territory stretching from the Akagera National Park in the north-east to the Virungas in the north-west. A week after Kennedy arrived at Juru, the RPA shifted their training camp and headquarters to Gishuro, just across the border in rebel-controlled Rwanda.

The camp was nestled between soaring mountains and shielded against aerial bombardment or attack – and there was water gushing down the slopes! The camp was about four kilometres from the frontline and the rifle and cannon fire in the distance reminded the recruits that they were about to enter a world where life was cheap and death ever lurking.

One of the first things the recruits did at Gishuro was to dig a network of *adaches* – holes or caves. They were about two metres deep and covered with branches. Soon the whole front was pockmarked with a series of *adaches* that not just protected the troops against mortar attacks, but could be used as makeshift cells to incarcerate captured enemy soldiers, spies and deserters.

In the mornings when it was still dark, the recruits were woken up. They crawled out of their caves and started running, maybe ten kilometres, during which they sang patriotic and liberation songs.

RPA, go forward.
RPA, be strong, have hope.
Habyarimana, where are you going to hide when the RPA comes?

After running, the recruits drilled. If there was food, they ate maize porridge; if not, they had a glass of hot water before continuing with exercises. The rest of the day was spent target shooting and receiving lectures on war tactics, followed by more running and drilling. At night, they sat next to fires, patrolled and sang more patriotic songs until they crept back into their *adaches*. When it rained, the caves were mudbaths, but the young soldiers made beds with grass, put down their heads and slept. After a while, everything – even the armouries – was in caves, some dug by prisoners of war who were executed afterwards in order to keep their locations secret.

'If you tried to escape or leave the camp, the punishment was death,' says Kennedy. 'Some tried to escape because of the harsh conditions, and they were captured and our commanders told us they were killed. We knew it could have happened to us as well. Once you are there, you stay there. You drill, salute, run, what, what. Sleep for one hour and then they wake you up. You only eat pap [maize porridge]. They beat you. You have to be strong. Some did not survive. I passed, of course. But many did not. I think God helped me. I grew up hard and now it helped me. Some died of cholera and the hard training. The commanders hit us with batons. If you dared to cry, they beat you more. If you got tired when you ran, they hit you again. The training prepared you for everything. At three o'clock they would wake you and put you in a drum full of water. It was cold, you were shaking, but they put you in the water. They taught us to resist torture. They did to us what the enemy could do to us.'

By the time Kennedy received his AK-47 and uniform – he got no shoes; he had to wait to take a pair from a dead enemy soldier – a month later, Xavier had already had his baptism of fire. He recalls: 'They attacked us. We fought back. We had to keep our trenches. Then we drove them back and followed them. We shot them. Many. We dug new trenches and then we advanced. We were so motivated that some of the wounded in the sickbay were crying that they wanted to continue fighting. They came to the front with their bandages. "Ha, where's my gun?" It was unbelievable. I was praying a lot, every day. A lot. But I felt strong because I was liberating my country.'

* * *

When the rest of Kennedy's compatriots were sent to the frontline, he stayed behind as he'd been selected to become both a military policeman and an IS member – both feared and revered units in the RPA. As a school-boy, Kennedy was groomed for his future role in the rebel army when he not only recruited support for the RPF, but gathered information in Burundi. He was educated, and could read and write. Not even Kagame could boast a matric certificate. Kennedy received further specialist train-ing that included intelligence gathering, interrogation and discipline.

According to Xavier, 'the other soldiers were afraid of intelligence because they watch you. If you step out of line, they're on to you. It is not any soldier who could become IS. Their education was high. They were the clever people. They did the dirty work. You don't know what they are doing, and they don't tell you. When you want to attack, they have to tell you the numbers of the enemy. They have to know everything. They were the ones who dealt with the prisoners. They asked them the questions. You are sometimes more scared of intelligence than you are of the enemy!'

Throughout my interviews with Kennedy, I try to marshal a mental picture of him during his early army years. No photographs of him from this time exist. Xavier and Kennedy only became friends in around 1996. 'He was a tall, sharp man and very clever,' describes Xavier. 'He knew how to make an assessment. He spoke like a politician. He was also very com-mitted. He was the model of the RPF soldier.'

19

Silent killers

The world over, from apartheid South Africa's Directorate of Covert Collection and Robert Mugabe's Central Intelligence Organisation, to the CIA, the KGB and Mossad, there's a murky and bloodstained side to military intelligence units. They are the dirty-tricks outfits, embroiled in hits, torture, disappearances, deception, executions, fabrications and lies. In my journalistic career, I've spent a lot of time with spooks and most exist in a delusional world of megalomania, paranoia and mistrust. Whether they have lived out their spy fantasies in Afghanistan, Iraq, South Africa or Rwanda, former sleuth-hounds continue to pretend that they live miles underground and their demeanour continues to smack of cloak-and-dagger.

It is the winter of 2011 when I meet a tall, bespectacled and elegant man with a scented whiff. Emile Rutagengwa is a former top RPA intelligence officer now living in South Africa. At one stage he lived and operated in Kagame's shadow. He says, 'I saw Kennedy for the first time in the bush. I think it was 1992. He was tall and skinny. He looked like a revolutionary. You look into someone's eyes and you can see if he is a revolutionary. It is that look. Someone who is ready to die and to sacrifice everything. If you have to fight, you fight. If you can't eat, you don't eat. He was ready to die for his country.'

When he deserted the army in July 1999 – five years after the RPF had grabbed power – Emile was a captain. He left, he says, because he was about to be sent to the Congo to head up a military intelligence unit. He would have been in charge of nothing more than yet another Kagame dirty-tricks outfit and death squad.

When we square our eyes on each other for the first time, Emile looks at me and says: 'I know you.'

'From where?'

'I took you to Nyarubuye. In May 1994. Do you remember?'

'What were you doing then?'

'I was your bodyguard. I had to protect you.'

* * *

I don't remember Emile, but how can I forget Nyarubuye, the Roman Catholic parish on the hill in Rwanda's south-eastern corner? Nyarubuye (the name means 'hard, stony place') continues to haunt everyone who went there. So many years on and I still find it difficult to write about it. I'll do so later. It is enough to know for now that when we arrived at the imposing red-brick basilica on that winter's day in 1994, the church compound was littered with thousands upon thousands of blackened, bloated and decomposing bodies discharging their metallic odour into the air.

Although our shared visit to Nyarubuye is a crude icebreaker, Rwandans generally don't open up to foreigners, tending to keep their tales to themselves. As a people they have endured more than most others on the planet and I suppose that for those who suffer so often and so incessantly, memories become unbearable and it's easier to just keep quiet.

That's the one side of Emile; the other is that a decade as an intelligence operative flying under the radar has left him a stealthy character who speaks in hushed tones and perpetually glances from side to side. He seldom meets twice at the same restaurant and prefers to convene in a parking area from where he'll whisk you away to another eating place where he orders a well-done T-bone with cheese sauce and an Italian beer.

Spooks usually suffer from delusions of grandeur and superiority, and Emile is no exception. 'If you want to be in intelligence,' he smirks, 'you have to be very, very intelligent.'

'How come?' I want to know.

'Because you must know who to trust and who not,' he adds with a mouth full of prime beef. 'Otherwise you're dead.'

Emile smells a rotting rat at every table. He warily peeps at a burly university student sporting a Blue Bulls rugby jersey who is holding hands and sipping semi-sweet wine with his blonde *poppie* and observes: 'You never know who they can hire.'

'I'm sure they're fine,' I assure him.

On the other side sits a dude tucking into a bowl of spaghetti bolognaise. He wears earphones connected to his iPhone and his feet are tapping to the rhythm of whatever is being propelled into his ears.

'He can't hear us,' I assure Emile.

* * *

Emile's father, Kalisa Boniface Rutagengwa (they have the same surname, which is unusual), was a lawyer and businessman in Kigali. 'Our house was nice, four bedrooms, and there was water and electricity. We were only four children and I was the firstborn. We had everything we needed. I always went to private schools, because it was so difficult for Tutsis to get to government schools.'

Born in the same year as Kennedy, Emile had a rather uneventful up-bringing, although he says he also suffered abuse as a Tutsi. 'I knew about this Hutu–Tutsi thing since I was young. Whenever you walked in the streets, Hutu children would shout things like *inzoka* – snake – at you. I asked my dad how we were going to live in this country, but he said to just stay out of politics and we would be okay. But I knew there was trouble.'

Three days after the October 1990 RPA invasion into Rwanda, soldiers took Emile's father away. 'They put them in the national stadium. There was no food and some died on the grass. They released my father after three months. They tortured him. I could see that we were not going to survive in that place. We were all going to die.'

In the days that followed the invasion, Emile decided to join the RPA. 'I asked my parents: "What's next? What are we going to do when the Hutu neighbours attack our house? These people are many and the police won't help us." I was just a boy but I saw the hatred that Hutus had for us. My father said, "Just stay away from politics. We will be fine." But I knew we were going to be killed and I wasn't going to wait for their machetes.'

In June 1991, days after he had written matric, Emile told his parents that he was going to a sleepover party to celebrate the completion of his exams. Instead, he and four friends – Bisangwa, Kayinga, Mitari and Kazungu (three were to die in the war) – made their way to Rwanda's southern border and crossed into Burundi, from where they travelled to Uganda to join the RPA.

This is how he remembers his first firefight: 'After my training, I went to the Virungas. It was very cold there and I had no jacket or proper shoes. I didn't even have gumboots. I had nothing on my feet. So I really needed boots. In those early times, there weren't enough guns for everyone. I had to make a plan to get a gun from a dead soldier. So I was in my first battle, just a civilian. We were 300, they were 600. I had to advance to find a gun. I was just making a noise, screaming, to disturb them, to frighten them. I found an AK with four magazines, a uniform and good shoes on a dead enemy soldier. So I returned a full soldier.'

Two months after joining, Emile was recruited into intelligence. 'You have to be trusted because it is sensitive information you deal with. You have to be intelligent. You have to be clever, you have to be creative. You have to be educated because you have to write reports. Of course, we also walked the *panya* roads to spy on the enemy. In the bush you have to be everywhere. And then you have to keep discipline.'

'And what does that mean?' I want to know.

'You punish and discipline. When you catch spies, you report them to higher authority. You get information and you re-educate some of them. Some wouldn't help you and would say: "Kill me." Then he must know ...'

'What about when your own soldiers deserted or committed crimes?'

'When you desert in the bush and they arrest you, you are in danger. And from there they have to decide what to do with you. Some didn't survive because they had a soft heart.'

'What happened to them?'

'You have to be strict if you run a rebel army. It is very tough. People who became undisciplined, they were severely punished. You cannot afford that.'

'Did you kill them?'

Emile shakes his head and holds his finger in front of his mouth. He is not going to elaborate. In the end, I interview Emile for three days and am none the wiser about his intelligence exploits.

I switch off the digital recorder. Sipping on his Peroni, Emile says he is planning to soon pen his autobiography.

'Oh yes?' I respond. 'That should be interesting.'

'And I already have a title for the book.'

'And what is that?'

'*Silent Killer.*'

20

Kagame's fighting machine

A troop of fresh recruits from Rwanda who had journeyed through Burundi, Tanzania and Uganda arrived at the rebel training camp of Gishuro. Military policemen and intelligence operatives searched their persons and bags. Kennedy, who had just graduated into the ranks of the rebel army's IS, ferreted out a listening device in the bag of one of the new recruits. Military policemen pounced on the young man, about as old as Kennedy, and threw him into an *adache* that was being used as a detention cell.

The prison caves, where deserters, spies, criminals and prisoners of war were incarcerated, were covered with branches before clay was packed on top to isolate the incarcerated from the outside world. Prisoners lingered like moles and snakes in their damp and muddy cavities and never saw the light of day – except when deserters who had done their time were released or when enemy soldiers and spies were hauled out to be interrogated or executed. Every second day or so, the guards chucked food and water down the sides. Some got sick and died. Deserters were kept for two or three months, except when troopers were needed at the front; then they would be taken out, given lashes and sent to fight.

After a few hours, the young man Kennedy had trapped was heaved from his cave and grilled and debriefed. He was half-drowned in a bucket of water. His interrogators threatened to shoot him. He refused to say anything, except that he had been recruited by government intelligence operatives in Burundi and dispatched to infiltrate the bosom of rebel operations in Gishuro. Kennedy and his co-inquisitors tied the man's hands behind his back and hung him head first from a tree. It is an excruciatingly harrowing method of torture that is widely known as the 'helicopter method'. It didn't prod his vocal cords either, and he was eventually marched away and shot.

* * *

It is March 2011 and Kennedy and I are sitting at my dining-room table, each with a glass of red wine and the micro recorder rolling. His eyes are cast downwards and he is fretfully wringing his hands.

'He was a handsome boy. I remember him because he had no fear,' he says, adding, 'I did some of these things myself.'

'So catching them with these devices was like a death sentence?'

'Exactly. There were many cases. There were boys who came from Rwanda and they were given devices. We found them on their bodies, in their bags.'

'Did you torture them?'

'Yes, this was no picnic. This was guerrilla war. You don't have judges, you don't have courts, so what are you going to do? Are you going to leave an enemy to come and destroy you? You destroy him before he can destroy you.'

'So who executed them?'

'There were squads responsible for doing that.'

'Who would make the decision for someone to be killed?'

'The officers. I had no rank.'

'Couldn't you have imprisoned them? Put them in the caves?'

'And then? Are they going to stay there for long? You need manpower to guard them … food to feed them … medicine to treat them. I know today it was unlawful according to international law. The things I'm telling you I have studied. I have debated these issues. Why do you think I want to work in international law? I want to be a voice for the voiceless.'

'What about captured enemy soldiers?'

'We did not care for enemy soldiers being brought in. The majority of them we killed.'

'And wounded enemy soldiers?'

'No, unless it was a big fish, a normal soldier didn't mean anything. It was a guerrilla war. We didn't have enough medicine to look after the enemy soldiers.'

'Did you feel sorry for them at the time?'

'At the time, no. They were enemies. They wanted to destroy me. That was justifiable. It was war and it was an order and the order didn't come from me. It was not my decision. It was part of my assignment. I had to give reports. I had to do it.'

'Do you think innocent people were tortured and executed?'

'Yes, exactly.'

'How do feel about the fact that you were part of this?'

'Of course it was inhuman, and today you will not convince me to do the same thing.'

'Did you think about it at the time?'

'No, I was a small boy. I was a junior soldier. What can you do when they tell you to do this? But don't put all these things in the book.'

'I'm trying to understand what happened and the position you were in.'

'Conditions were harsh. I was just a soldier. I was nothing. Even the firing squad, if they said shoot them we would shoot them.'

'How do you feel talking about this?'

'I don't feel comfortable. I'm telling you things that I've not told anybody. It is almost too terrible to talk about. If I had known these things, I would not have joined the army. I regret anybody who died at my hands.'

He is silent for some time and then says, 'I don't want all these things in the book and then people read this and they start remembering me as a killer.'

'Unless you play open cards, we cannot write this book,' I counter. 'If you're going to say to the world that you were a soldier in this rebel army and did nothing wrong, do you think people are going to believe you? You can't sit there and tell me you don't want it in the book. We can tell it in a certain way; we can explain it.'

'Do you have to say how we punished them?'

'Yes, otherwise we must stop here. I'm not going to be part of a cover-up for you.'

'How are people going to treat me?'

'These events are very important because they made you the person you are today. We are going to put it into perspective.'

'Please. That is what I'm asking you to do.'

* * *

Two young RPA soldiers accused of raping a woman in a village were hauled in front of IS. According to Kennedy, the IS men weren't convinced that the woman was telling the truth and there was no medical evidence and no witnesses, and the accused professed their innocence. The camp commander sentenced them to death. The junior officers were instructed to assemble their troops to bear witness to the execution of the sentence. The condemned were tied to a tree; a firing squad lined up, cocked their AKs and fired twenty-one bullets into the damned duo.

'It was an example to each and every one of us,' says Kennedy. 'How could you rape a woman? I watched and didn't mind because by then they had also become the enemy. Most of us came from good families and we didn't have this thing of rape in our heads. That was not what we were fighting for. They were shot to pieces.'

'And if they were innocent?' I ask him.

'This was a liberation war. There wasn't Red Cross or anything like that. We know today that there were a lot of injustices. But there was a code of conduct which they broke and the commander decided that they should die.'

Kennedy maintains that the RPA was among the most disciplined rebel armies ever. Indeed, it had a reputation not just of being a swift and lethal fighting force, but for demanding a high level of orderliness and obedience from its cadres. Rape and sexual assault by RPA rebels were virtually unheard of.

Kennedy says they only seized livestock and produce from peasants when they were hungry and had to eat. 'When you capture a place, you will harvest the cassava. We were not allowed to eat the food from the enemy because it could have been poisoned. But we took food from the peasants. We took even their cows and goats.'

* * *

By 1992, Kennedy was a member of A Company and stationed in the Virungas near the government stronghold of Ruhengeri. Fighting a war in the Virungas must have been a living hell. It is cold, wet, muddy and inhospitable. Once inside the forest, nature breaks out in a state of madness and seems to be in constant and exuberant eruption. The flora is so tightly packed that there isn't space for mortal souls.

'The camp was just *adaches*,' recalls Kennedy. 'We were living underground. Whenever you capture a place, you dig caves. Even when you go and fight with the enemy, you dig a small, temporary one where you can sleep with your gun. When they shoot mortars, the fragments go over you. We were digging a lot. We were like animals. We were always full of mud. It could rain from morning to evening. Sometimes it was a blessing because it would clean you a little bit. We were dirty like pigs. It was just us and our guns and our bullets. Sometimes when you kill an enemy and he has new boots, you take them. We only had gumboots and your feet could rot in those. So when you kill an enemy, you remove everything. You wear their uniform and their shoes. You would be proud because others would know that you've killed.'

'And the locals, how did they treat you?' I ask.

'The peasants were not friendly in Ruhengeri. Some were killed in the crossfire but some even had guns. When you passed, they would be hiding in the banana plantations and they would shoot at you. We shot them. They were told to fight the *inyenzis*. Even the kids, we didn't trust them. A child could be cultivating, but next to him was a gun and when you passed he could shoot you. So we shot them.'

'Did you hate Hutus?' I ask Kennedy.

'I didn't think a Hutu was a good person. In my eyes, Hutus wanted to kill Tutsis.'

For most of his time in the volcanoes, Kennedy had to walk nightly reconnaissance missions that took him beyond enemy lines. 'My eyes were always red. No sleep. Even now, I don't sleep more than four hours. I wake up at four in the morning. My wife always wants to know why I wake up so early. We were walking patrol between the two frontlines, looking for a way to penetrate their defences. You had to get intelligence about the weapons they had, the manpower they had, what their strength was. It was very dangerous. So every night we had a confrontation. We killed them, they killed us. When you engage, you're like a dead person. You don't think. You go into automatic.'

Night after night he scoured the *panya* roads in search of FAR positions. Many of these *panya* roads have existed for centuries and are shared by man and animal alike. Various clans, tribes and villages have their own that at some point cross one another. If you haven't grown up on these paths, you may think you are still on track but instead you have wandered off in completely the wrong direction. The most tricky rat roads are those in forests because the flora is so jammed together that you can easily lose direction and, instead of it getting thinner and starting to shrink, it just swallows you deeper and deeper into its innards.

'We had to know their strength,' says Kennedy of the enemy. 'I've been shot at many times by them, but usually you cannot reply; you must just get away. If you shoot back, they know where you are. We were usually small reconnaissance groups of three or so. One night, at three in the morning, we were looking for a place to break through. They were on top and it was very steep. We had to pass under their trenches. One of us stepped on a stone. They started shooting. We fought for thirty minutes. None of us were hit. We crawled out and managed to get away.'

21

An ordinary Rwandan

Africa has many scourges and plagues – diseases, corruption, natural disasters, poverty, AIDS – but none as repugnant as the warlords and rebel leaders who set about enlisting private armies to loot, rape, kill, pillage and, ultimately, snatch the ruling reins. Of course, there have been legitimate rebel fighting forces such as South Africa's African National Congress, Mozambique's FRELIMO, Zimbabwe's ZANU/ZAPU, Sudan's SPLA and Namibia's SWAPO, but in general rebel armies are nothing more than rabbles of bullies and bandits that terrorise locals and stuff the pockets of their overlords.

They usually sprout in countries with vast and untapped resources – think diamonds in Angola and Sierra Leone, oil in South Sudan/Darfur, rubber in Liberia and just about every natural resource in the Congo – and start with a senior army officer, politician, businessman or confidant of the ruling elite who feels that he didn't bag his fair share of the spoils. He decides on a name, usually flaunting the word 'democracy', and copies and pastes a set of programmes or principles from the internet (he never reads it himself). And there you have it: life has been given to yet another African liberation movement.

That done, the warlord recruits an army, which is much easier than one would imagine. African metropolises are swamped by unemployed youths who are ripe for the picking and will do anything for a decent place to sleep and a warm meal. In the villages, guileless boys and men are even easier to entice into a rebel army. The preferred age of enlistment is between twelve and twenty. They don't ask questions; they kill. And once the killing starts, there will be even more boys to 'shelter' in your army before cajoling them to the frontline.

Weapons are cheap and plentiful and, in some places in Africa, are easier to come by than a decent meal or proper healthcare. Government armouries are badly secured and those who hold the keys have probably not been paid in months. And there you have it: the continent's latest killing cabal is ready to commence its campaign of terror and slaughter. The cadres are instructed to fend for themselves and are not just permitted to abuse their guns and power, but are encouraged to tyrannise the populace.

Warlords have butchered their way to riches and power up and down the continent, from Jonas Savimbi in Angola and Laurent Nkunda in the Congo to Charles Taylor in Liberia and Foday Sankoh in Sierra Leone. They have reduced land and man to rubble and left an ineradicable memory in the minds of millions.

Although not quite in this league, there exists today a vast body of evidence implicating the RPA in a range of human rights abuses and war crimes committed in northern Rwanda before the 1994 genocide, including reports by human rights organisations and the UN, eyewitness accounts and confessions by former rebel soldiers.

Human Rights Watch (HRW), for example, concluded that between 1990 and April 1994 the RPA was responsible for a host of serious human rights violations. They killed and attacked civilians – among others in a hospital and a camp for displaced peoples. They forced hundreds of thousands of Hutus to flee either to Uganda or to camps in the interior of the country where they were at the mercy of warring factions and forced to eke out a miserable existence. HRW documented cases where unarmed Hutu civilians were forced to produce their political party membership cards. Those who belonged to the ruling party were summarily executed.

Amnesty International has also reported on scores of deliberate and arbitrary killings, extrajudicial executions and disappearances of captured combatants and unarmed civilians. Human rights organisations have reported RPA massacres and killings in the communes of, among others, Bwisigye, Cyumba, Cyungo, Kibali, Kivuye, Kiyombe, Mukarange, Muvumba, Ngarama, Butaro, Cyero, Nyamugari, Shonga and Kanzenze. The list is vast.

Rebel raids on enemy positions, barracks and towns were often accompanied by the looting of villages along the way. Marauding rebels seized livestock and crops, especially maize and potatoes, leaving locals without food.

* * *

One of the most damning indictments of Kagame and the RPA comes from the Rwandan humanitarian of *Hotel Rwanda* fame, Paul Rusesabagina. This stocky and soft-spoken Hutu hero rose to prominence after the genocide when evidence emerged about how he had shielded 1 200 Tutsis from the genocidal killers. He was then the manager of the luxury Hôtel des Mille Collines in Kigali. When the mass killing commenced, Tutsi survivors flocked to his hotel. For three months he pleaded with and bribed the executioners to spare the refugees in his hotel. The Hollywood epic reflecting his heroism is probably the most lasting and lucid impression Westerners have of the Rwandan calamity.

Rusesabagina, whom I interviewed in Brussels in 1999, is for me the embodiment of an ordinary Rwandan man: upstanding, decent, good-natured and astute. He is untarnished by the bloodletting in his country and a voice of reason and uprightness in a wilderness of greed, mercilessness and political conniving. Among his host of awards and commendations are the US Presidential Medal of Freedom (received in 2005) and the Tom Lantos Human Rights Prize (a medal bestowed on him in 2011).

In November 2006, Rusesabagina presented the world with a compendium of RPF crimes committed since the invasion in October 1990. He writes: 'The overall goal of this document is to lift the cloud of mystery and secrecy hanging over the Rwandan tragedy. It is to fight impunity and help bring equitable justice to Rwanda: whoever killed a Tutsi must pay, whoever killed a Hutu must pay, whoever killed a Twa must pay, and whoever killed a foreigner must pay.'

What follows is a list of crimes perpetuated by the RPA and Kagame. Rusesabagina says that of these, a number of atrocities committed since October 1990 were the result of the 'RPF army which hated and hates Hutus, and wanted and wants to kill them massively'. He claims Kagame himself gave direct orders to fire on crowds of displaced people.

'The provinces of Byumba and Ruhengeri [where Kennedy served] did not experience the wave of genocidal killings that engulfed the rest of the country in 1994, because they were already under RPF control. Yet, the vast majority of families currently living in these areas are made up of widows and orphans, who tell stories of their husbands and fathers having been killed by the RPF. The simple question is this: why has the international community remained blind in the face of such blatant brutalisation of human life? From 1990 to 1994, a reported 400 000 people have died in these areas. Who killed them?'

When I put Rusesabagina's accusations to RPA officer Emile Ruta-gengwa, he pensively contemplates his answer before saying: 'People didn't believe we were Rwandans, they thought we were Ugandans. So the first thing that happened when we arrived at a village was people screaming that the Ugandans are coming. They made noise. So if you make noise, you are the enemy. So people died. Some of my friends were killed by civilians. There were civilians with the soldiers. So how do you know who is a civilian and who is a soldier?'

Although Rusesabagina is equally scathing of the Habyarimana regime and its policy of hate, the authorities in Kigali hit back hard at his allegations. They first attempted to rubbish his valiant conduct during the genocide, accusing him of exaggerating his claims and alleging that he charged survivors and refugees money in return for protection. They then accused him – without a shred of evidence – of being a believer in Hutu Power ideology and of having close ties with the architects of the genocide who are still hiding out in eastern Congo.

Rusesabagina was finally targeted in accordance with Rwanda's draconian 'sectarianism' and 'genocide ideology' laws. They protect the government from anyone questioning the official version of the genocide. Any person who asks that Hutus who perished in the genocide be remembered and honoured alongside their fallen Tutsi countrymen is branded 'a revisionist and a denier of the Rwandan genocide'. To raise questions about RPF atrocities against Hutus, or mention the killing of Hutu civilians, is equated under law with denying the genocide and begs a lengthy prison sentence. Should Rusesabagina return to Rwanda from exile in Belgium, he faces arrest and long-term imprisonment for saying, among other things, 'All sons and daughters of Rwanda who perished in this tragedy were a terrible loss to humanity and must be equally mourned, regardless of their ethnicity.'

* * *

Lieutenant Aloys Ruyenzi was one of Kagame's personal bodyguards and an officer in the RPA's IS. A veteran of Museveni's military campaign against Obote, Ruyenzi was among the RPA rebel fighters who crossed from Uganda into Rwanda during the first invasion of October 1990. In 2001, he fled to Norway, from where he made a statement about rebel atrocities. In 2010, he testified before the ICTR in Arusha about Kagame's complicity in a host of human rights abuses.

'I had the misfortune of working in his escort, where the climate is abominable,' he says in his statement. 'There is a permanent climate of terror and mistrust, as everybody spies on everyone else. I was an intelligence officer, but I knew very well that I was myself being spied on. The intelligence officers do not carry out ordinary military intelligence work. They are a squad of criminals. Its sole mission is killing opponents and other unwanted elements.'

Ruyenzi says Kagame is 'of quite a bad character' and that he 'can spend a whole month without smiling … He ordered at numerous occasions to kill as many civilians as possible. This took place in many areas in Byumba, Ruhengeri and elsewhere, and long before the Tutsi genocide.'

The Rwandan government's response was to question Ruyenzi's authenticity. They admitted that he had joined the rebel army in 1990, but said his tenure was plagued by 'continuous indiscipline' and claimed he was never a 'close bodyguard' of Kagame. They admitted that when he deserted in 2001 he was a lieutenant, but failed to explain how he was promoted to an officer when he 'faced continuous disciplinary reprimands'. They also neglected to address any of his claims.

Ruyenzi's statement caught my eye not just because of the value of his testimony, but also because he was an intelligence officer who cast some light on the shadowy RPA underworld that had sucked Kennedy deeper into its belly as the war progressed.

22

Apocalypse coming

In August 1993, the guns on both sides of the conflict fell silent when Habyarimana, Kagame and several Hutu political parties signed a peace agreement in the northern Tanzanian resort town of Arusha. The so-called Arusha Accords included protocols on integrating the two warring armies into a single defence force, a right of return for Rwandan refugees and the resettlement of displaced persons.

The accords crucially laid out a timetable for installing a broad-based transitional government consisting of representatives of all Rwanda's political parties, including the RPF. They also made provision for a UN peacekeeping force to be deployed in Rwanda. The Arusha Accords took more than a year of bickering and bargaining to thrash out. A previously declared ceasefire had been broken before the ink on the paperwork had dried, and therefore the reaction to Arusha ranged from cautious optimism to being viewed as a political charade by two adversaries who had already embarked on a near-certain path to war.

'For me, there was hope at that time. Maybe Rwanda was going to be a good country for everyone,' says Xavier Ngabo. 'I was thinking about my family every day. What had happened to them? I thought if Mama had died, maybe I will still see the kids. I said God, please help me that if they kill the boys at least the girls will survive. They often killed the parents and left the children. I was hoping that some were still alive.'

An ailing economy, international pressure and military advances by the RPA compelled Habyarimana to put his pen to paper at Arusha. He resisted the agreed-upon implementation of the accords at every step until international pressure forced his hand. He knew he was committing political suicide and that the ever-influential Hutu Power faction within his ranks would never agree to share power with Tutsis.

In the run-up to the signing of the accords, Léon Mugesera, a vice-chairman of Habyarimana's MRND, made a speech in which he said, 'The mistake we made in 1959 is that we [the Hutus] let you [the Tutsis] get out safe and sound. Your country is Ethiopia and, soon, we will send you to your home via the Nyabarongo [River] on an express trip.'

Mugesera, a close friend of the president, was a voice for extremists in the regime and supporters of the ruling party recited his speeches around the country. He demanded death for the *inyenzis*: 'What are we waiting for to execute the sentence? Don't let them get away. Destroy them! Drive them out! Long live President Habyarimana!'

At the time, Rwanda was governed by a multiparty coalition and the minister of justice was a member of the Liberal Party, the only opposition party with some Tutsi representation. He ordered an arrest warrant for hate speech for Mugesera, who turned to the army for protection. The minister was fired.

A few days after the signing of the accords, Rwandans woke up to a new voice on the air: Radio-Télévision Libre des Mille Collines (RTLM). Extremists within Habyarimana's party had used the cover of multiparty politics and freedom of speech to set up the radio station as a means of inciting the populace against Tutsis. The station was funded by members of the *Akazu* and openly called for the extermination of the *inyenzis*.

By this time, Rwandans had become accustomed to a new sight on the streets of Kigali: Hutu Power youths wearing multicoloured trousers and tunics and sporting pop hairstyles and dark glasses. They cavorted around on motorcycles and waved posters splashed with images of Habyarimana. It was they who became known as the *interahamwe* – those who attack together – and who were instrumental in the engineering and realisation of genocide. Funded by extremist businesspeople, they were secretly trained as 'civil defence' units. The economic slump of the eighties had rendered scores of youth jobless and they were easy pickings to swell the ranks of the *interahamwe*. These carnival killers were organised into neighbourhood cells that compiled lists of Tutsis in their area. They were instrumental in organising and carrying out some of the earlier genocide 'dress rehearsals'.

* * *

When the RPA invaded Rwanda in 1990, the FAR had only 5 000 men under arms. By the time Arusha was signed, its ranks had swelled to more than 20 000. The tiny central African nation became in the early nineties one of the biggest arms purchasers on the continent. At the end of 1992, as peace negotiations commenced in Arusha, South Africa sold 20 000 grenades, 3 000 R4 rifles, Browning machine guns, grenade launchers and more than two million rounds of ammunition to the Rwandan government. More ominously, between 1992 and 1994, companies linked to Hutu Power ideologues imported 580 000 machetes (the weapon of choice in the genocide) from, mostly, China.

The RPF also scrambled to prepare for its final assault to seize power. According to former RPA officers, 300 tons of war materiel was cached in Rwanda in the summer of 1993. According to Rusesabagina, RPF sympathisers in Kigali had caches of weapons in their residences and were training their own youth militia.

Xavier says the respite from hostilities gave him and his infantry buddies valuable time to play soccer, attend English classes and listen to lectures that painted a utopian Rwanda under RPF leadership. 'We heard that even though it was peace, Tutsis were still dying in my home area. It somehow gave me hope because it meant that some Tutsis were still alive. I thought maybe there's a chance that I would see my mother and brothers and sisters again.'

In November 1993, Emile Rutagengwa was one of 600 RPA soldiers who arrived in Kigali to take up their stations in Rwanda's Parliament building, the Conseil National de Développement, under the provisions of the Arusha Accords. His stint in Kigali gave him a chance to see his parents, who had thought he was dead. After he absconded to the RPA in 1991, a FAR military officer knocked on their door and informed them that their son had died trying to leave the country.

'When they saw me, they just cried,' recalls Emile. 'They were very proud of me. I was no more a boy, I was now a man. My mother said, "You are only 600 men here. You are too few. These people are going to kill you." I said, "No, Mommy, we have guns, we can defend ourselves. But I am worried about you and I want you to leave. There's no hope." "No," she said, "we're fine. The United Nations is here. They will protect us."'

It was the last time Emile would see them. When the mass killings started, the families of RPA soldiers were the first to be targeted. 'We knew about the planning of the genocide. The *interahamwe* were trained not far from our barracks. At five in the morning we could see them running. Civilians were being trained, for what? We could hear what they were singing: "Away with the Tutsis. Death to the Tutsis." The radio was playing songs about killing Tutsis.'

* * *

In early 1994, Kennedy – then based in Byumba – and his intelligence compatriots were dispatched on top-secret reconnaissance missions. They had to venture beyond enemy lines to determine where the rebel army could break through in the event that they launched a full-scale assault on Kigali.

Night after night, riflemen Kennedy Gihana, Masasu Nindaga (he later became a general in the Congo during the Kabila regime) and Steven Kaitare wormed their way up and down *panya* roads to detect army positions, determine troop strengths and estimate the size of their armouries. 'The three of us were very close,' says Kennedy. 'We understood one another. They were my best friends. Masasu came from the Congo, but he was Rwandan. Kaitare was also from Uganda. We slept together, fought together and ate together. We did everything together. Both later died. These were suicide missions. You always knew you might not be coming back.'

The trio skulked through and around enemy lines as far as Mugambazi, from where one can see the lights of Kigali. 'We moved at night and hid during the day. The enemy was mostly on the hills. We passed where the enemy didn't expect us to pass. In the valleys were villages that were not friendly so we sometimes had to move in civilian clothes. All the time we were getting intelligence. We slept in the bush. Sometimes you didn't sleep. We had a little plastic bag with maize and a bottle of water. When the enemy heard a noise at night, they shot. We didn't shoot back. We just tried to get away. One day we walked into a patrol, but they were only two. We shot them dead. We got away and took cover. We were instructed that rather than get caught, we should shoot ourselves. Instead of being taken hostage, we had to kill ourselves, even if we were wounded and couldn't get away. You shoot yourself or ask your friend to shoot you.'

By the beginning of April 1994, the RPA was ready to pounce. A passage to Kigali had been plotted, troops were on standby and arms caches in Kigali had been set up. According to evidence presented many years later to two French investigative judges, two Russian-manufactured ground-to-air missiles were dispatched from Kampala in Uganda to RPA headquarters in Mulindi in northern Rwanda. Once there, they were concealed among food supplies intended for the 600 rebel soldiers in Kigali and were then transported to the capital for a top-secret operation.

At the same time, the *interahamwe* were distributing the imported Chinese-manufactured machetes to their henchmen. The lists with the names of Tutsis had been drawn up and RTLM was urging its listeners to literally cut down Tutsis and their *ibyitso* – accomplices – once and for all.

* * *

Back in January 1994, the force commander of the UN Assistance Mission for Rwanda (UNAMIR), Lieutenant General Roméo Dallaire, notified his superiors in New York that he had a reliable informant within the senior ranks of the *interahamwe* who assured him that the extermination of the Tutsis was at hand and that Kigali was flooded with weapons.

Dallaire warned the UN that genocide was being plotted in the highest echelons of government and emanated directly from Habyarimana's camp. New York's response was ludicrous: they instructed Dallaire to inform Habyarimana, which he duly did. His informant disappeared and the preparations for genocide intensified. When Dallaire asked for permission to raid arms caches, he was told it wasn't part of his mandate.

Rwanda was on the edge of a calamity. On both sides of the political divide, the scheming and conniving of the hardliners were in overdrive. No one was prepared to share power, says the famed author on Africa, Ryszard Kapuściński, because by then it was clear that there was not room enough in pocket-sized Rwanda for two peoples so fatally at odds with each other.

He says the Kingdom of Banyarwanda was plagued by a tragedy as profound as the Israeli–Palestinian conflict. But unlike the Israelis and Palestinians, Hutus and Tutsis speak the same language and practise the same culture and religion. What divided them were greed, myth, hateful politics and abominable politicians who flaunted catchwords like 'democracy', 'unity', 'free and fair elections' and 'multiparty politics' but who were ultimately driven by amassing and securing absolute and unchallenged power. As they shook one another's hands and sat down in negotiating forums to sign peace agreements, they were already stealthily plotting how to politically and militarily outwit their foes. They knew all the talk was pie in the sky and that Rwanda's destiny would ultimately be determined over the barrel of an AK – or, in this case, over the blade of a machete.

* * *

The transitional government was never implemented. On 6 April 1994, Habyarimana and his Burundian counterpart, Cyprien Ntaryamira, took to the sky in the Rwandan president's Mystère/Falcon jet – a gift from his friends at the Élysée Palace in Paris – and flew to Arusha to discuss the implementation of a broad-based transitional government in Kigali with Tanzanian president Ali Hassan Mwinyi and representatives of the neighbouring states.

A fierce debate rages to this day about whether it was FAR soldiers at Kanombe military base who aimed two missiles at the aircraft as it was about to land at Kigali's Grégoire Kayibanda International Airport or if it was Kagame's henchmen based in the capital who sneaked out of their barracks under the cover of darkness and fired off their Russian-manufactured missiles.

Most fingers initially pointed to Colonel Théoneste Bagosora, a former Rwandan military officer with links to the *Akazu*. Years later, prosecutors at the ICTR failed to finger him as the triggerman, but defence teams for the accused equally couldn't muster enough evidence to nail down Kagame as the culprit.

Subsequent attestations by former Kagame army officers and disgruntled political lackeys have accorded more weight to the arguments compromising the RPF leader. Every one of them, though, had fallen out with their former political master or was in exile and had ulterior motives in spilling the beans.

Whoever assassinated the two presidents also pushed the country over the precipice.

The Apocalypse had dawned.

23

Genocide

It is nine o'clock at night on 6 April 1994 in northern Rwanda. It is drizzling and a layer of cloud has descended like a coal-black blanket over the region, blotting out any light from the stars and moon. In a military base masked by misty-peaked mountains, RPA commanders order their troops to assemble in full gear for a top-priority briefing. Some fighters are huddled around damp and smouldering fires; others slumber in their concealed *adaches*.

Within minutes, 400 troops of the rebel army's A Company shuffle into file. Most are armed with AK-47 assault rifles; others with Belgian FNs and South African R4s that they have captured from FAR soldiers. Among the troops is Kennedy Gihana, gangly and lean-bodied with gaunt features. He is clad, like the rest of his compatriots, in a striped camouflage uniform – called *mukotanyi* – and gumboots. The latter are a necessity in order to negotiate the muddy and slippery paths. Kennedy is carrying a Kalashnikov RPK light machine gun (LMG), a devastating tool of war that spits its mortal slugs at a speed of 600 a minute. It is a variant of the dreaded AK-47, but is equipped with bigger magazines, a longer barrel for improved accuracy and a bipod for stability. Without deploying the pod, it kicks like a mule on steroids. Soldiers are selected for their strength, mobility and endurance to man an LMG.

A stern-faced company commander, Colonel Shaka, breaks the news in a muted voice. President Habyarimana is dead, along with the president of Burundi and several of their top advisers. He informs the men that RPA commander Major General Kagame has personally ordered the troops to be ready to march, engage the enemy and crush them.

For many months now, the rebel leadership has warned that the Arusha Accords are nothing but a scrap of paper and that the Kigali regime is deceitful and conniving. With the imminent collapse of the accords, the 600 RPA soldiers stationed in a military base in Kigali are in mortal danger. The priority of the RPA is thus to reach the capital to reinforce the Kigali contingent.

For the remainder of the night, the troops prepare for battle. Each soldier is given an extra supply of bullets. Kennedy has three curved magazines each holding forty rounds and a tin box containing many hundreds more.

* * *

It is almost exactly seventeen years later, and in my dining room in Johannesburg, Kennedy shakes his head and lets out a long, soft whistle. 'This was war. Finally, it was real war. I can't remember what went through my head, except that we knew that this was it. This was going to be the final battle. We were going to liberate our country and nothing would stand in our way. Nothing.'

'Were you scared?' I ask him.

'No, there wasn't time to be scared. We were ready to fight. We were put on standby many days before the crash and were told to be ready to fight. We were excited and even happy. Finally, we were going to the capital.'

* * *

At the base of 101st Battalion near Byumba, a friend rouses Xavier Ngabo and tells him the president is dead. They attend a briefing where the colonel says, 'You guys, things are going wrong in Rwanda. They are killing Tutsis. We have to stop the killing and save them. Tutsis are dying like cockroaches.' At that moment, Xavier knows he will never see his people again. They will all be killed; nobody is going to survive. This was the decisive battle.

* * *

A few hours after the plane crash, and under cover of darkness, A Company is on the move. Kennedy, his LMG draped over his shoulder and the tin box of bullets clutched in his hand, slogs in the vanguard. In front of them is a demilitarised zone, but beyond that skulk divisions of FAR, deeply lodged in their trenches and recently emboldened by the acquisition of additional hardware and troops. The column of rebel soldiers avoids major routes, plying the *panya* roads that Kennedy and the rebel army's intelligence operatives have so meticulously and carefully mapped in the preceding months.

Kennedy: 'It was raining heavily, but that was good because we could use it as a cover. We wore gumboots and there was mud everywhere. We couldn't expect any support from behind or supplies coming to us. Everybody carried as many bullets as possible, and grenades and things. Some of the government soldiers were spoilt and lazy; they couldn't climb the high mountains. They were waiting for us on the big roads but we passed next to them. We walked around villages, not through them. The fighting started on the second day.'

The RPA attacks in three main thrusts across an eighty-kilometre front and sweeps with lightning force across the countryside.

Xavier: 'Soon after we had left, we were fighting the FAR. We beat them and continued. God was on our side. The enemy was on the hills and we had to take them. We fought from hill to hill. We liberated one position after another. They were running! They had some defences that tried to stop us, but we went forward. Many of them died. There were *interahamwe* with the soldiers. They were also armed. We had to kill them as well. If they had guns and you met them, even if they were wearing civilian clothes, you shot them. If they had joined the battle, what did they want?'

Kennedy: 'We were now encountering sections of the enemy and we were fighting. Anything we met, we shot and moved forward. We had only one thing in mind: forward. We didn't even take a break. We just marched. We did not stand or rest, we marched as fast as we could. It rained non-stop for three days. When you lifted your leg, it was full of mud and the gun was heavy. We were not taking prisoners, nothing. Women, kids, nothing. Our aim was to reach Kigali. We knew the killings had started. We knew that every Tutsi was a target.'

A day or two later, Kennedy is promoted to the rank of corporal. 'I was promoted in the bush. I could command a section of up to thirty soldiers. I was also the intelligence staff of A Company and was carrying the big machine gun. Everybody looked up to me. I was respected.'

* * *

In Kigali, Radio Rwanda announces that Habyarimana's plane has fallen in flames over the city. Hutu extremists take charge of the decapitated regime and the genocidal engine slowly jerks to life. The chief conspirator is Colonel Bagosora.

Senior ruling-party politicians and their families are evacuated to a military camp, but leading opposition lawmakers are instructed to stay at home. They are on the death list and the elite presidential guard is ordered to dispatch them. Top of their list is Prime Minister Agathe Uwilingiyimana, a moderate Hutu favouring the power-sharing agreement with the RPF.

Around the capital, government soldiers, police and the *interahamwe* set up roadblocks and the machetes get to work. By mid-morning, some of the roadblocks are human abattoirs; lines of bodies snake down the sides of the roads and litter the capital's streets. Soldiers and the *gendarmerie* (paramilitary police force) command the roadblocks and *interahamwe* do the chopping and slashing. Enthusiastic youths soon join in the bloody fiesta and drag the bodies to the roadside. Some of the women are exposed, their legs spread, raped before they were finished off. Some of the victims are still alive, softly groaning as they await death.

Trucks roam the streets, stopping at roadblocks to pick up their grisly cargo. Bodies are tossed upon bodies and driven away to be buried in mass graves where they will lie in crumpled heaps until covered with lime and soil. Some are still alive, but it doesn't matter. They are dead enough. On this, the first day of genocide, an estimated 8 000 people are killed. By day four, the death toll would rise to 32 000, by day twelve to 112 000 and by day twenty-five to 200 000.

Government soldiers surround Uwilingiyimana's house. She phones the UN and requests an escort to the national radio station to address the nation. When the Blue Berets arrive, the presidential guard fires on them and takes the contingent hostage. As FAR soldiers take the fifteen captured peacekeepers to a military camp, Uwilingiyimana and her husband are shot dead.

At the FAR base, the presidential guard separates the Ghanaians from the Belgians. The Africans are taken to safety, but the Europeans are tortured and then executed. Belgium withdraws its troops from the UN peacekeeping mission. Foreign embassies shut their doors and evacuate their nationals. Days later, the UN Security Council, on which the Rwandan government has a seat, slashes the UN mission from 3 000 to 270 men.

With the UN a mere onlooker, the killers are left to carry out their task of extermination unimpeded, and the massacres start in earnest. The presidential guard kills several opposition politicians, moderate ministers and the president of the Constitutional Court, all supporters of the Arusha Accords.

Interahamwe, armed with lists of Tutsis and Hutu traitors, round up those under sentence of death. By now, RTLM is reminding its listeners that every living Tutsi is a threat, as are their children and even their unborn babies. 'Fight them with the weapons you have at hand. You have arrows, you have spears! Go after them! Death, death to the *inyenzis*! You must act fast. Force them to come out! Find them at whatever cost!'

The genocidaires have plotted something akin to a team sport. Everybody has to take part. No one is allowed to sit on the sidelines. In order to accomplish a Tutsi-free Rwanda, there have to be neither witnesses nor accusers nor bystanders. Every Hutu is called upon to do his national duty and murder Tutsis. Some excitedly join the ranks of the killers, motivated by a mixture of hatred and greed. There are those who genuinely believe Tutsis are going to kill them and take their land. Others use genocide as a pretext to settle old feuds, loot possessions and increase the size of their plots. Then there are those – their numbers run into tens, even hundreds, of thousands – who reluctantly take part in the killings, some of them under duress or out of fear for their own lives. Rwanda is a patriarchal society where authority is difficult to ignore. When those in positions of power call the masses to action, most obey.

For 100 days in 1994, killing Tutsis is the law of the land. Young and old, rich and poor, ignorant and educated adhere to the call and take up their machetes. Relatives kill their next of kin, teachers their pupils, doctors their patients and clergy their flock. Most people die not as a result of bullets or bombs or rocket launchers, but of machete cuts, *ubuhiri* gashes, hammer blows, and spear and knife wounds. An immense amount of manual labour goes into the genocide.

In journalist Jean Hatzfeld's brilliant journal of the killers, *Machete Season: The Killers in Rwanda Speak*, an elderly Hutu says: 'Some hunted like grazing goats, others like wild beasts. Some hunted slowly because they were afraid, some because they were lazy. Some struck slowly from wickedness, some struck quickly so as to finish up and go home early to do something else. It was each to his own technique and personality. I chose the ancestral method, with bow and arrows, to skewer a few Tutsis passing through. As an old-timer, I had known such watchful hunting since my childhood.'

The hate radio is not just urging Hutus to rid the country of Tutsis, but is directing the massacres. It tells the *interahamwe* where the *inyenzis* are hiding; it names people to be exterminated; and it spurs on the populace to hunt down the cockroaches. 'Death! Death! Graves with *inyenzis'* bodies are still only half full. Hurry and fill them to the top!'

Hutu genocidaires see themselves as the true sons and daughters of the soil and it is their mission to clear their land of an alien presence. Hutus are not killing their fellow countrymen; they are getting rid of colonial invaders. RTLM encourages the killers to send the Tutsis back to Ethiopia by way of the Nyabarongo River, which winds through Rwanda before discharging into Lake Victoria. The river becomes a waterway of death. Thousands of yellowing bloated corpses spill into the lake and wash ashore. First to arrive are the corpses of men murdered while trying to stave off the marauding killers. Second are the slain women and children, and last are the babies, many of whom don't carry wounds as they are simply tossed alive into the river.

* * *

Never has it been truer that evil triumphs when good men do nothing. Two days into the genocide, Dallaire, the UN's mission commander in Rwanda, again cables headquarters in New York and warns his superiors that there is a well-organised and deliberate campaign of terror against Tutsis being carried out. He says he believes that with just 5 000 well-armed men, he can stop the killings and restore order to Kigali. New York reminds him in no uncertain terms that his priority is to protect his own men, not to save Rwandan lives. UNAMIR watches helplessly as the killings spread.

Dallaire then asks New York to arrange for the hate radio to be shut down. The UN doesn't have the means to jam the signal and so makes a formal request to the United States to do so. The Pentagon studies the issue and concludes that the operation will be too costly – $8 500 an hour for a jamming aircraft to fly over the country – and might violate the autonomy of an independent state.

The reaction that is most wanting is that of Kofi Annan, under-secretary-general of the UN's peacekeeping operations (and later UN secretary-general). An African himself, he reckons to his eternal shame that sending more troops to Rwanda will be too costly in terms of both time and money. In the first four weeks of genocide, the systematic and continuing slaughter taking place in Rwanda is not once discussed at length in UN Security Council meetings. It takes the UN six months to brand the killings premeditated genocide.

As bodies accumulate next to the roads and the first visuals of the killings reach the outside world, newly appointed Rwandan interim president Théodore Sindikubwabo describes the violence as a spontaneous outburst of rage sparked by 'sorrow and aggressive feelings of frustration' after the killing of Habyarimana. Prime Minister Jean Kambanda says there is 'a certain frustration among people, a certain vague anger that made it impossible for people to keep control'.

It seems to strike the right chord and is exactly what the world wants to hear. It is much easier to pretend that this dot on the African continent – where there is nothing that anybody wants – is haunted by a collective madness and incessant hatred. Hutus killing Tutsis and Tutsis killing Hutus is an inevitable and ghoulish national pastime.

The world ignores compelling evidence that the genocide is being orchestrated from the very top. Kambanda is shown on Rwandan television inciting the populace to kill Tutsis. He travels to the university town of Butare (where the killing got off to a slow start) and urges Hutus to join the campaign to exterminate Tutsis. 'Don't be onlookers when the rest of your brothers are doing their national duty,' he lambastes them as he dishes out guns. 'Exterminate the vermin in your midst.'

The killings are more bloody and effective than those of Nazi Germany's Holocaust. The machetes and *ubuhiris* of the *interahamwe* and the ordinary people they incite produce far more rapid results than Hitler's gas chambers. The genocide is many times more intense than the ethnic cleansing in Serbia, Croatia and Bosnia during the early 1990s, yet Western powers poured more than 50 000 troops, an arsenal of high-tech weapons and billions of dollars into the Balkan conflict.

In the space of a hundred days, 800 000 people are massacred – which computes to 333 murders every hour, or just over five a minute. Of those killed, 300 000 are children. Another 100 000 children are separated from their families, orphaned, lost, abducted or abandoned. A quarter of a million women are widowed. Tens of thousands more Rwandans will die in the aftermath of the genocide in cholera-infested refugee camps in neighbouring Zaire and in subsequent raids launched by the killers from their hideouts. In addition to the children who are slain or orphaned, 95 per cent of the country's next generation will witness or experience brutality. Many of the survivors are nothing but living dead. Never before has rape been used as a weapon of war to such an extent as in Rwanda. Four women are raped every minute of every day for the 100 consecutive days of genocide. Many are raped several times.

As the killings intensify, Nigerian author and Nobel laureate Wole Soyinka remarks that Rwanda is clinically dead as a nation.

24

A mother and her baby

Kennedy's stony eyes scour the village, mostly emptied by the killers and abandoned by its terror-stricken inhabitants. Even the surrounding fields and hills, usually exploding at this time of year with radiant spurts of daisies and amaryllis, are lying fallow. Kennedy's LMG has by now acquired the nickname 'Rambo' and on this day, the third of the Rwandan genocide, the amalgam of man and machine promises to deliver more deluges of death.

A shot rings out from a banana plantation. A rebel soldier whimpers and falls over. Kennedy flings himself to the ground. In a blink, he erects the LMG on its bipod, pushes the butt into his shoulder and discharges a crackling burst into the plantation. The 7.62-millimetre bullets reduce the banana trees to shreds. The gunman scampers away. While Kennedy gives cover by spraying his fire through the plantation, other rebels heave themselves from the ground and give chase.

Kennedy follows a few seconds later, his hefty gun dragging him down. At the border of the plantation, and with a valley beckoning at its edge, rebels force the shooter to a halt. He throws his AK aside and sticks his hands in the air. There are several other young men around him, and a young woman, hardly out of her teens, lurks on their flanks with a baby on her back. Next to the band of men lie a few machetes that they probably tossed aside seconds earlier. Their hands are also in the air.

The gunman's narrow, ghoulish red eyes dart from one rebel soldier to the next; he mumbles something about mistaking them for FAR soldiers because their uniforms look alike. He babbles how happy he is that the RPA has arrived to liberate their area. His hair is matted and he reeks of beer and stale sweat.

A rebel levels his AK on the captive's chest. The latter stutters into silence. He gapes at his executioner and slowly drops his hands in front of his chest as though he wants to ward off the bullet. A single crack rings out. The high-velocity bullet catapults him backwards and he dies before his body hits the ground. There is pandemonium among the other captives. They beg and wail. One falls to his knees, his hands stretched out in front of him. Another prays. Unperturbed by their pleas for mercy, the rebels mow them down.

The air reeks of gunpowder. The eyes of some of the dead are wide open and blood seeps from gaping wounds in their bodies, forming red puddles on the black soil. The woman is lamenting and imploring mercy.

The rebels fleetingly scan one another. Some look away, their eyes drifting across the valley. One or two step back, almost disassociating themselves from the chore at hand. Kennedy is standing at the front of the group, still clasping his LMG.

The baby bawls. The woman stops screaming, her terror-stricken face etched with the knowledge of her fate. In this godforsaken place, at this time, being a woman or a child offers no protection, not even from the rebels. Being with the *interahamwe* is a death sentence. Nobody is taking prisoners.

The executioner lifts his AK. A single shot rings out. The woman's lifeless body plummets to the ground. As the echo of the gunshot floats down the valley and dissipates over the furthest hill, the air fills with the squall of the baby. The bullet has slid through the mother's body but not even grazed the tot.

The rebel's finger again curls around the trigger, his eyes locked on the tiny target on its mother's back.

* * *

It is almost exactly seventeen years later, and in my dining room in Johannesburg, Kennedy holds his head in his hands. His body shakes. He takes off his glasses. It is raining – one of the last showers of the summer – and for some time, the only sounds are the drops lashing the old tin roof and his soft whimpers. I study the sobbing man. My initial disgust gives way to pity. After so many years, the big man has let go of a tormenting secret. I want to get up and put my arms around him and comfort him, but I let him grieve in silence. After several minutes, Kennedy looks up, takes a deep breath and stares at a Vietnam War poster adorning the wall behind me. It is as though he is too ashamed to look me in the eye.

'I'm tired now,' he says. We take a break. I promised earlier in the day to cook him traditional South African food and I assemble a *smoorsnoek*, a Cape Malay dish of smoked fish, rice, potatoes, tomatoes and peppers.

Kennedy tries not to eat red meat. He suffers from chronic active gastritis and oesophagitis – a severe and bleeding ulcer. He says his body is worn out from many years of eating badly or not at all, having nowhere to sleep and trying to survive.

I give him a glass of red wine (I'm not sure how good that is for the ulcer), which he has taken a liking to since meeting me. He prefers it semi-sweet, though. We eat in almost silence. He says he is tired and I take him home after lunch. We chat on the way about politics and law and he comes to life again. He tells me he saw a news item on Al Jazeera during the week about the Russian ambassador in the UN's Security Council opposing stronger measures against violence-ridden Syria. He says he wants to cry when he sees the bodies of young people lying in the streets of Damascus while the world looks on with folded arms. He doesn't mention our earlier conversation around the dining-room table, but just before I drop him off he says, 'You don't know what it was like to have been there, my brother. And you must thank God that you don't have to think about things like that every day of your life.'

* * *

That night, I listen to what Kennedy has told me earlier in the day.

'The *interahamwe* were shooting at us. And we shot back. Every place we liberated we had to do an operation, hunt them down. They were hiding in the forests, in the banana plantations. We were hunting them. We killed lots of them. We knew the good people had already left or were dead. To see kids being killed … that anger. They were cut with machetes. Some were not even dead. It made me mad. It made me ask: why should this one live? Or why should that one live? That's why everybody that was not a Tutsi was the enemy. That is why we shot each and every one in front of us. Because of our anger, we did not ask who was *interahamwe* and who was not *interahamwe*. As long as they were Hutu. Women, whatever …'

Talking about the woman and her baby, he said, 'We shot her but we could not leave the kid, because the kid could not live alone. This kid was on her back and who would take care of it?'

'Why did she have to die?'

'We killed her because she was an enemy. She was a Hutu. It changed the way I looked at the world. I have nightmares. I remember it very well. I have nightmares, and not only because of that one.'

'But were you not doing exactly what they were doing? They were killing people because they were Tutsi and you were killing people because they were Hutu.'

'Yes, but if you didn't kill them, they would kill more people. As the war continued, we killed more.'

'Do you ever think of that day?'

'I still think about the baby we killed. Every night. That baby was not fighting us. But all Hutus were the same. They were either soldiers or *interahamwe*. All of them. They ran away and we shot them. All of them. Then the baby. It is in my mind now. All I can do is to ask God for forgiveness.'

Kennedy Gihana ... orphan, cattle herder, rebel soldier, wanderer, street child, security guard, LLM graduate

'Don't write everything I tell you ... What will people think of me?' – Kennedy and the author, Johannesburg, June 2012

Ten years after walking from Rwanda to South Africa, Kennedy receives his LLM degree, Pretoria, April 2011

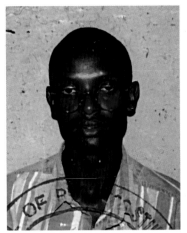

The oldest photographs of Kennedy, taken while he was a RPA soldier in Rwanda in the mid 90s

With RPA soldiers during the assault on Kigali, May 1994

RPA rebels pounding government positions with heavy machine guns, mortars and RPG rocket launchers, May 19●

The scene that confronted me upon my arrival at the Roman Catholic mission of Nyarubuye in south-east Rwanda - thousands upon thousands who had been shot, hacked, clubbed and stabbed to death. Filmed in May 1994

Reporting from the Roman Catholic mission at Nyarubuye in Rwanda. My head was a confused mess and I cannot remember what went through my mind

Paul Kagame defends Rwanda's role in Zaire at a press conference in 1997

Moving with RPF soldiers across the volcanoes in northern Rwanda, March 1999

he Nyarubuye skulls, five years later and neatly stacked in a genocide museum. Filmed in March 1999

Tony Karamba, our rebel guide in 1994, returns to the Roman Catholic mission at Nyarubuye five years later

Genocide accused Enose Nsabimana emerges from a akeshift prison in the south-east of Rwanda. Filmed in March 1999

Enose Nsabimana, clutching the skull of the neighbour he had clubbed to death during the genocide in 1994

Xavier Ngabo

The hole in which Xavier's mother, Beatrice Ndebereho, was buried

Exhuming Beatrice's body, December 2009

The exhumed skeleton of Beatrice Ndebereho

Xavier with his mother's remains

Villagers line up for a *gacaca* court hearing in an effort to find the remains of Xavier's father, Edward Mushatsi, December 2009

The house that was built on top of Edward's makeshift grave

Xavier and community members gather around Edward's remains, April 2010

Xavier and his aunt wash Edward's bones

Kennedy and Goreth on their wedding day, December 2010

The bride and groom in traditional dress

The traditional wedding, and another change of clothes

Kennedy, Lisa and Goreth

...nnedy in conversation with Veronica Kirabo during his return to Uganda in 2011

Kennedy greets his long-lost friend, Dominique Kashugi

...nnedy with Dominique's family in front of their home in southern Uganda

The boyhood friends at the spot where Kennedy spent his childhood with his grandparents

Kennedy greets long-lost friends in Kabonela, Uganda

Drinking traditional beer with locals in Kabonela

Kennedy with his aunt Getruida and some children in her house in Uganda

With his former teacher, Rwabuduri Kahira, at Bigada Primary in southern Uganda

With his beloved long-horn Ankole cows

Kennedy greets his sister, Nyinawumuntu Matsiko

Kennedy shows Nyinawumuntu and her husband, Yassir Matsiko, pictures of his newborn

25

Madness

The rebel swoop on Kigali is today saluted as one of the greatest wartime assaults in African military history. The rebels were unstoppable and three days after setting foot on the *panya* roads in the north, the first RPA soldiers seized territory on the outskirts of the capital.

It is exactly seventeen years later, and in my dining room in Johannesburg, Kennedy squares up to me once again. It is the day after he has laid himself bare and, incidentally, 6 April. Across Rwanda, survivors are lighting candles to commemorate the day, seventeen years ago, when Habyarimana's plane was shot down and their country descended into hell. It is usually a burdensome day for Kennedy as it evokes memories of the depravity that enveloped him and his complicity in it. We spend most of the morning trying to track down the whereabouts of Xavier Ngabo, but, by teatime, the micro recorder is rolling again.

'When we passed Mugambazi, from where you can see the lights of Kigali, we started seeing more bodies on the road,' says Kennedy. 'Two here, three there and lots of fresh blood. It was scary. We were listening to *Radio des Mille Collines*. They called on every peasant to stop cultivating and kill the cockroaches. There were no Tutsis left in Mugambazi. We didn't see any. I started counting … you went into one house, you counted ten people. Their bodies were piled like sacks of maize on top of one another. You asked yourself whether anybody would survive. Hutus hunted Tutsis as though they were animals. Our orders were to fight and kill; to kill the killers. And we were killing them nicely because we were shooting them. Many innocent people died as well, of course.'

'Were you ever wounded or injured?'

'One day we were passing and an *interahamwe* shot at us with an arrow. I was very slim, so it passed through my trousers. They were hiding everywhere, that's why we shot everything standing.'

'And you had no mercy for them?'

'No, for what? And anybody that was with them, whether it was a woman or what, we just shot them.'

'Were they begging when you found them?'

'No, the *interahamwe* went mad. It's because of all the blood. Some didn't even have guns. They only had arrows, but they were standing in front of the guns. We killed them. Others said they didn't do anything, but where were you going to put them? And you could never believe what they said.'

In the wake of the UN's incapacitation and the impotence of the international community, Kagame and his rebels are hailed as the liberators of Rwanda, the thin bright line of justice that conquered the legions of evil. The world is so repulsed and sickened by the images of genocide that they ignore the tens of thousands of Hutu civilians that died at the hands of Kagame and his cut-throat troops. The rationale is that the government and its cronies were committing genocide; Kagame and his 'disciplined' fighting machine were stopping it.

Although the killings committed by the RPA should never be permitted to obscure the massacres executed by the genocidaires, the rebels nevertheless mowed down civilians and summarily executed suspects. To this day, many ignore the compelling and indisputable evidence of RPA atrocities and still refer to the 800 000 victims as Tutsis and so-called moderate Hutus unwilling to participate in the killings. They refuse to acknowledge that thousands upon thousands of innocent Hutus perished because they simply happened to stumble into the gunsights of RPA rebels or were at the wrong place at the wrong time.

'Why do you think the RPA was regarded as such a disciplined army?' I ask Kennedy.

'We were young guys who came from school and from the villages where we were well brought up by our parents. There was also our code of conduct. If you misbehaved, they shot you. Without even investigating. They just shot you.'

'But what about the civilians that you killed?'

'The soldiers followed orders to the letter. Of course, you didn't question that which your officers told you to do. You obeyed, otherwise you were killed. You say "Yes sir" and you kill. We were killing everybody: men and women and kids. Nobody was left to tell the story.'

* * *

The most telling indictment against the RPA comes from a damning UN investigation that was deviously suppressed for years. Five months after the Rwandan president's plane was shot down, a team of UNHCR investigators found that areas around Kigali and several other prefectures were the scene of 'systematic and sustained killing and persecution of the civilian Hutu population by the RPA'. Dubbed the 'Gersony Report' after its author, it concludes that the rebels were guilty of the large-scale killing of men, women and children, including the sick and the elderly. Robert Gersony estimates that between April and August 1994 the RPA killed up to 45000 civilians. Gersony presented his notes and findings to the UN, but was then ordered by Secretary-General Boutros Boutros-Ghali to write no report and to speak to no one. His notes were, however, leaked to the media.

* * *

'Hutus were murdering Tutsis,' continues Kennedy, 'and that was why anything standing in front of you that looked like a Hutu was the enemy. You could not think properly because all you saw were rivers of blood running. We were not used to that. We shot a person and he died quickly, but they used machetes, sharp sticks, hammers, everything. I cannot describe what kind of weapons these guys used. Into the vagina of a woman, cutting her body open and killing an unborn kid. It was shocking to see that a human being could do this. There was a devil there and that is why you didn't negotiate with them. You shot them. You could see him raising his hands but you were not sure whether he had a good intention. You shot him.'

* * *

HRW also concluded that the RPA slaughtered tens of thousands of civilians during the genocide and that the killings were directed by the highest command. Its estimation is that between at least 25000 and 30000 civilians were killed by rebel soldiers. 'These killings,' they say, 'were systematic, widespread and involved large numbers of participants and victims. Commanders of the army must have known of and at least tolerated these practices.'

* * *

'Near Kigali we started using some roads and they were full of bodies,' recalls Kennedy. 'We were not talking because our aim was to shoot and to fight. Bullets and bombs were flying over us. Mortars, whatever, came from heavy weapons on top of the buildings in the city. We came to Kabuye, which is a suburb to the north of Kigali near the sugar factory. There's a swamp. It was full of bodies floating all over. Jesus! Some had already started smelling. We were also being killed and there was no time to bury anyone. It was chaos.'

'What is the worst thing you saw?'

'Just outside of Kabuye, we found a family. It was on a hill. We found them in the yard of a house. They were all on one stick. All seven of them, starting with the father and ending with the mother. The kids were in the middle. It was like a kebab. The oldest child followed the father. The youngest kid was next to the mother. It was a baby. The stick went through their bodies and it was lying in the yard. That was the cruelness of those guys. The hatred! Those memories have stuck in my mind. It made me want to kill as well. I wanted to do to them what they were doing to us. But now that I've grown up, I see that I could have done it differently.'

* * *

In his compendium, Paul Rusesabagina provided an equally scathing indictment of RPA atrocities. According to him, 20 000 civilians died during the RPA offensive on Kigali. He specifically mentions Kabuye and Mugambazi – where Kennedy fought – and talks about a mass grave with 500 Hutu corpses, tens of Hutus who were called to a meeting and killed with grenades, and thousands more who were massacred in a church.

* * *

'All this killing, what did it do to you?' I ask Kennedy.

'Until the end of the road, I didn't think a Hutu was a good person,' he replies.

'But didn't you also see Hutus that were killed by the *interahamwe*?'

'These stories only came after the war. The majority of dead Hutus were killed by our soldiers.'

'Did you think all Hutus were involved in the genocide?'

'Yes, I did. In my eyes, Hutus wanted to kill Tutsis. That's what was said on *Radio des Mille Collines*. It called on all Hutus to kill all Tutsis. We listened to that radio. We heard how Prime Minister Kambanda gave guns to Hutu civilians and told them that when they saw Tutsis, they must kill them. When you hear that every Tutsi should be killed, you fight like a demon, like a crazy human being.'

* * *

The RPF has been remarkably successful at keeping the lid on their atrocities, and few former rebels have dared to speak out. It's in any case perilous to spill the beans in Rwanda; you'll disappear and be plonked into a shallow grave before your words have melted into the nearest hill. In present-day Rwanda, it is illegal to say that Hutu civilians other than 'moderates' also died in the genocide – never mind blame the president and his gung-ho fighters for their demise. Most of those who blabbed are now in exile, having been motivated by self-preservation or the lure of asylum or refugee status. Their testimonies have been rubbished in Kigali as seditious fabrications.

I don't believe Kennedy has told me everything, but I think his candour is nonetheless remarkable. His connivance in war crimes is lodged like a black malignant growth in his soul, and I hope his professions to me are just the start of his voyage of healing. He tells me repeatedly that the time is now for each and every Rwandan to admit his or her complicity in human rights abuses and to forgive, absolve and get on with rebuilding one of mankind's most scarred and damaged societies. I salute him for his valour.

Kennedy is far more forthcoming than anyone else I have ever interviewed. I don't quiz Xavier about the killings, because he has a wife and child in Rwanda and plans to return to his homeland one day. When I ask Emile Rutagengwa about RPF atrocities, he ponders the question for some time before saying, 'I can't say the RPA didn't kill people. RPA also killed civilians.' I prod, but he simply shakes his head and smiles. Maybe he'll reveal his involvement in his memoirs. Rumours about his mercilessness as an intelligence operative abound.

Kennedy, along with millions of other Rwandan survivors and perpetrators, will go to his grave with pictures of unimaginable horror seared into his mind. He will never be able to forget them, erase them or blank them out. They are with him every second and every minute and every hour of every day.

Imagine being confronted with this: 'There was a girl, she was seventeen or eighteen. We found her lying at the roadblock. Instead of killing her, they had taken an iron, put it in the fire and burnt her inside her private parts. And before they did that, they had raped her. She didn't say anything. She was like a dead person. We took her to the sickbay. I don't know what happened to her. I think of it every day … the bodies, the piles of bodies. All those bodies, killed in a different way. One's hands were cut off, the other's legs; you found others who had been put in a tree like a kebab. They took pregnant women and they cut their stomachs open and then removed the unborn kids from their stomachs. These women were still alive when they did that. You asked yourself: how painfully did these people die? It drove me mad. A life is worth nothing. Life is valuable in the eyes of God, not in the eyes of a human being. Life is nothing.'

Charred in Xavier's memory bank are equally indelible frescoes of horror. 'It was two o'clock,' he says. 'The church was on the road from Byumba, not far from Kigali. The bodies were still fresh. Then I knew: my people are finished. Some people were still moving. Those who were cut by machetes were still crying. There were men and women and children. The baby was killed with a machete, cut up. The mother was still alive and held on to it. I didn't see anyone with bullet wounds. They used just machetes. This was how my father was killed. It made me very sore to see this. These killers were taken by another spirit. They were the devil. They attacked us with machetes. Because of this hatred they couldn't control themselves. They were told our guns couldn't kill them and that our bullets were working like grain or beans. That's how mad they were. The *interahamwe* had to die because they were killing the people.'

* * *

One day, long after we have finished our interviews, Kennedy produces a washed-out and fading black-and-white identity photo of himself that he says was taken in the mid-nineties. It's the oldest existing photograph of him. The man in the picture certainly doesn't resemble the man sitting in front of me. Instead, I see a hollow-cheeked, almost gaunt face with a thin moustache. What strike me are his eyes: expressionless, dark and empty.

26

The living dead

Many of the living in Rwanda – survivors, victims and perpetrators – are condemned to an eternal grave. Rwandans call them *bapfuye bahagaze* – the living dead. They have been sentenced to live out their days with ghouls and bogeymen knocking and ticking and running amok in their skulls.

One such soul is an elderly farmer by the name of Enose Nsabimana, a father of five and grandfather of twelve. I meet Enose only once, and for not more than an hour or two. His story has stayed with me as the epitome of the sadness and devilry that engulfed Rwanda in the autumn of 1994, and the embodiment of what happens to an ordinary man when evil lays hold of his soul.

It is 1999 and I am on my sixth visit to Rwanda to compile a documentary on the fifth anniversary of the genocide. A guard unbolts the gate to a makeshift prison, nothing more than a former army warehouse that has been converted into a jail by covering the two windows with iron bars and installing a steel gate.

A blanket of pink-clothed prisoners greets me. They are packed together so tightly that it is virtually impossible to determine whose leg belongs to whom and what foot is attached to which body. Stooped down on stick-thin legs a few feet from the door is a senile-looking man, gazing straight ahead of him with manic eyes. A grey beard covers his withered face. The guard calls his name. He totters towards the voice and a ray of sun illuminates the human skull he clutches in both his hands.

The guard marches the man, clasping the skull close to his chest, to a tiny office where an army officer says: 'This is the prisoner. You can now speak to him.'

'What's your name?' I ask him through my Rwandan interpreter.

'Nsabimana Enose,' he answers in Kinyarwanda.

'And whose skull is that?'

'Augustine.'

'And who is Augustine?'

'It was my neighbour.'

'And what happened to him?'

'I stroked him on his head with a big stick.'

'And why are you holding his skull?'

'I want to show it to the court.'

'Where did you get the skull?'

'I got it after we buried him,' he says.

'Why did you kill him?'

'Augustine was an *inyenzi*.'

'And how do you feel about killing him?'

'I've got a big pain. Even my heart doesn't pump well.'

As we end the interview, Enose asks me if I am going to speak to the state prosecutor.

'Yes, I am. But why?'

'Tell him I'm waiting to show the skull to the judge. He must hurry up because I want to bury Augustine again.'

I call the guard and tell him to take Enose back to the cell. Once inside, he herds into a corner, where he slumps down and almost disappears in the mass of flesh and bones that packs the makeshift prison.

'That's how he sits,' the guard says. 'Day in and day out. He doesn't move. Sometimes he talks to the skull. And if we try to take it away, he fights with us.'

* * *

I speak to the state prosecutor in Kibungo a few hours later. He has Enose's file in front of him. 'He made a full and signed confession that he killed Raturamaruga Augustine. He hit him with a studded stick on his head somewhere in April 1994.'

'He seems mad,' I remark.

'He wasn't when he made this confession. We found him with the skull and he admitted to the murder.'

'You don't call a man holding a skull mad?'

'What are we supposed to do? Release him?'

'Put him in a mental asylum.'

'We don't have asylums. He'll have to wait his turn to stand trial.'

'That could take a hundred years!'

'Then he'll have to wait,' the prosecutor says. He shoves the file across the table to me. 'Read his confession. No doubt he's guilty of murder.'

* * *

For most of his life, Enose contentedly tilled his tiny terraced cornfield in the pastoral province of Kibungo in eastern Rwanda, and tended to his banana plantation and three Ankole cows. But towards the middle of 1993, things changed when his youngest son, Elizaphan, joined the *intera-hamwe*. Enose couldn't read, but Elizaphan told him about the 'Hutu Ten Commandments', published in the *Kangura* (a Kinyarwandan word meaning 'wake up') newspaper. Elizaphan explained that the commandments declared every Tutsi an enemy and commanded Hutus to join hands against them. Hutu men who married Tutsi women were traitors.

This bothered Enose, because Augustine was Hutu, but his wife Rose was a Tutsi. Their three children were classified as Hutu. Enose and Augustine had been living a few metres from each other for as long as he could remember. They shared pots of banana beer and their wives had a stall at the market where they sold onions and tomatoes.

'And what about Augustine and Rose?' Enose asked his son.

'They are also on the list,' Elizaphan admitted.

'What can Augustine do?'

'He'll have to exterminate his *inyenzi* and cleanse himself,' answered Elizaphan.

'And the children?'

'They are *inyenzi* bastards!' Elizaphan exclaimed. Before he left that day, he gave Enose an *ubuhiri*. The older man didn't want the studded club, but his son insisted. 'You will need one, because we will all have to help exterminate the *inyenzis*.'

Enose warned Augustine about the looming peril and, just before the genocide, he sent Rose and the children to Burundi. When Enose woke up on the morning of 7 April, he switched on the radio and heard that Habyarimana was dead. He ran next door, where he found Augustine in a sombre mood. He had also heard the news.

'My time has come,' Augustine lamented.

'No, no, no!' Enose pleaded with him. 'You must leave. Immediately!'

He helped his neighbour scratch together a few pieces of clothing and packed him some food. 'Where will you go?' he asked.

'I'll hide in the forest and then try to get to the border. I greet you, Enose,' said Augustine.

'*Imana aguhe umugisha* [God bless you], Augustine. Go well.'

The killings came to Kibungo a few days after the presidential plane was shot down, and soon Tutsis were extremely hard to come by. Those who had not been massacred had fled into the mountains and forests, where they were hunted down by Elizaphan and other *interahamwe*. Enose's own village had been emptied of *inyenzis*. Many of the murdered Tutsis had once been his friends.

Frederic Nyilinkwaya and his family were killed in their home. Théresa and her children were hacked to death at the market. Ephiphanie Mukakabanda, his wife and five children were intercepted at a road-block just outside the village, dragged to the side of the road and cut up with machetes.

Enose watched the *interahamwe*, wearing crowns of banana leaves and spurred on by the screech of a whistle, drag a young man into the village after finding him hiding in the forest. As they surrounded him with their machetes, he was on his knees begging – not for his life, but for the mercy of a bullet. One of the *interahamwe*, who had a gun, asked him if he had money to pay for the bullet. He didn't. The killers descended on him like a pack of wolves and continued to hack at his body long after he was dead.

With all the Tutsis gone, talk in the village turned to the advance of the RPF. According to RTLM, the Tutsi rebels were killing Hutus in the villages and towns they had taken. The radio urged listeners: 'A hundred thousand young men must be rapidly recruited so that they can rise up and kill the Tutsis. We will exterminate them all. So look at a person and see his height and how he looks. Just look at his pretty little nose and then break it!'

The *interahamwe* intensified the hunt for survivors to make sure there would be no witnesses to tell their stories by the time the RPF reached Kibungo.

As the sun rose over the mountains, casting a mandarin glow down the misty valleys, Enose woke to a commotion in front of his home. It was a group of men, feverishly babbling all at once. He recognised Elizaphan's voice, and then heard someone pleading, begging and crying. He identi-fied the voice as that of Augustine, his neighbour. Enose rushed outside.

Augustine was lying in the road with his hands tied behind his back and his face a bloody mess. 'We found the *inyenzi*!' Elizaphan barked trium-phantly when he saw his father. Augustine's face lit up when he saw his neighbour.

* * *

'He thought I could help him,' explains Enose.

'What did you do?' I ask.

'There was nothing I could do. He was an *inyenzi* and he was finished,' Enose says, adding, 'Augustine was not my friend any longer.'

* * *

Augustine had never made it to Burundi or Tanzania. He may have heard *interahamwe* were waiting for fleeing Tutsis at border crossings, where they cut them down. He probably decided to hide in the forest until the killings subsided. When the *interahamwe* found him, he told them that he had money at home and would pay them to save his life. He didn't have money; he was merely trying to prolong his life for an hour or two.

'He's yours, old man,' a soldier said to Enose. 'Kill the *inyenzi*!'

Elizaphan spurred his father on. 'Come on, it's now your turn. Where's your *ubuhiri*? Fetch it!'

Enose went into his house and fetched the studded club. All the while, Augustine was crying and pleading for his life.

* * *

'My mind didn't think,' says Enose. 'I just knew I had to do it.'

'Did you say anything to him?' I ask.

'Nothing. But he spoke to me.'

'What did he say?'

'He asked me to save his life.'

27

The trenches

Every soldier who has languished in a trench describes it as a living hell of blood, mud and bone. There are a multitude ways of dying in a trench – sniper fire, bayonets, shell fragments, stray bullets, grenades, disease, exposure – and precariously few ways to live. Wherever soldiers are damned to trenches – the Somme in France, Gallipoli in Turkey, the Western Front in Europe – their lives are mired in hunger, misery, inclement weather and imminent violent death. Rwanda in the autumn of 1994 is no different.

As the rebels attempt to take control of the hills surrounding the capital, Kennedy and members of A Company are condemned to trenches for almost a month as they launch an assault on Mont Jari, a 2000-metre-high mountain located ten kilometres to the north of Kigali. The battle for Jari was to become known as one of the greatest and most decisive clashes of the Rwandan civil war and would pave the way for the RPF to march into a blood-soaked Kigali and claim victory.

The battle is a far cry from the guerrilla tactics employed by the rebels during their failed 1990 invasion. This is nothing but a merciless conventional duel – attrition warfare where death is a constant companion to everyone on the line. Day after day, the green mountainside spurts with dirt as bullets slam into it and the trench-incarcerated fighters become trapped by long, elongated plumes of dark soil as mortars and bombs burst around them.

* * *

Kennedy and I speak about Jari for more than a day. He babbles incessantly about the mountain as though he's almost relieved to escape scrutiny of his exploits during the first ten days of the genocide. His speech is interspersed with drawn-out whistles, head shakes and the odd '*Jissus!*' (an Afrikaans expression of amazement that comes from the word 'Jesus'). He starts by drawing me a map. 'Here is the road from Byumba. Here is Kigali. And this here, this is Mont Jari. When you are on that mountain, you control the city. There were lots of government soldiers. There were barracks on top, and there were trenches that were dug by the French. People could walk in them. We were ordered to take the mountain.

'We fought and we captured bit by bit. But many soldiers were already dead. Our commander called Kagame and said we had to leave the mountain because the kids were finished. Kagame told him that he would fight until he was dead too. We were told that we would fight until the last of us was dead. The enemy was too many for us, they pinned us down. The first few days 300 to 400 of our soldiers died.'

'Did some of your friends die?' I ask.

'We were not thinking of friends because at that time everybody was like a relative to you. We were overwhelmed. Half of our soldiers were already dead. One of our soldiers had to fight ten of them. We fought day and night. There was no sleeping at all. How could you sleep when they shot at you from all directions? It smelled like hell. The smell was a mixture of bodies and gunpowder.'

'What stood out for you?'

'That we were not going to survive. We could not manage it. There were too many enemy soldiers. And all the time they were shooting us with big guns from the buildings in the city. One of them had this gun with four barrels, an anti-aircraft gun. We had many wounded but no medics. Many died in agony. They were calling for help. You felt as if you had betrayed the wounded because you couldn't help them. At night, we carried the dead and wounded down the mountain in the mud, the rain and the darkness. We delivered the wounded to the sickbay down below in a banana plantation. But the majority were already dead. The bodies of the enemy were just lying there. They couldn't fetch them. We just buried ours in a small hole. The whole mountain smelled of death.'

Xavier Ngabo soon joined Kennedy on the mountain. 'Mont Jari was like something from a movie,' he says. 'It was unreal. Many died, but many more of them than us. The enemy is in his trench, you are in your trench. We even screamed and shouted at one another. "You think you are going to get us out of here? Fuck you! You're gonna die!"'

'Some of us were blown up because of the mines in front of their trenches,' recalls Kennedy. 'Legs were flying all over. I wasn't scared of dying but I was scared of the mines. You died badly. I prayed to God that a bullet would take my life rather than being taken alive or stepping on a mine. If they were to capture me, I would have been interrogated, tortured and killed. There were, of course, no prisoners of war. We kept the top commanders, but the normal soldiers … what do you do with them? If our soldiers got captured, we never saw anybody coming back.'

Speaking about FAR soldiers, Xavier says: 'They had helmets that protected them against the fragments. Some of our soldiers took those helmets. The boots they wore were very valuable. We only had plastic boots. It got very hot inside your boots and water got inside. I remember when I tried to take the boot off it was stuck to my foot! Then you had to make a small hole in the boot to get your foot out. That's why the shoes of the enemy soldiers were very valuable. Their uniforms too. They were new and they had belts and bottles for water. I got a good uniform but it took a long time to get the right boots because I wore number tens.'

'It was bullet to bullet, RPG [rocket-propelled grenade] to RPG, hand grenade to hand grenade,' says Kennedy. 'And then they had mortars and cannons. Let me tell you, my brother: we were flying! The bad thing was when we ran out of bullets. With your last bullets you waited for an enemy to come as close as possible before you shot him so that you could take his bullets. But sometimes they also ran out of bullets, and then it was up to bayonets and knives. A guy came for me and wanted to hit me with his gun. None of us had bullets. He was more powerful than me. My friend Kaku shot him on top of me. He still had bullets. That's what I remember of that night.'

* * *

It is 1 May and soft rain sweeps through Rwanda, turning Mont Jari into a misty, hazy outcrop on the outskirts of the capital. Kennedy has been in a trench now for eighteen days.

'In all those days we didn't eat, sleep or wash properly, but there was anyway no time to think about those things. When you are a rebel, you are like a dead person. You are like a ghost. Your eyes turn from white to red, like the colour of that car,' Kennedy says, pointing to a red car driving by the coffee shop where we are having breakfast on a Sunday morning in Hatfield, Pretoria. 'At night they brought samp from below and you'd eat it and drink dirty water. You didn't sleep because the enemy could take you alive. You just waited and then you fought.'

Steven Kaitare is entrenched next to Kennedy. Each has his own trench, separated by no more than ten or fifteen metres. Kennedy and Steven have been bosom buddies ever since they made their way to Juru Camp together, trained side by side, shared the fear and exhilaration of their first battle and mapped the *panya* roads as IS in the days preceding the genocide. Now the friends confront death and mayhem on Jari.

In a last, desperate attempt to root out the rebels from their trenches, FAR aims an arsenal of heavy artillery at the lines of rebel soldiers. Heavy cannons pound the rebels from their positions in Kigali while enemy soldiers lob mortars on the rebels from their dugouts around the mountain. Kennedy says bullets sounded like flies above his head. A mortar explodes near his trench and a piece of shrapnel penetrates his wrist. He bandages the wound and fights on. The rebels can do little more than to keep their heads low and wait for the bombardment to end. The wounded accumulate, but the rebels have to wait for nightfall to slither from their trenches and crawl through enemy lines with their injured comrades on their backs towards the sickbay below.

Early the next morning, the shelling starts again and continues throughout the day. Bombs explode around Kennedy. One bursts almost on top of him. Mud rains down on him. He waits a few seconds, lifts his head and peeks from his trench. The shell has fallen on top of Steven and almost blew him from his bunker. He is still conscious, making murmuring sounds. 'Kennedy! Kennedy!' he whimpers. The rebels have been trained not to go and help in situations like this because when the enemy hits the target, they will keep their aim and wait for help to come. Then they fire off another round, which is sure to hit the new target.

Kennedy clambers out of his trench and crawls towards Steven. As he emerges in the open, a shell bursts close to him. He presses his body on the ground and covers his face. He waits a few seconds and crawls on. He reaches the dying man. The bottom half of his body has been ripped away by the blast. 'The *mujingas* [stupid people] have shot me,' he burbles before he dies in Kennedy's arms. He waits till nightfall before he digs a shallow grave for his friend and bids him farewell with a short prayer.

'I think about him a lot,' says Kennedy. 'He was a very courageous boy, a very happy guy. He liked jokes. He sang the patriotic songs. We fought next to one another all the time. He was a brave soldier. But we were all brave. We were all on the frontline.'

The next morning, long before sunrise and with Jari cloaked in darkness, FAR pounces with every man, gun and bullet they possess. Soldiers, laden with grenades and rockets, arise like ghosts from their trenches. The whole night, however, the rebels have been scouring the curved horizons for the enemy. Captured and tortured enemy soldiers have disclosed the imminent attack. The rebels are running out of bullets and have to wait for the FAR soldiers to be almost upon them before pulling the trigger. The fighting continues throughout the day and by the afternoon, bodies litter the mountain. Sections of the rebel lines are overrun and many of Kennedy's compatriots are mowed down.

Rebel reinforcements arrive later in the day. Among the soldiers rushing to A Company's rescue is Lieutenant Emile Rutagengwa.

Emile: 'We had to go up as they shot down at us. We lost many, many people on Jari. Lots of my friends died right next to me. But you have to try to forget things like that so that you can live a normal life. You look at where you are now and you wonder, For what? Why did I do all of this?'

Kennedy: 'By ten that night both sides were out of bullets. The guys were taking their bayonets out. But my Rambo had no such thing. Many of the enemy soldiers had G3 rifles and they also had no bayonets. We fought with our hands. We killed one another with our bare hands. You tried to get your hands around his throat so that you could strangle him.'

Emile: 'Now it was hand-to-hand combat. And it was difficult, because by then we all had the same uniform. Our commanders said we should take the one sleeve off so that we could know who the enemy was. But you didn't always know who was who. We fought with knives, sometimes they had bayonets. And the enemy was good with this, they were well trained. I saw terrible things.'

Fighting on Jari continues for another ten days, but more rebel platoons arrive on the mountain and the RPA surrounds the capital. They sever FAR supply lines to their soldiers on the mountain, and by mid-May the enemy retreats, fleeing to the central provincial city of Gitarama where the interim genocidal government is already based. The remnants of A Company assemble to be rearmed and then give chase.

'When we went down that mountain, we looked around to see who had survived,' Kennedy says quietly. 'We were shocked. There were very few left. There were 143 of us in my company that went up Jari. Now we were only twenty-three.'

28

Nyarubuye

By the tens of thousands, they flood to the houses of God, where they squat in a corner or an open space with a crucifix gazing down upon them. They feel safe because during previous orgies of bloodletting the marauding masses respected the sanctity of churches. This time, however, the killers ignore the glaring gaze of the Virgin Mary. When priests and bishops and nuns abandon their flocks, it's an invitation to the *interahamwe* to convert Rwanda's churches into the country's Auschwitzes.

One such place is the red-brick Roman Catholic basilica of Nyarubuye, set on a rocky outcrop in south-east Rwanda near the Tanzanian border. A few days after Habyarimana's plane is shot down, thousands of Tutsis descend on the church. Some say there were 3 000; others put the number as high as 5 000 or even twice that. Among them is Valentina Izibagiza, a Tutsi who is living with her four brothers and three sisters in Kibungo when the killing erupts.

As death closes in on Kibungo, a delegation of mainly Tutsis turns to the *bourgmestre*, Sylvestre Gacumbitsi, for help. He advises them to seek refuge at the Catholic mission at Nyarubuye. They believe him because Tutsis found sanctuary there during previous attacks in the fifties, sixties and seventies. Refugees start arriving at the church on 13 April. By then the priests have gone, leaving their congregation at the mercy of the killers.

The refugees have hardly settled into their sanctum when thousands of men march towards Nyarubuye. The column consists for the most part of villagers and peasants from surrounding communes, armed with sticks, machetes and *ubuhiris*. Among them is Enose Nsabimana, carrying the studded stick that his son Elizaphan had handed him a fortnight before. Earlier in the day, Enose and the other villagers had been picked up by an army truck and taken to a spot not far from the church, where soldiers and members of the *interahamwe* addressed them. '*Inyenzis* are hiding in the church,' the men were told, 'and we are going to exterminate the vermin once and for all.'

* * *

'Why did you go to Nyarubuye?' I ask Enose.

He drops his grey head in thought before speaking. 'Elizaphan told me to go. He said, "Father, do you remember the *ubuhiri* I gave you? Go fetch it and come with us because there is an important task at hand." I took it and went, even though I didn't know how to use it.'

* * *

Gacumbitsi presides over the slaughter. He instructs the police and soldiers to shoot, and then the peasants to move in and hack, slash, club and bludgeon the *inyenzis* to death. 'There must be no survivors and no runaways,' the *bourgmestre* instructs. He divides the villagers into several groups. Enose joins a group of peasants, mostly older men, outside the church to make sure that nobody escapes.

By three o'clock on the afternoon of 15 April, the church is completely surrounded by soldiers, police, *interahamwe* and villagers. They tell the refugees that those with money should hand it over and they will be spared. A few come forward, but they are killed anyway.

Gacumbitsi gives the order to attack. It starts with soldiers throwing grenades into the compound. Gacumbitsi sets the tone by shooting a Tutsi. Then the soldiers and *interahamwe* open fire. One of the leaders says: 'They are snakes and the only way to kill snakes is to smash their heads.' Inside the church it is chaos; everyone is running around, screaming and trying to find a place to hide.

Soldiers gun down those who attempt to flee. Villagers skulking with machetes, spears and *ubuhiris* pounce on the few that manage to slip through the first line of attack. They hack and club their victims to death.

* * *

'Did you hit anyone with your stick?' I ask Enose.

'No,' he says. 'I was too slow.'

* * *

As the killers swoop on the thousands, Valentina creeps into a tiny cubbyhole at the church entrance. It is so small that nobody bothers to check if anyone is hiding there. Children are thrown against the walls; some fall very close to Valentina, others almost on top of her. Towards the end of the day, more men arrive and stick knives in the wounded to make sure they are dead. By this time Valentina is lying underneath several people, and they assume she too is dead.

Killing is much more labour-intensive than most anticipate. Victims resist, crawl away, and use their hands and arms to shield themselves from the blows that rain down on them. Others simply refuse to die.

From her hiding place, Valentina recognises one of the soldiers as a neighbour. She creeps out and begs him: 'Can you find it in your heart to forgive me for being a Tutsi? Will you spare me?' He spits on her and calls a villager over to club her to death. They smash her hands with a club until her fingers break. Her skull is bleeding and the pain is terrible. She passes out and they leave her for dead.

As night falls, only a few hundred have been finished off. The killers cut the Achilles tendons of some and leave them to wail and cry and maybe die during the night. In the meantime, they retreat to feast on Primus beer and the barbecued meat of cattle they've looted from their victims.

* * *

Enose could hear the lamenting of the people inside the church.

'What did you do?' I ask him.

'Nothing,' he says. 'We made jokes and drank beer and ate meat.'

* * *

The killers report for duty early the next morning. It takes another two days of slashing, hacking and clubbing to exterminate all the *inyenzis*. When it seems that everyone is dead, the *interahamwe* bring dogs, which begin eating the corpses.

Valentina stays among the rotting corpses for forty-three days. For the first few days she is in terrible pain, but eventually she loses all feeling, along with any sense of being alive. She manages to crawl out now and then to drink rainwater.

As the killers flee before the lightning-fast advance of the rebel army and cross the border into Tanzania, Valentina and a handful of survivors emerge from their holes and hiding places. The stronger ones light fires and scour the area for bananas and wild fruit, trying to stay alive while waiting for death to take them as well.

* * *

At the same time that Kennedy and the rebels emerge victorious from Jari, I am in Rwanda to report on the genocide, and rebel soldiers whisk me off to a massacre site in the south-east corner of the country. Emile Ruta-gengwa is in the Land Cruiser with me.

We leave the capital in an army convoy and head east along the main road, normally a major artery gridlocked with people, trucks, cars, buses and taxis. But Rwanda is now a place where nothing moves except for roadside grasses that gently bow in the soft breeze. The usual sounds of Africa – a cacophony of ebullient voices, pumping music, frenzied traffic, barking dogs and screaming children – that always hover in the background are absent today. The only sign of life is a kaleidoscopic range of wild flowers that have burst forth in the last week or two as a result of incessant rain. As the diesel growls up the stony hill leading to the church, swarms of white butterflies play host to us.

We first stop at the clinic dispensary, a few hundred metres from the church. I smell death long before I see it. Thousands of flies take to the humid air when we walk in. Seven or eight female corpses are stretched out on their backs in a neat row. Shreds of colourful sarongs still cling to their blackened and bloated bodies. Flesh peels off their white cheekbones and rib bones poke like chopsticks from their hollowed chest cavities. Swarms of maggots wriggle around the bodies and pools of black bodily fluids stain the bare cement floor. Their skirts are hitched up around their thighs. They were raped before they were killed.

The dispensary is a crude prelude of what awaits us in the church. My head is a confused mess. We drive in silence to the imposing red-bricked basilica. I am forced to press a cloth to my nose as I get out of the car because of the four or five or six thousand decomposing bodies discharging their metallic odour into the sky.

How does one describe the stench, the rotting flesh, ballooned bodies and vacated bowels? Is it really necessary to know all the detail? What do you say about a mother and her two children huddled together where they were clubbed to death? The corpse of an elderly man still clutching a Bible? What about the cleaved skulls, heads severed from their torsos, hands without fingers, arms without hands, legs without feet, toddlers crushed or hacked almost in half and body parts strewn everywhere? Or the lone figure in front of the altar, cut down, his feet chopped off as he crawled towards the crucifix?

The scene unfolding in front of me is, ultimately, indescribable. In *The Zanzibar Chest*, Aidan Hartley writes: 'I can't put my finger on exactly how death smells. The stench of human putrefaction is different from that of all other animals. It moves us as instinctively as the cry of a newly born baby. It lies at one end of the olfactory register. A man who has been dead for seven days reeks of boiling beans, guava fruit, glue, blown handkerchiefs, cloves and vinegar.'

* * *

I return to the church a year after the massacre. Nyarubuye has been declared a genocide memorial and the bones have been left untouched. The surrounding fields have been cultivated, there is human life on the terraced slopes, and villages and markets are hives of activity. The air is filled with a fragrant breeze and birdsong. The stench of a year earlier is gone. Rotten flesh has been reduced to white skeletons. Even the tormented faces are nothing more than bleached skulls.

* * *

Like Auschwitz in Poland and Tuol Sleng in Cambodia, the red-bricked basilica on a rocky outcrop in Rwanda is an eternal reminder of the insanity that enveloped a tiny nation while the world looked on. Since then, a host of dignitaries and statesmen and -women have visited Nyarubuye to pay homage to the dead and have their pictures taken among the skulls and bones that are now neatly stacked in parish buildings next to the church. In March 1998, American president Bill Clinton became the first Western head of state to visit Rwanda and expressed regret for not intervening during the genocide. It was a rather contrived apology as he never left Kigali's international airport and spent no more than a few hours on Rwandan soil.

Among the more sincere pilgrims to Nyarubuye were Archbishop Desmond Tutu and Lieutenant General Roméo Dallaire, the man who had warned the world long before the president's aircraft was shot down that extremists were plotting genocide. He left Rwanda broken, disillusioned, haunted and suicidal, but bent on telling the world how he and his mission had been abandoned and betrayed by the international community and UN bureaucrats who refused to give him the men and the means to stop the killings.

'I know there is a God,' writes Dallaire in his book, *Shake Hands with the Devil: The Failure of Humanity in Rwanda*, 'because in Rwanda I shook hands with the devil. I have seen him, I have smelled him and I have touched him. I know the devil exists and therefore I know there is a God.'

- As for the Arch, he hardly made it to the church entrance before he crumpled into a heap and sobbed.

There is little to comfort the survivors of Nyarubuye, except perhaps that the architect of the massacre has been brought to book. Justice caught up with *bourgmestre* Gacumbitsi in 2001, when he was arrested in Tanzania and handed over to the ICTR. The court heard that Gacumbitsi was one of Hutu Power's most efficient genocidaires and was instrumental in ensuring that Tutsis in the south-east of Rwanda were almost completely annihilated. He not only incited Hutus all over the area to kill, but also encouraged the *interahamwe* to rape and 'enjoy the *inyenzis* while they could still scream and kick'. In November 2004, Gacumbitsi was convicted of genocide, rape and crimes against humanity, and sentenced to thirty years' imprisonment.

Valentina survived against all odds. She was admitted to hospital with her hand chopped in half and two deep gashes in her neck. One of the wounds became infected and medical staff thought she would die. She didn't. The physical wounds healed and her emaciated frame eventually swelled and she grew into a healthy young woman. She became the voice of those terrifying seconds, minutes, hours, days and weeks at Nyarubuye.

BBC journalist Fergal Keane was one of the first to show Valentina to the outside world, dubbing her 'the Rwandan girl who refused to die'. He writes: 'There comes a point in the telling of a story where the existing vocabulary of suffering becomes inadequate, where words wither in the face of an unrelenting darkness. As a reporter I found this the most difficult story of my career to tell. As a parent I listened to Valentina's story with a sense of heartbreak. I marvelled at her courage but felt deep anger that this should happen to any child.'

Nyarubuye continues to haunt everyone who saw it. Many years on, I still find it difficult to write about it. Eighteen years ago, for one brief moment I was exposed to the ultimate horror of man's depravity that soldiers like Kennedy, Xavier and thousands of others witnessed on a regular basis. Can you even imagine what havoc it played with their sense of decency and empathy?

29

The road to Gisenyi

By the middle of June, the RPA rules most of the country and commands vital sectors of the capital. The killings have slowed down, simply because there are not many Tutsis left to kill. As the rebels surge through the country, churches, houses, halls, hospitals, schools, banana groves, army barracks, pits, rivers and vacated roadblocks reveal their horrifying secrets.

Embedded journalists – of which I am one – are whisked under escort to slaughter sites from where they beam the images of genocide into living rooms around the world. It stirs swells of emotion and heaps of condemnation, but fails to spur the international community into any significant action.

Less than two weeks after the death of the president, HRW labels the killings genocide and demands that the UN and the international community meet their legal obligation to intervene. The Genocide Convention of 1946, passed by the UN's General Assembly in the aftermath of the Holocaust, compels member states to intervene in cases where a population is being annihilated. The Clinton administration actually forbids the use of the dreaded g-word and the United States and others jargon themselves out of liability. The furthest Washington goes is to say that 'acts of genocide may have occurred' in Rwanda.

(Years later, then UN secretary-general Boutros-Ghali said in an interview that he had various meetings during the genocide with the American and British ambassadors and urged that action be taken to stop the killings. This is how he described their reaction: 'Come on, Boutros, relax. Don't put us in a difficult position. The mood is not for intervention, you will obtain nothing. We will not move.')

In Kigali, evidence is emerging that UNAMIR is not just understaffed and ill-equipped, but is literally being starved by New York. The Ghanaian contingent has run out of food, drinking water and fuel. Furthermore, they have to deal with a football stadium full of Tutsi refugees. Only a stone's throw from the UN headquarters, children are dying of dysentery and diarrhoea; cholera has broken out and there are cases of malaria. The soldiers have no medicine to treat anyone.

Dallaire needs 100 armoured personnel carriers to be effective on the ground. The United States has vast and unused fleets of post–Cold War vehicles. The Pentagon commits fifty, but inexplicably changes its mind and comes up with a price tag of $4 million, which they insist has to be prepaid. Then they want another $6 million for transportation. The personnel carriers eventually arrive in Uganda stripped of machine guns, radios, tools, spare parts and training manuals. The United States has literally supplied the UN with tons of expensive and useless rusting metal.

* * *

In and around the capital, Kennedy and his rebel compatriots are rounding up the remnants of the FAR and their *interahamwe* collaborators. In Katenga they lay an ambush for retreating enemy soldiers.

'They walked into the ambush. We mowed them down. I had Rambo, my machine gun. It had a big barrel. It was lethal. It fired unbelievably. But it was also heavy. We didn't take any prisoners,' Kennedy says.

'What did you do with wounded government soldiers?' I ask.

'We finished them off.'

'Were those orders from your commanders?'

'Not really. You took your initiative.'

'But you know today that you cannot do that! It is illegal according to international law.'

'Yes, but at the time I didn't even know that there was a law like that. To kill an enemy at the frontline, that's no crime. We obeyed orders and we didn't question our commanders. We were guided by them.'

* * *

A few days later, Kennedy, now a member of 9th Battalion, is at the front of a rebel column plodding the *panya* roads back to the former northern rebel hotbed of Byumba. The FAR soldiers have retreated to their stronghold of Ruhengeri in the north-west. This is their last footing of resistance, and Kennedy and his compatriots have to dislodge them. Once in Byumba, rebels footslog along the Virungas to attack the enemy from the rear while other RPA units prepare for an assault from the front. One of the FAR bases, Kuwait, is a secret underground facility a few kilometres outside Ruhengeri.

Kennedy: 'I was at the front. I was never behind. We stormed Kuwait at three in the morning. They were trying to get out of their underground hole and we shot them. We mowed them down. Two days and they were out of Kuwait barracks. They fled to Ruhengeri, where other RPA units were waiting for them. We followed them. We were shooting them all the way to Ruhengeri. We killed many.'

With defeat inevitable, the FAR in the north-west take flight to the south in an effort to make it to the lake town of Gisenyi from where they can vanish into Zaire. The rebels are in hot pursuit. Kennedy is standing on the back of a truck with his LMG settled in his hands and his finger curled around the trigger. The road from Ruhengeri to Gisenyi, which passes through Xavier's hometown of Mukamira, turns into a slaughterhouse.

* * *

'We followed them,' continues Kennedy. 'They were running. We were shooting. They had mixed with civilians and that is where thousands died. The civilians were also fleeing. It was chaos on that road. FAR soldiers took off their uniforms to look like civilians. They threw their guns away or buried them. We killed thousands. They couldn't even run into the bush because we were also in the bush.'

'What about those who handed themselves over?'

'No, we took no prisoners. It was a fantastic victory. The whole operation took two days.'

'What did the road look like?'

'It was raining. There was no sun. There were men, women and kids on the road, carrying things on their heads and backs. We were not to kill women and children because they were running away. The soldiers had gotten rid of their uniforms so it was difficult to distinguish who was who. Every man was an enemy. It wasn't easy for men to survive. This fighting was the last kick of the dying cow. The civilians were terrified, hiding in the banana plantations. They were screaming. There were bodies everywhere. Some had not even finished dying. The road was a mess. It was full of bodies. Kids, women, soldiers, everything. We were in high spirits. Nothing could stop us. The war was over.'

* * *

A hundred days after Habyarimana's plane was shot down and the mass killings commenced, the guns fall silent. Kagame declares the civil war over and the next day in Kigali a government of national unity is sworn in. The president is a Hutu, but Kagame claims the vital positions of vice-president and minister of defence. He's the real power behind the throne. (Almost twenty years on, he rules the country as his own personal kingdom and with the same iron fist that galvanised his forces to victory.)

But this is no elated conquest. No new government has ever faced a greater challenge with fewer resources. On every front, a crisis looms. The country has been looted and the new administration inherits a wasteland. There is a country but no state. There is no power, water or telephones. Government ministers have no staff, offices, equipment or vehicles. Only two members of government have any experience in running a department or administration. Most of them, in fact, had never even been to Rwanda before the genocide. There is no money in the banks, hospitals are starved of medicine, markets are empty, livestock have been plundered, and doctors, lawyers, teachers and other professionals have either been killed or left the country.

Rotting bodies are everywhere; hospitals, schools and churches are stinking mortuaries. In the whole of Rwanda, there are only six judges to deal with tens of thousands of genocide-accused incarcerated in choked prisons. The streets of Kigali are almost empty. Only a sixth of the original population of 300 000 remains in the capital. Whole communities have been annihilated. The population is divided and the RPF is mistrusted by most. Above all, people are traumatised and in shock. We will never know the true number of dead, but the world has settled on a figure of 800 000.

* * *

And a new calamity looms: a sea of soot-faced outcasts trapped on a volcanic sheet of ragged rock. As the rebels enter Kigali and capture bigger towns around the country, a million Hutus, fleeing before the RPF advance and spurred on by *interahamwe* and FAR troops, flood into neighbouring Zaire with whatever they can carry in their arms, balance on their heads or push in carts. Bureaucrats and businessmen pile household goods, radios, television sets, kitchen equipment, their families and in-laws into their cars and join mile upon mile of people filing along the road from Kigali to Gisenyi.

The refugees settle on lava rock that stretches for many miles from Goma along the Rwandan border. Within days, six refugee camps, each bigger than most cities in the region, rise from nothing. It is an almost delusory image that meets international aid workers and journalists: kilometre upon kilometre of blue-canvas shanties cloaked in the smog of cooking fires. Within days, people start dying. Cholera is unleashed on a million souls trapped on an expanse of stone with nowhere to go. Between 30 000 and 40 000 die in the three or four weeks before the disease is contained.

Death becomes an almost pedestrian event. Those who have died during the night are rolled up in straw mats and left next to the road for collection. The hard rock makes it impossible to bury them and bull-dozers are brought in to dig mass graves where corpses lie in crumpled heaps until they can be covered with lime and soil.

30

The survivors

It is a few days after the dawn of the new Rwanda and Xavier Ngabo, now an army clerk based in Gitarama in central Rwanda, is given leave to go home. He arrives in Mukamira after lunch. It is a drizzly day with cushions of mist tossing down Mount Karisimbi and rolling through the villages located at its edge.

He saunters into a bar, orders a Primus beer and contemplates his pilgrimage back home. He recognises a young man – a Hutu – who grew up with him.

'I heard you were in the army,' the friend says, 'which is why you survived. Every Tutsi in Mukamira is dead.'

Xavier stares outside at the fading and greyish day and asks the question of which he knows the answer. 'Do you have news about my family?'

His friend shakes his head. 'You are strong, Xavier, because you survived the war and now you must be strong again. Your family is no more. There are no Tutsis left in Mukamira.'

He tells Xavier that the *interahamwe* were well prepared so the killings started on the seventh of April and by the eighth every Tutsi was dead. They had lists and threw roadblocks around the village to prevent anyone from escaping.

'How did my mother and brothers and sisters die? Please, can you tell me?' Xavier pleads.

'I don't know how they died but I know they are dead.'

'And what happened to them? Where are they buried?'

'That I don't know either, but don't go there now. It's too late and it's dangerous. There are still *interahamwe* hiding in the villages. Come back later again.'

Xavier returns to Gitarama and commences his monotonous army chores: 'People were enjoying the victory of the RPF and I had to pretend that I too was happy. I was laughing but I knew it was going to be difficult for me to have a life. I hadn't completed my education and I had no family left. I felt a deep pain, a pain I have been living with since 1991. And I couldn't show this pain to anyone. Part of it was that I hadn't been able to bury my father and mother or any of my family. Where were their bones? They were lying there somewhere or were under the ground mixed with others. I had to find them in order to give them a proper burial.'

Two weeks later, Xavier returns to Mukamira, this time with a military escort that swoops on the village to arrest his father's killers. His family home has been razed to the ground. It is literally as though the three-roomed dwelling perched in the shadow of the eucalyptus grove never existed. The trees have also been cut down. The family's land is no longer demarcated. One section is now part of Boniface's plot, while another portion has been incorporated into the property of another of the slaughterers. The killers have expunged the existence of Xavier and his family from the face of the earth. The soldiers surround Boniface's house but discover he is already in prison, not just for Xavier's father's killing, but for several other murders. He was an *interahamwe* leader in the area. Fati is visiting someone in the south-east, while the others are somewhere in the vicinity.

* * *

'Everyone in that area was involved in the killings,' says Xavier. 'All of them were *interahamwe*. Fati and his friends had guns and they manned the roadblocks. The men killed and the ladies looted. Someone got the bricks, others got the roof, that one cut the trees down and another took the furniture. One takes the table, another the chair and that one the radio. One wants the broom and this one says, "Excuse me but the pots and pans are mine." We didn't have much but they took everything. After they had looted, they divided the land among themselves. I tried to ask a neighbour who wasn't involved why they had broken down our house but he didn't answer me. Nobody wanted to talk. There was a silence.'

'Why didn't the killers go to Zaire to hide like the others?' I ask him.

'They didn't leave because they were not afraid. They had killed all the Tutsis. They felt safe.'

It is agonisingly taxing for Xavier to talk about his family. He blathers in intervals and grapples through whimpers to find words – English is his third language after Kinyarwanda and French.

'This has been very painful for a very long time. You are the first person I have told all these things. I tell you my life, which I've always kept a secret because it is too painful. I was sixteen or seventeen when my father died.

With machetes! I couldn't share it with anyone else because the pain is too deep.'

The only neighbour who embraced Xavier with open arms was Marciano, an elderly Hutu woman who had been his mother's dear friend. She told him the soldiers and the *interahamwe* arrived at seven o'clock on the morning after the president's plane was shot down. She watched them hammering on the door of Beatrice's home before bursting in.

'The soldiers shot my brothers and sisters inside the house. The youngest was nine. My mother escaped and ran to Marciano's house, where she said to her: "My husband and my children are no longer, so let us pray together so that I can die peacefully." Marciano is a believer, a strong woman. So she prayed with my mother. When the soldiers and *interahamwe* arrived, my mother was at peace. She wanted to die and told them so. They took her away. Marciano heard the gunshots after a few minutes, so she knew my mother was dead. My mother was the last Tutsi survivor of that village. Each and every one was by then dead.'

* * *

Xavier isn't alone in his torment. Across Rwanda, many have had to come to terms with the fact that they are sole survivors on a continent where life revolves around family. One such person is Emile Rutagengwa, who years later recounts in a stealthy and reserved tone how three days after the fall of Kigali he went home to face the fate of his family. Among the first Tutsis to perish were professionals and intellectuals and those who had sons in the rebel army. Emile's father, Kalisa, was guilty on both counts: he was a lawyer and his son a second lieutenant in Kagame's army.

'There was nobody in the house but there was blood everywhere,' remembers Emile. 'There was nothing left; everything had been taken. They shot Mama where she was hiding behind the cupboard. The family survived for one day by hiding with our Hutu neighbour in his house but went home at night to sleep at their own place. That's when that neighbour phoned the soldiers. They killed my mother, father and three brothers and sisters. I could see they suffered a lot.'

Their bodies were tossed onto the back of a truck and driven away, probably to be deposited in a mass grave. The ratting neighbour fled to Zaire. The killers of Emile's family will probably forever remain incognito – inglorious and obscure figures in striped uniforms that belted from

house to house to dispatch those who happened to carry the wrong identity card.

'You will not believe it, but about 300 of my extended family on my
mother's side and 180 on my father's side were killed,' Emile tells me. 'I
have one aunty who lives in Germany. She has been there for forty years
and I haven't seen her for a very long time. I have one uncle who lives in
Rwanda and he's a businessman. The rest are all dead. The children, the
old people, everyone.

'Things are very bad for me every April. I can't work, I can't go anywhere and I can't do anything. It's like a funeral for me. I look at my family's
photos. It was a beautiful family. And it wasn't just my mother and father
and brothers and sisters. My grandfather was killed by people who worked
for him for more than twenty years. He gave them cows, helped them
to get married, everything! The killers of my grandparents are in prison to
this day. But they don't know where the bodies are. They killed, but other
people took the bodies away and buried them. I tried to speak to the killers
but they said, "No, it wasn't us". I now have to accept that I will never see
their bones and that I have to move on.'

* * *

I ask Xavier how many of his extended family survived. He ponders the
question and belches out a shriek of laughter. 'You know how we Africans
like to make children, so there were many before the genocide.' His dour
expression returns before he adds: 'My immediate family were all killed
and virtually every one of my extended family. Very few survived. Most of
my uncles and all my aunties are dead. Two uncles were outside the country so they survived, but their families stayed behind and they were killed.
All my cousins are dead. The niece who brought me messages, Charlotte,
is also dead. If I had a family tree, I would be one of the last branches. My
child is a little branch. But there are no other branches. That tree was cut
down like one of the eucalyptus trees around our house.'

* * *

Soon after Xavier's visit to Mukamira, Boniface's co-executioners – Fati,
Jean-Paul, Bandora and several others – are also arrested, charged with
murder and incarcerated in Mukamira's prison. Rwanda's eighteen prisons
and 200 detention centres are human rights calamities. The prison system

was designed to house 12 000 inmates, but 125 000 genocide suspects are eventually behind bars. Inmates have to find a place to sit or stand between the legs of others, take turns to sleep and wait for friends or family to bring food. Hundreds of prisoners require amputations, as their feet literally rot in the damp of the prisons.

In an effort to find the bones of his parents and give them a decent burial, Xavier pays a visit to Mukamira's prison. Boniface, decked out in Rwanda's distinctive pink jail garb, is brought to him.

'Hello, Boniface. How are you?'

The prisoner doesn't answer, but shock registers on his face at the sight of Xavier.

'I want to cooperate with you because I want to get the bones of my father,' Xavier continues.

'It wasn't me and I don't know anything,' Boniface replies. 'Where were you when your father died? Did you see me do it? No, you didn't. So how can you say it was me?'

'Fine, you stay just where you are. Goodbye, Boniface.' With that Xavier asks the guard to take him away.

31

The new Rwanda

'And so, how did the war end for you?' I ask Kennedy.

It is over seventeen years later, and in my dining room in Johannesburg, Kennedy wrings his hands and plays with a pen. 'That's the problem, my brother, because the war never ended for me.'

'How come?'

'It just carried on. It never stopped. The genocide was finished, but the war continued. I fought twenty-four hours a day, seven days a week. Since I joined the RPA, I never had a day off.'

* * *

The mass exodus of Hutus to Zaire during the last days of the war plays beautifully into the hands of the extremists. The masses provide perfect cover for the *interahamwe* and FAR soldiers to feign the role of desperate refugees and bleed international-aid hearts. But the chaos also provides a perfect base for Hutu Power to regroup, recruit new disciples and plot the final phase of Tutsi extermination. The same mayors who oversaw the genocide and the same *interahamwe* who wielded the machetes during the mass killings are still in charge. Refugees who speak of returning to Rwanda are branded traitors, and many are killed.

Lieutenant General Dallaire realises the camps have become recruitment centres for further genocide and are being organised as replicas of the Hutu Power state. He warns that the presence of the genocidaires in the camps has the potential to ignite a catastrophe throughout the Great Lakes region that will be even worse than what has already come to pass. He proposes that the UN and the international community separate the genuinely displaced from the killers. The refugees should go back to Rwanda and the genocidaires be brought to justice. At a meeting with ambassadors to discuss his plan, the French and Americans reject it as unworkable.

As Rwanda regains a sense of normality and Kagame is hailed as a visionary and 'new breed' of African leader, the extremists and genocidaires in Zaire launch raids into north-west Rwanda to ultimately complete the programme of genocide, kill witnesses and destabilise the new regime.

The border between Rwanda and Zaire becomes one of the most dangerous places in the world. Kennedy and many like him are condemned to survive at the forefront of an increasingly dirty and harsh border war that will eventually ignite the continent's own 'world war' and lead to the demise of millions. RPA units are deployed in Zaire to hunt down the remnants of the FAR and *interahamwe* that have regrouped. Rwanda's north-west is once again plummeted into war and the Virungas remain an overgrown amphitheatre where both man and beast are trapped in a battle for survival.

Kennedy commands a platoon of around thirty soldiers that scours the muddy *panya* roads within the interwoven and crammed jungle of the Virungas in search of militia and *interahamwe*.

* * *

What were the conditions like? I ask Kennedy.

Sniggering, he says, 'It was always raining. It never stopped. There was water and mud everywhere. We wore plastic gumboots. Some of the other soldiers lost their toes because they rotted in those boots. We had to climb the Virungas to set ambushes. We had to wait through the night for the enemy to arrive. There were still lots of *interahamwe* and they killed survivors every day. We had to hunt them down before they could kill.'

'Did you arrest any?'

'I was the IS for the company so any captured *interahamwe* would be brought to me. We got information by threatening to kill them. They told us they were preparing for another war. Some even had guns in Rwanda that they hid when they ran away.'

'Were they willing to give you information?'

'Of course you forced them. We tied them. We beat them. Nobody we captured left alive. Once they spoke, we killed them. There were no prisoners; what would you do with them? After they gave you information, you killed them.'

Before I can talk, he says, 'There are so many things here. I don't want you to write them.'

He wrings his hands. With eyes cast down, he wants to know how I'm going to depict this chapter of his life in the book. Exactly as it happened, I tell him. But is this really necessary? he wants to know. I tell him it is because I have to write his story as honestly as I can. He slowly nods his head as he casts his mind back to events he has attempted to forever entomb in the remotest sanctum of his memory.

'I was just a peasant soldier,' he continues. 'I didn't think at the time it was wrong. We were still at war. That was my frame of mind. I now know these guys were under our control and we should have treated them as prisoners of war. We could have screened them while they were in prison. Then the innocent should have been released.'

'Did any beg you for mercy?'

'Of course. Even now, I am not comfortable. Because I knew some of them were innocent. They were just ordinary peasants.'

'After the RPF took power, you had prisons and courts. What happened to those prisoners?'

'I can tell you now I never took any person I captured or arrested to Kigali.'

'At the time, the genocide was over, the RPF was in government and the president was a Hutu. Did you still regard Hutus as the enemy?'

'All those people we arrested were Hutus. They still tried to ambush us, they were killing civilians. Those guys were bad guys as far as I could tell.'

Kennedy and his comrades-in-arms were ruthlessly coerced by their commanders to prolong their war exploits without any regard for their mental or physical well-being. 'Soldiers started getting sick. There were lots of mental illnesses because some couldn't take it any longer. There were political commissars who gave us political education to motivate us. But we didn't learn a thing about human rights,' Kennedy explains.

'Did the RPA in any way attend to the mental health of their soldiers?'

'I'm sorry to say, but that is a white mentality, not an African mentality. That's how it works in Europe, not in Africa. In Africa nobody cares about you. If you die, they recruit another one. I had never heard of a psychologist before I came to South Africa. Maybe Kagame knew because he trained in America, but he didn't pass it on to his soldiers. They had no interest in our mental health.'

The portraits of torture and execution that Kennedy paints in my dining room are by now almost clichéd and routine. They evoke author Hannah Arendt's observation at the post–Second World War trial of Nazi Holocaust conspirator Adolf Eichmann of how utterly normal he was. One would have expected one of the chief architects of the *Endlösung der Judenfrage* (Final Solution to the Jewish Question) to be oozing evil. Yet at his trial, Arendt was struck by how normal Eichmann appeared; a mild, dull and simple human being that could have been anyone. This was for her more frightening than anything else: his ordinariness.

There is, of course, no comparison between Kennedy and Eichmann, but it strikes me over the days of our interviews how commonplace and mundane killing became to him and his cohorts in the RPA. They killed without reservation or challenge.

'Do you remember some of these people?' I ask him of his victims.

'I remember many of them. I can especially remember some of the ladies.'

'What do you remember?'

'There was a lady selling beer next to the road. We got information that she was selling beer but at the same time was cooperating with the *interahamwe*. I arrested her with fifty guys. I arrested them during the week and on Friday I put them on the truck. At night we drove them to the military base. Then we killed them.'

'Including this woman?'

'Yes.'

'Why do you remember this woman?'

'She cried a lot. Every soldier around there knew her.'

'What did she look like?'

'She was very young. She pleaded.'

'Do you think she was innocent?'

'Of course nobody believed her. I now think that she was innocent like other people.'

'Why did you at the time think she was guilty?'

'You got information. You could not verify or scrutinise that information. It was very difficult.'

'So she was killed?'

'Yes, and what pains me was the death they were dying.'

'How did they die?'

Kennedy looks down at the dining-room table and mumbles: 'We didn't shoot them.'

* * *

His hands are clasped around his head, his shoulders are drawn together, his body is quivering and he is crying uncontrollably. I allow Kennedy to grieve. I don't prod and probe about how his captives died. Do we really need to know how they were put to death? Does it matter whether they were strangled or clubbed or poisoned? It was wrong, vile and evil.

When he stops, he lifts his head, gazes in front of him and says, 'I did all of this for what? I have blood on my hands for nothing. I killed for nothing.' Once he has regained his composure, he continues. 'Their bodies were just thrown into a mass grave.'

'Isn't a mass grave dangerous because others could discover it?'

'And so what?'

'How could you do things like that? A person like you?'

'When it is war, it is war. It was orders. I was young, we were in a war. Every man who was not in our army was an enemy. Everyone who was not with us was against us. At that time, I didn't think she could be innocent. And she died with many others. On an operation, if a woman runs away, you shoot her. And you also shoot the kid, because the child cannot remain alone.'

'But a woman might be running away because she's scared, not because she's guilty!' I argue.

'Yes, for sure, but how could you know? We were young. It was a daily thing, it was normal. Yes, that was sad, but how would my colleagues take me if I didn't do it?'

Hit squads throughout the world have their own peculiar vocabulary when they damn someone to die. From apartheid South Africa, Pinochet's Chile and Franco's Spain to present-day Syria, homicidal outfits never use the words 'murder' or 'kill'. People are 'taken out', made to 'disappear', or permanently 'removed' from society.

Kagame's squads never used the word *ubwicanyi* – killing – either. 'We would say: take them where they belong. That's how we spoke among one another,' says Kennedy. 'Or in Swahili we would say: *kumufanyiya* for one or *wafamyiye* for many. It means "to do work on him" or "to do work on them". When we said that, it meant to go and kill them. It was a military code we used. There was no documentation. They just disappeared.'

32

Doing evil

In Aleksandr Solzhenitsyn's classic *The Gulag Archipelago*, he writes that 'in order for men to do great evil, they must first believe they are doing good'. People commit wrongs because they consider them to be just. This explains how a regime, a dictator or a führer can set up something as debauched as a death camp and get guards to meticulously follow their orders.

Tyranny triumphs not just because ordinary people blindly and mechanically follow orders, but also because they consider their deeds to be for the greater good. And, of course, the more uneducated, isolated or ignorant the guards or soldiers are, the easier it is to mould their beliefs and get them to heed your every call.

Evildoing is not the preserve of a small minority of demented individuals. It lurks within all of us. That is why it is utterly absurd for me or you to say that we would never have done what Kennedy did. Who knows how we would have acted had we been in his shoes at the time? In all probability, exactly the same.

American historian Christopher Browning's book *Ordinary Men: Reserve Police Battalion 101 and the Final Solution in Poland* provides the clearest example of the fallibility of ordinary men and how easy it is to be swept away by torrents of evildoing; how ordinary people succumb to social pressure to commit acts that would otherwise be unthinkable.

Browning says that in March 1942, around 80 per cent of all Holocaust victims were still alive. A mere eleven months later, 80 per cent of all victims were dead. During this period, able-bodied soldiers were dispatched to the Russian front, which prompts Browning to ask: 'Where had they found the manpower during this pivotal year of the war for such an astounding logistical achievement in mass murder?'

A study of Nazi war-crimes archives revealed the activities of Reserve Battalion 101, a unit of about 500 men from Hamburg, Germany. Too old to be drafted into the regular army, they were predominantly working-class and lower-middle-income men with families and no history of crime – as ordinary as they come. They were sent with very little training to Poland to scour remote villages in search of Jews in hiding.

The 101st Battalion commander told his troops at the outset that any individual could refuse to execute men, women and children. According to records, half initially refused. But by the end of their mission, social pressure and indoctrination had prodded 90 per cent of the men into killing Jews. In just four months, they murdered 38 000 Jews and condemned another 45 000 to their deaths at the concentration camp at Treblinka. Many proudly took photographs of themselves with their victims and didn't even attempt to hide what they had done.

It raises the question of why 10 per cent did not participate. But then, most of us are not part of that 10 per cent in any case. I also wonder how many of the 10 per cent would still have refused to kill if they were ordered or coerced. Not many, I presume, because ignoring a command during war can land you up in chains or with a bullet hole in your forehead.

* * *

Have you ever heard of the so-called death marches of camp survivors back to their towns and cities in the Reich? As the Allied Forces advanced during the closing days of the Second World War and liberated concentration camp inmates, 500 000 Jews embarked on a journey back home. Many were weak, frail and in bad health. In *The Death Marches: The Final Phase of Nazi Genocide*, Daniel Blatman chronicles the journey. He estimates that half of the survivors died on their way back to their towns and cities: hunted down, sniped and killed by ordinary German citizens who were so indoctrinated with Nazi dogma that upon their thousands they became killers, despite not ever being ordered to behave in such a fashion. They killed Jewish survivors in cold blood, in ones and twos, often tens, and sometimes hundreds at a time.

* * *

In the seventies, a Californian psychology professor conducted a study that was to become a cornerstone of social psychology. In what is now famously known as the Stanford Prison Experiment, Philip Zimbardo set up a mock prison in the basement of Stanford University's psychology building. He selected twenty-four young men, chosen after undergoing psychological tests and clinical interviews to ensure that they were as healthy and normal as possible. Zimbardo assigned each subject to be either a prison guard or an inmate. He got the local police department to arrest the inmates and the prison conditions were as realistic as possible.

The researchers were initially concerned that the participants wouldn't take the experiment seriously enough. They needn't have worried. The two groups quickly started to behave like their real-life counterparts. After little more than a day, an inmate had to be released because he was suffering from acute depression, uncontrollable crying and fits of rage. After another few days, four more inmates had to be set free after showing similar reactions.

But it was the behaviour of the guards that was most telling and disturbing. Zimbardo had to abandon the experiment after six days because of the pathology he was witnessing. Otherwise pacifistic young men started behaving sadistically, inflicting pain, humiliation and suffering on the inmates. Some of the guards even reported enjoying doing so. Zimbardo was alarmed at his own behaviour as that of prison superintendent. He began to walk, talk and act like a rigid institutional authority figure far more concerned about the security of his 'prison' than the well-being of the inmates. He surmised: 'The Evil Situation triumphed over the Good People.'

Thirty years on and after much more research and observation, Zimbardo concludes: 'We are not born with tendencies toward good or evil but with mental templates to do either. Any deed, for good or evil, that any human being has ever performed or committed, you and I could also commit – given the same situational forces.'

* * *

If you wonder how Kennedy could have perceived his depraved actions to be justified, this is what Kagame said after the RPF assumed power in July 1994: 'The only thing we plan is to kill more of those who cause problems … Sometimes it is easy to identify who is armed and who is not. Sometimes it is difficult.'

There is ample evidence of RPA abuses and killings in the north-west in the months and year following the genocide. The infamous Gersony Report claims there is credible evidence that in the Gisenyi area Hutus were arbitrarily arrested and executed. HRW reports that the RPA generally treated the populace as collaborators of the genocidaires, killing 'thousands'. Amnesty International says the killings in north-west Rwanda became 'almost a banality in the lives of ordinary Rwandese'; civilians were living in a state of fear; and thousands were removed from detention centres and executed.

'How many people do you think you might have killed?' I ask Kennedy. 'I didn't count, but it was many. Many.'

33

Rwanda's Alcatraz

Kennedy is about to taste his own medicine: what it means to suffer the wrath of Kagame's fighting machine. It is the end of 1994 and Kennedy has now been trudging the mire and mud of the Virungas for six months. It is almost three years since he joined the RPA and, for more than a thousand days, the young man has done non-stop battle for Kagame and country. He has not had a single day off or any period of rest.

At the time, and for many years after, it is impossible for RPA soldiers to get demobilised or discharged from the army. For as long as the new regime needs you, you will subsist over the barrel of a gun and scrape a meagre soldier's existence in the sludge of the Virungas.

* * *

'In 1995, selected soldiers were withdrawn and the next thing they were studying,' says Kennedy. 'You then heard they have a relative who is high up in the army or politically connected. You had to stay behind and fight. All I wanted to do was study. I'd given my life to the liberation of my country and now I was stuck.'

Although his experience was similar, Xavier takes a different view. 'I was in the army because it was a safe place and I had nowhere to go. I wanted to complete my secondary education but it wasn't easy. Those who went to study were the ones who had connections. You couldn't just leave the army. You had to stay and fight. But even if I could leave, where would I go? At least I got clothes, a place to stay and a little bit of money.'

* * *

It is December 1994 and Kennedy asks permission to take a few days' leave.

'Why?' his commanding officer wants to know.

'My mother lives in Butare, *bwana* [sir], and the last time I saw her was in 1988 when she left Uganda and moved back to Rwanda. And then there are my grandparents. The last time I saw them was before I went to the army. They were then very old and I need to find out if they made it to

Rwanda after the genocide. I only need a few days, sir, and it is very important to me.'

The officer matter-of-factly refuses his request and orders Kennedy to kit out for another patrol in the jungle.

A few days later, Kennedy sneaks off the base. He is dressed in civilian clothes and has a small bag slung across his shoulder. He plans to be away for only a few days and has arranged with platoon mates to cover for him. He will stay with a friend in Kigali, where he has never set foot. From there, he will travel to the southern university town of Butare and onwards to eastern Rwanda. He reckons that if his grandparents Francis and Kamabera have made it back, they will most probably have settled with their cattle there. Most Tutsi returnees from south-eastern Uganda settled in this area after the genocide because it offered excellent grazing.

Kennedy stays in Kigali for a day before boarding a minibus for Butare. As he is settling in for the two-hour journey, they come up to a roadblock, manned by RPA soldiers. They search the minibus and spot Kennedy.

'Who are you?' they demand to know. He doesn't know what to say. 'Who are you?'

'I'm a soldier,' Kennedy admits.

'Why are you in civilian clothes?'

'I'm on leave,' he responds.

'Where's your *kibali* [pass]?'

They ask the same question twice before he admits, 'I don't have one.'

The soldiers, their guns levelled at his chest, surround him. A military policeman cuffs him and orders him to sit down next to the road. He waits an hour or so. Eventually a van with armed soldiers picks him up and drives him to the psychiatric hospital on the outskirts of Kigali that has in the meantime been converted into a military detention centre. All the inmates are soldiers, mostly deserters.

Kennedy knows he's in trouble. Big, big trouble. He has deserted the frontline and there's no bigger crime than that. Kennedy and the others are incarcerated for two weeks in one of the wards before they are frogmarched onto trucks and driven away.

He thinks he's going back to his unit at the foot of the Virungas, but the trucks pass Mount Karisimbi and continue on to Gisenyi on the banks of Lake Kivu. It is dusk when they finally stop at a small harbour on the outskirts of town and the deserters are ordered at gunpoint to board military vessels. As the sun casts a saffron lick across the lake, the diesels roar to life and the boats point towards the void on the other side of the horizon.

Some detainees fear they are going to be dumped into the middle of the lake to drown. They beg and plead for their lives. Kennedy says nothing, awaiting his fate at the hands of his compatriots. Eventually, he spots a light or two in the distance. When they get closer, he realises that it is an island. This is where they dock and disembark.

Kennedy and the others are marched to a vacant stretch of land where they huddle together and wait for daybreak. The island is a military base; the remnants of artillery pieces and mortars are strewn around, left behind by the FAR when they fled a waterborne attack by rebel soldiers towards the end of the civil war. The soldiers are ordered to start digging *adaches*, obviously to serve as their future shelters.

An officer assembles them and tells them that they are military prisoners on the island of Iwawa, a restricted and classified military base in the middle of Lake Kivu. 'This is where you will stay until we decide that you have been rehabilitated and are fit to rejoin your respective units. Don't even think of escape,' he warns, 'because land is many miles away and you will drown – if we don't find you first and shoot you. Watch out where you walk because there are landmines around the island that the enemy planted before they fled. And don't drink the lake's water, because it is poisonous.'

Without a charge ever brought against him, Kennedy is incarcerated at Rwanda's own Alcatraz. Most dictatorships and military regimes have their Siberian gulag equivalents, where dissidents and insurrectionists are condemned to live out their days or until they conform and accede to programmes of re-education. Kagame's strategy of punishing his renegade soldiers – those lucky enough to live – is to retrain and re-educate them on a small island littered with mines and rife with malaria. Kennedy and his group are the first arrivals at Iwawa. A month later, there are several hundred disobedient soldiers. None of their families know where they are. They have simply disappeared.

'I was living in a cave again. You cut grass and you slept on it. In the morning, we started looking for wood because we had to cook our samp. That's all we got. Samp. I was cut off from the world. We were just moving ghosts. We were treated like criminals. If you didn't follow the rules, you could get ten, twenty, up to forty lashes. They just gave us blankets and maybe a piece of soap to wash with. We had to wash in the lake, and that's where the majority got blown up. So you asked yourself: am I ever going to be a human being again and am I going to get married and be normal?'

Kennedy is on Iwawa for eight months, surrounded by nothing but the silvery shimmer of Lake Kivu's methane brew, the bluish outline of the Virungas beckoning in the distance. Iwawa haunts him as much as the baby on its mother's back or the interrogation and execution of innocent civilians. The inmates at Iwawa undergo basic military training all over again, boosted by political commissars who bombard them with the wonders and awe of their new political masters in Kigali. The inmates have no radios, can't read newspapers and have no contact with the outside world.

'People died on this island. They died of malaria and they died because of the mines. People were blown up next to me. Their legs were gone! They called a boat to come and take them away. I even had to carry them to the boat. People tried to escape, but they died. They drowned. That's how desperate they were. Once a week there was a doctor and if you were seriously sick they would take you to the mainland.'

The inmates on Iwawa have a song they frequently sing:

Inyangira a kanyoni Nkigurukira (I wish I could be a bird)
Nkaja gusura ababyeyi (To fly and see my parents)
O' wanyanja we (Oh sea why don't you dry out)
Wakumye inkiyambukira nkaja gusura Ababyeyi (So that I can cross
    and see my parents)

'I didn't know for how long we were going to stay, so that made the punishment worse. When you are sentenced, you can count the days. But there we didn't know. You just saw the sun coming up and going down, day after day. Why did I join the RPF, because those who had stayed behind were much better off than us. They had completed school and now they had positions and were living nicely. This created a big hate in me towards the RPF. There was now nobody looking after me. It took my life away; that's why I don't like to talk about this. It still hurts. I then knew it was only me and God. I was alone.'

Some of the inmates have influential parents or family and it isn't long before they leave the island on the boats that bring the commissars for their lectures or the doctor on his weekly visit. Once home, the Iwawa returnees obviously blab about their ordeal and soon the island is an open secret in Kigali. A newspaper dares to publish details of Kagame's penal colony and, although promptly shut up, questions are now being asked.

In July 1995, a VIP disembarks from a military boat docked at Iwawa for an unannounced visit. It is Prime Minister Faustin Twagiramungu, described as a 'moderate' Hutu and appointed by the new regime in a ceremonial position to illustrate to the world that this is a government of true national unity.

Twagiramungu does a tour of the island and assembles the inmates. When he enquires about the conditions they are living under, they pour their hearts out to him. Back in Kigali, the prime minister announces the closing down of the facility. A few weeks later, inmates receive new uniforms and are transported back to Gisenyi. Kennedy rejoins 9th Battalion, which is now stationed at Kibuye, further east along the shore of Lake Kivu. Twagiramungu resigns shortly after closing down Iwawa and goes into exile. He says in his letter of resignation that he called a crisis cabinet meeting to discuss the ongoing killing of civilians by the RPA, but Kagame threatened him.

Kennedy's desertion brought to an end any aspirations he may have once had to advance in the Rwandan military. He was about to be promoted to sergeant and the next rank would have been lieutenant, but his misdemeanour put paid to that. A deserter will never be officer material and Kennedy is doomed to live out his life in the army's lower echelons. It probably also put an end to his exploits on the frontline because a renegade soldier cannot be trusted with the disposal of innocent lives. Ironically, it also saved his soul – or what was left of it.

* * *

Iwawa faded from public scrutiny for many years after the hapless prime minister unexpectedly stamped his limited authority. A far-flung outpost such as this, however, is too valuable for any dictator to simply discard.

Since the early 2000s, foreign visitors to Rwanda have been delighted with the orderliness of Kigali. It lacks the choking shambles of Nairobi or Kampala, the streets are neatly swept, there are no sprawling slums and, for a country of orphans, there are surprisingly few grime-caked and sooty-fingered street kids soliciting handouts. Iwawa saw to that. In April 2010, the *New York Times* told the story of fourteen-year-old Gasigwa

Gakunzi, a boy from a poor neighbourhood of Kigali who was arrested for loitering. The next thing he knew he was carted off to Iwawa and confined alongside 900 beggars, homeless people, loiterers, street children and suspected petty thieves. None had ever appeared in court, but had instead been banished to Iwawa without the permission of their parents and families. According to the *New York Times*, Gasigwa spent his days learning patriotic songs and how to march like a soldier.

Kagame lashed out at the paper, describing the story as 'pathetic' and tellingly ordering his internal security minister to deal with the issue. A day or so later, the government newspaper and state television introduced readers and viewers to cheery singing and clapping young men at the Iwawa Rehabilitation and Vocational Skills Development Centre, established to equip young Rwandans living on the street with skills such as carpentry and sowing to make them employable.

The incarceration of juveniles and the homeless at an off-limits detention centre without the permission of their families or the consent of a court screams against every grain of decency and legitimacy. Unperturbed, however, Iwawa held its first 'graduation ceremony' in 2011, when 752 'graduates' marked the end of more than a year of 'learning and rehabilitation' on the island. One of the 'graduates' who was paraded to the media excitedly exclaimed: 'I spent all my life running away from the government. In my new life, I will instead be coming closer to the government in whatever I do.'

The happy event was, however, marred by an accident in which six guests returning to the mainland after the ceremony drowned when their boat collided with a military vessel. It's safe to assume that these were not the first to be condemned to a watery grave off the island. And don't be surprised to find AK-wielding Iwawa graduates in striped uniforms prowling and looting the Congo on behalf of president and country.

34

Getting out

Post-genocide Rwanda is visibly better run than its neighbours and loved by international donors, yet mass killings in the region continued through the nineties and into the new millennium. The conflict in Rwanda spread into the sprawling rainforests of eastern Congo, culminating in two civil wars that cost millions of lives. There is no prettier sight on the planet than Africa's Great Lakes, but the tranquil and shimmering waters of Lake Kivu and the towering splendour of the forest-clad Virungas disguise the human cataclysm that perpetually lurks in their shadows. In the past fifty years, more people have violently perished here than anywhere else on earth.

Within two years of grabbing power, Kagame's Rwanda looks remarkably similar to pre-genocide Rwanda. The lessons and warnings of 1961 and 1973 have long been forgotten. Once again, the old order stands on its head. Habyarimana has in many ways been replaced by the new ruler. The promise of a government of national unity has dissipated as quickly as the fog on Mount Karisimbi in the mid-morning sun. By 1996, fifteen of the twenty-two chiefs of ministerial staff, sixteen of the nineteen permanent secretaries and 80 per cent of the country's mayors are Tutsi and RPF members. The vast majority of faculty staff at the national university is Tutsi – as are 80 per cent of the students. Virtually the whole of the army and the police force and 90 per cent of judges are Tutsi.

* * *

Kennedy is now confined to barracks, and for the rest of 1996 he does nothing more than the odd paperwork, smoke and drink copious amounts of Johnnie Walker Red Label (the officers drink Black Label). His life is uneventful and drearily predictable.

In July, he finally gets leave to find out if his mother, Teddy Uwamaria, is still alive. He travels to the commune of Runyinya, just outside of Butare. Very few Tutsis have survived, and his mother and her family are not among them. Kennedy also travels to the eastern highlands to search for his grandparents. He spends a few days in the area and literally walks from village to village looking for them. Some of the older people tell him they are both dead. Kennedy has to accept that he will never see them again.

He realises his only passport to freedom is an education. At the end of the year, he travels to Kigali to see Major Dr Richard Sezibera, the permanent secretary in the ministry of defence. He is one of the most esteemed officials in Kagame's administration and the general's personal doctor.

'Sir, I beg your permission to go and study,' Kennedy implores. 'I am thinking of political science. Even if there is no money, I will pay my own way and then come back and loyally serve you.'

'Don't worry, you will study, but not all senior soldiers can go and study,' was the major's reply. 'You have to wait.' Wait until when, Kennedy wonders.

He spends most of 1997 behind a desk at military intelligence headquarters in Kigali. He works in the counter-intelligence section where he 'continues to hunt those opposed to the government'. One of his tasks is to make sure that newspapers don't spread anti-government matter. Publications have to submit their stories for the next edition for approval and censorship. If there is anything dissenting in the reporting, an officer phones the editor and orders him to set it right. At least Kennedy is now living in a room outside the barracks and earning around 15 000 Rwandan francs (R200) a month. During the course of the year, he even meets a young girl by the name of Isha, whom he fancies and contemplates marrying.

* * *

'But with what?' he laments. 'I was a lowly in the army and how would I get money to marry her? I had nobody to help me. I was on my own. I knew that an education was my only hope. Otherwise I would have died in the army. With an education, I could get a good job, marry, have a family and have a future. And be a decent citizen,' says Kennedy.

'What did she look like, this girl? Was she nice?' I ask.

He titters and says: 'Why do you always want to know about them? I was a military man, an intelligence man, and we arrested lots of women who were trying to get information from men. So I didn't trust them. But then I met Isha. She was still young and at school. We agreed that we were going to marry after all this studying. We were not really boyfriend and girlfriend and we never slept with each other.'

* * *

Back in Gitarama, Xavier was also attempting to study to obtain his matric qualification. 'I couldn't become an officer but I couldn't study either,' he tells me. 'I was desperate. I went to the major. I said, I am not talking to you as my commander, but as my big brother. You are the first and the last person in the army that I will explain what happened to me. I told him my family was dead and how they died and how alone I was. If I had first finished my matric, I would not have been able to fight in the war and help stop the genocide. Now I had to salute a second lieutenant who was much younger than me. It was painful. I was twenty-something and I had three more years at school to do. I told him I didn't mind going to school with children. I just wanted him to assist me. He agreed that I had a case but he said I should wait. He said maybe next year or so.'

* * *

The Indian government gives 400 bursaries to young Rwandans to study in that country. Kennedy sits for two days in front of the office of the minister of education, a medical doctor whom he knew from his days at the rebel training base at Juru. He eventually sees the minister's secretary. He pleads once more and is told to leave his details. He doesn't hear anything. He is now bitter, disillusioned and intent on turning his back on the country he once fought and killed for. He decides to leave Rwanda.

'In Rwanda you needed education, connections or rank,' explains Kennedy. 'I didn't have connections or rank or education. There was no place for me. I was bitter when I looked around me and saw other young people having a normal life. You feel inferior because you don't have money or a car and can't do what they do. I had no future in the army. I had done enough killing. I had had enough of war. What I had done and seen was enough. I wanted to have another life. But of course I was sad to leave. I risked my life. I lost friends.'

Throughout 1997, Kennedy plots his demobilisation from the army. It is not easy; Rwanda is engaged in full-scale war in Zaire. In 1996, four civil wars were being fought either in part or entirely on Zairian soil. Towards the end of that year, these cataclysms finally converged into a large-scale regional conflict, yet smaller ones continued to rage.

It had all started in October 1996, when the Rwandan army attacked and forcibly closed down Hutu Power–dominated refugee camps in the Kivus in eastern Zaire. *Interahamwe* and former FAR soldiers, as well as large numbers of terror-stricken Hutu refugees, fled deeper into the forests. The RPA gave chase, slaughtering indiscriminately. Innocent civilians died by the thousands. In early 1997, the Zairian kleptocrat Mobutu was overthrown and replaced by the equally devious Rwandan-backed Laurent-Désiré Kabila, and Zaire became the Democratic Republic of Congo.

The honeymoon soon ended when Rwanda accused Congo's new despot of supporting Hutu rebels and Kagame invaded the Congo again. The following five years of war drew in armies from six nations and a dizzying cast of more than twenty rebel groups and warlords. Hostilities quickly descended into the mass plunder and looting of Congo's untapped mineral wealth and natural resources, and millions died. A UN report eventually accused Rwanda of wholesale war crimes, including genocide, during the years of conflict in the Congo. Depending on whose figures you believe, the death toll was anywhere between three and seven million.

* * *

Kennedy visits the army's demobilisation commission, which mostly deals with soldiers without legs or with chronic disease. He tells a panel that he cannot continue as a soldier and is war weary. They refuse his request and send him back to base. He returns a few months later and opens his heart to an army captain, and for the first time in his military career he seems to have found a listening ear. He is added to a list of soldiers to be demobilised and a kidney problem is given as the reason.

In September 1997, Kennedy lines up for a military parade in Mutara attended by Kagame. The vice-president tells the passers-out that they have done their country proud and are the nation's future leaders. He shakes Kennedy's hand and presents him with a letter of gratitude carrying his signature. (Kennedy has his letter to this day.) After serving in the army for more than five years, he receives the royal payout of 40 000 Rwandan francs (about R500) and corrugated-iron sheets to build a house, which he sells.

With no more than between 100 and 200 dollars in his pocket, Kennedy prepares for his journey. He has a small sling bag containing one spare pair of jeans and a T-shirt. He puts his matric certificate and Kagame's letter in a plastic bag and ties it around his waist. He doesn't have a passport. ('Why?' he would say to me. 'That's a Western thing. In Africa we walk through border posts.')

Before he leaves, he visits Isha and tells her he's going somewhere where he can study and be 'someone'. 'Will you be patient and wait for me?' he asks her. 'Of course I will,' she says. 'Come back to me.'

In January 1998, Kennedy crosses over the Rusumo Bridge that spans the Kagera River from Rwanda to Tanzania. He tells the guards on both sides that he's visiting a relative in the Rwandan refugee camp in Tanzania. It was over this bridge nearly four years earlier that tens of thousands of petrified refugees fled before the advancing RPA rebels. Among them were the killers of Nyarubuye and prefectures across south-eastern Rwanda. They had dropped their machetes, knives and sticks in piles at the bridge before scurrying into the welcoming arms of the international aid community that assisted them to erect, within days, yet another city in the troubled Great Lakes.

∗ ∗ ∗

'I wasn't sure which direction to take, but I was excited because, for the first time in my life, I was a free man,' Kennedy recalls.

'And where were you going?'

'I didn't know. I had no plan. I was just going to take the *panya* roads and get to a place where I could study.'

Kennedy leans back in his chair and shakes his head. 'This is now the start of a new chapter of my life. I thought the hardship was going to be over and that I would study and lead a normal life. If only I had known. If only.'

As Kennedy babbles about his journey, I'm thinking of a famous Rwandan proverb: 'You can outdistance that which is running after you, but not what is running inside of you.'

35

Seven million steps

Whenever I tell Kennedy's story, the one pivotal event of his life every-one fixates on is his long walk to education. It overshadows any of his other triumphs or tribulations. It is his footslog across and down half of the continent that captivates the imagination and is the one aspect of his tumultuous existence that people crave to know more about. They are enthralled by the idea of a human tramping thousands of kilometres through inhospitable terrain infested with robbers, rebels, serpents, pre-dators, bugs, viruses and disease, and visited by plagues, heat and rain. And if visions of those aren't enough, crooked cops, bent officials and trigger-happy soldiers will surely do the trick.

We forget that the continent's inhabitants are intrepid travellers and have been a moving, trekking and roving lot for centuries. Thousands of Africans journey to Senegal every year, where they board dinghies to cross the Atlantic in an attempt to reach the Canary Islands or the European mainland. Others cross the Sahara to set foot on the shores of the Medi-terranean, from where they can almost touch Sicily or Malta. Still others, Eritreans, Sudanese and Ethiopians, trek across the perilous Sinai in search of a dream in Israel or beyond. At Africa's war-ravaged Horn, Somalis pile into wooden fishing boats and paddle as far as Tanzania's southern coast or Mozambique's northern shores. They are dropped on a beach, from where some make their way to a refugee camp and others plod onwards to South Africa. Many don't live to tell their tales.

If you measure the main routes, Kennedy travelled a distance of 5 680 kilometres from Kigali through Tanzania, Kenya, Malawi, the northern part of Mozambique and Zimbabwe to South Africa, and onwards to Johannes-burg. He mostly avoided the main routes because of perils in the form of outlaws and uniformed thugs that lurked along the way. He stuck to *panya* roads zigzagging across or running alongside the major arteries. Despite taking buses at the beginning and end of his journey, it is safe to say that he walked in the region of 5 000 kilometres. I've tried to calculate how many times he would have had to put one foot in front of the other to enable him to get to Johannesburg. An average man takes around 1 400 steps to walk a kilometre. Kennedy therefore took more or less seven million steps to reach his destination.

It took him six months to reach Johannesburg. He stayed in some places for a few days or even weeks, walking between forty and fifty kilometres a day. By the time he reached Arusha in northern Tanzania, he had no money left. Unscrupulous lawmen and grafting officials awaited him at every border post, which he had to cross not just without visas but without a passport either. He did this without a cent in his pocket.

* * *

One would expect Kennedy's journey to be an epic event; a tale of extreme survival and endurance; the story of one man's triumph over virtually every adversary that the continent has on offer. I interview Kennedy for eleven days, altogether sixty-five tape-recorded hours in Johannesburg and Pretoria. We converse for many more hours in Uganda and throughout the writing of this book. The transcripts of the formal interviews amount to 170 pages. One would therefore expect his transcontinental journey to occupy a healthy chunk of our dialogue. This is unfortunately not the case. We speak for no more than an hour or two about his walk to South Africa. The transcript of his trek is barely six pages. And believe me, I try every trick in the book to draw as much out of him as I can.

'So how did you cross the border posts?' I ask.

'You just pass. You walk through. I know Swahili very well, so I told them I was going to buy something on the other side. I was an intelligence soldier so I was able to assess the situation. I waited for the right moment and walked through.'

Most Africans regard border posts as nothing but a colonial legacy that has resulted in barbed wire carving up tribes, families, societies and nations. Crossing borders is therefore just another nuisance and hazard on their junkets across the continent. Crossing frontiers was the least of Kennedy's concerns.

'Were you ever robbed?'

'No. I had nothing anybody wanted.'

'Were you attacked by wild animals?'

'No. I saw them, but they left me alone.'

'Did you ever land up in prison?'

'I was arrested but I wasn't kept for long.'

'How did you stay alive? What did you eat?'

'It's this thing in Africa we call *ubuntu* that helped me to survive. Whenever you see smoke, there are people. I would ask for a place to sleep and they would show me a place to sleep. That's how people are in East Africa. They give you cassava. Or maize meal or whatever they have. You eat. The next morning you say thank you and goodbye and you move on.'

'What were the main problems you had?'

'When I got south to Malawi and Zimbabwe, people were not so friendly any longer. Swahili didn't help me. I had lots of problems at the border posts and the soldiers got me.'

'Did you ever get sick?'

'No, my body was very strong in those days.'

'Did anything really bad ever happen to you?'

'No. I just walked.'

'Lions?'

'They were far away.'

'Snakes?'

'Many. I grew up with them. I wasn't scared.'

You get the picture. For Kennedy it was the same monotonous exploit day after day. There were no great feats or tales of stinging scorpions, coiled cobras, broad-shouldered hyenas, bulldozing elephants, leaping lions, stamping rhinoceroses, delirious bouts of malaria, dirty police cells or AK-touting robbers.

Kennedy was a veld boy, and for the first thirty-plus years of his life he seldom had the opportunity to sleep on a mattress. He would stretch out his body on a flat piece of ground and within minutes it would go limp, flop, relax and sink into sleep. Three meals a day was a luxury he had never tasted. Resigned, he would patiently await his next meal or nourish himself with wild fruit or berries, whatever was on offer.

It is important at the outset to remember that the young man who embarked on this journey on the eve of his twenty-seventh birthday was a fit and rugged soldier who had already endured the worst that Africa had to offer. Kennedy had plied vast distances by foot his whole life and had for years persevered under extreme conditions. He could easily walk fifty kilometres a day, put his head down on the outskirts of a village or in the veld, solicit a piece of cassava, wake up the next morning and walk another fifty.

He left Rwanda with a single pair of sneakers. By the time he reached southern Tanzania, the soles were threadbare and he had to resort to locally manufactured sandals made out of abandoned car tyres. Distance had little meaning for him. He didn't know how far Nairobi or Dar es Salaam was and it didn't matter. In front of him was space, boundless and empty, but also promise, and that's where he was heading.

* * *

In the first days of 1998, Kennedy crossed into Tanzania, took a bus to the lake city of Mwanza and from there traversed on foot along the shores of Lake Victoria, Africa's greatest lake and the second-largest body of fresh water in the world. The Victoria basin is home to thirty million people and the lakeside is littered with fishing villages that are often nothing more than a collection of mud and woven-branch dwellings separated by muddy lanes. The talk among the assemblies of shirtless fishermen fixing their nets or oiling their outboards in the searing heat is of catch and cash, of the falling numbers of catfish, lungfish, tilapia and the prized Nile perch, highly favoured on Europe's gastronomy tables.

After crossing another border and plying the corridors of green hills and scattered woodlands of south-western Kenya, Kennedy arrived in the capital, Nairobi. Another of those sprawling and evolving African cities where fluid throngs of newcomers set up rickety shanties fronting opaque skyscrapers, Nairobi is a mixture of Rolexed businessmen, perfumed women in designer apparel, street vendors selling anything from airtime to watches, and dishevelled juveniles with eyes dreary from sniffing glue. Hooting, fume-emitting taxis weave around polished German saloons, and 4×4s whisk khaki-clad tourists to safari wonderlands. Like everywhere else on the continent, life is on the streets and it is one of crowds, traffic, bustle, chaos, noise and colour.

Kennedy booked into a fleabag hotel but decided not to stay long. Kenya was at the time a favoured destination for former FAR officers and *interahamwe* fugitives. It was also a happy hunting ground for Kagame's death squads that were tracking not just genocidaires, but also his political enemies who had been forced into exile.

Most notorious was the assassination of Seth Sendashonga, an eminent Hutu-turned-rebel who became minister of the interior after the genocide. He could not accept the RPF's complicity in post-genocide massacres and murders. Sendashonga documented hundreds of incidences of reprisal killings and sent his findings to Kagame, who failed to respond. He fled into exile and settled in Nairobi. Armed with lists of names and addresses of murdered Hutus, Sendashonga calculated that Kagame's soldiers had massacred around 150 000 people between July 1994 and April 1995.

He also signed his own death warrant. In 1996, the day before the French newspaper *Libération* published his dossier, he was ambushed and wounded. He identified one of the two attackers as his former body-guard in Kigali. The other was an official from the Rwandan embassy in Nairobi.

'I was scared in Nairobi,' says Kennedy. 'It was not a friendly place. There were lots of *interahamwe*. I didn't want to stay there.' He decided to move south to Tanzania. Not long after he had left, on 16 May 1998, Sendashonga was shot and killed in his car by gunmen armed with AK-47s, shortly before he was scheduled to testify before the ICTR. The Rwandan ambassador in Kenya, Alphonse Mbayire, was fingered as the mastermind behind the killing. He was recalled by his government in January 2001, only to be killed by unidentified gunmen in a bar in Kigali a month later.

36

Towards the Promised Land

Kennedy was now on the plains of the Masai, the tall and handsome spear-wielding herdsmen wrapped in red kikoi who roam vast distances with their cattle in search of water and grazing. This is the crater floor of Africa's Great Rift, where rolling grassland eventually ascends to mist-draped volcanic highland and the magnificence of snow-capped Kilimanjaro. This is the land of umbrella-shaped acacia and a million cavorting, frolicking, galloping wildebeest and zebra. It accommodates the greatest number of antelope in the world, but also shelters the most significant concentration of large predators on earth.

Serengeti, Ngorongoro, Masai Mara and a patchwork of other reserves are wildlife islands surrounded by a rising tide of humanity that walls their edges. In villages, tales abound of yellow-toothed lions with scruffy and matted manes grabbing women fetching water or attacking children who have fallen asleep under trees. One of the greatest dangers for lone travellers is older lions that have lost their agility and speed and have been cast out of their prides. This is when they start hunting people.

'I saw lots of elephants and buck,' Kennedy tells me. 'I grew up with wild animals, so even as a boy I wasn't scared of them. There were days when I had no food. I sometimes walked with an empty stomach from early morning till the night. It didn't matter that I had no food because I knew someone would eventually give me something to eat. I had no blanket. I'm a soldier, you don't need those things. I could lie down anywhere and sleep.'

He stayed in Arusha for a few days and spent his last money on essential supplies before hitting the 500-kilometre road to Dar es Salaam, Tanzania's commercial and political centre (although not the capital; that honour belongs to Dodoma, a dreary town in the middle of the country). It took Kennedy two weeks to ply the *panya* roads between the two cities.

Dar was a haven for Africa's liberation movements. Zimbabwe's ZANU/ZAPU, Mozambique's FRELIMO, Namibia's SWAPO, South Africa's ANC and Angola's MPLA all skulked and plotted from their hideouts in the city. Despite this, Dar es Salaam – the name means 'haven of peace' – is a far gentler, flatter and friendlier city than Nairobi and the gateway to the tropical islands of Zanzibar and Pemba. Its boulevards are wide and palm-fringed, but beyond its magnificent colonial and newer upmarket suburbs loiters just another African city, where almost identical dwellings stretch for kilometre upon kilometre and indistinguishable neighbour-hoods blend into one another.

'I liked Dar and stayed a whole month,' says Kennedy. 'I first lived with the homeless and slept on the streets where there were many other people. I later befriended some Rwandan guys and hung with them. I carried water and other things for people and they gave me a little money. There was enough food and I was never hungry. I ate pap and those small fish that you mix with green banana or peanuts. I could survive in Dar, but there were no opportunities to study.'

The guys that Kennedy hung out with told him that if he wanted to study, he would do well to head for South Africa. 'I had heard of Mandela and the ANC. And I learnt at school about the Zulu kingdom, the Nguni people and things like that. When I was a boy at school in Uganda, they took a small part of our school fees as a donation for the ANC. So I was contributing to the struggle. We knew about the elections in 1994 and listened on the radio. It was during the genocide, but we listened. A free-dom fighter became president! It was fantastic. I heard in Dar that there were lots of jobs in South Africa and opportunities to study. People said I must look for a white person to pay for my studies. There were also organisations that could sponsor me. There was even a bus between Johannesburg and Dar. But of course I had no money. I had to walk.'

* * *

It was the beginning of March when Kennedy left the mangroves and palms of Dar es Salaam and headed down the T1 national road towards Moro-goro, an attractive town trapped between two soaring verdant walls of mountain that had once concealed a secret ANC military camp. The T1 is a lingering and dreary artery that stretches for 800 kilometres like a sheeny black snake. A bus trip from Dar es Salaam to the Malawian border takes twenty-four hours. The road climbs up to African savannah, with its vast rolling plains of acacia and scrub. In March, heat waves whirl and twirl on the searing asphalt. The horizon is blotched and smudged. It is during sweltering times like this that Africa descends into silence and drowsiness. People become motionless, animals freeze and activity grinds to a halt.

The only relief is a downpour every second day or so, when the clouds split apart to quench the thirst of man, beast and land. Kennedy rested during the day and walked at night.

'There's a big national park I had to walk through,' he recalls. 'At night I walked with fire. I made a torch. I took grass and tied it with banana rope. I put coals in the middle and that's how I walked, hoping that wild animals would be scared. I came across some tourists who were there to look at the animals and who gave me food. My belief in God protected me on this journey. Jesus and the angels were walking with me. I held my rosary in my hand and I prayed a lot.'

Sometime in April 1998, Kennedy reached the border between Tanzania and Malawi, the warm heart of Africa and home to some of the biggest smiles on the continent. His attempt to get through the border post was thwarted by a Malawian guard who sent him back to Tanzania, so he walked awhile along the bank of the mighty Songwe River that divides the two countries.

'The villagers had small boats. A young man asked me if I had money and I said no. He wanted twenty dollars to row me across. I told him, "I'm from Rwanda and I have no money and can't cross at the border post. But you have a boat, so please help me as an African man and get me across." He did so without any charge.'

Kennedy reached the Malawian city of Lilongwe ten days or so later and found Rwandan Tutsis on the streets who introduced him to Hassan, a Tanzanian Muslim and restaurateur in the capital. He gave Kennedy a room with a mattress and hot water – 'my first proper cleaning in many months' – in exchange for his services scrubbing dishes in the kitchen. Hassan also arranged a false Tanzanian temporary travel document for him.

Kennedy left two weeks later carrying even less than he had at the outset of his journey, as his small shoulder bag had been stolen in Lilongwe. All he had was the plastic bag containing his matric certificate, which he tied around his waist, a hundred dollars that Hassan had given him and a piece of paper with a Tanzanian's telephone number in Johannesburg, a man Hassan thought might be able to help him. By now the veld had turned the colour of khaki and crackled underfoot.

Kennedy crossed into Mozambique and walked for two days through the Tete Corridor. 'The easiest route would have been through Maputo, but I didn't know it and nobody told me. At the Zimbabwean border it was very difficult. It's a big border post with lots of security and it was very difficult to pass. But they are so corrupt. I tried to pass but they refused. You needed money to pass. I gave the immigration officer fifty dollars but he said he wanted more. I had to give him seventy dollars. He escorted me through the post and then I started walking. There were small towns and it was different from the other countries. The roads were big and there were nice shops. Most of those shops belonged to white people. It was cheap. A loaf of bread cost only two Zimbabwe dollars. It was an organised country.'

It took him five days to walk to Harare, where he slept for a few days on the streets before heading south towards the Beit Bridge that spans the Limpopo River on the border between South Africa and Zimbabwe. A journey of around 600 kilometres, it took him just over two weeks to walk. He stopped in a village just before the border post and was shown a spot where he could sleep. Minutes later, a moonless night the colour of soot descended over Africa. Ahead of the impenetrable darkness lay the end of Kennedy's journey and the beginning of his new life.

* * *

Beitbridge is one of those monstrous African trans-frontier posts that are a ceaseless maelstrom of grinding and shifting human and mechanical traffic. Like a sausage machine it sucks them in on the one side – traders, tourists, travellers, outlaws, asylum seekers, the trafficked and the traffickers, new-hopers, no-hopers – and spits them out on the other. On its periphery has risen a sprawl of vendors and markets where everything and anything can be bartered and traded. There are ventures of every sort: shops, importers and exporters, insurers, makeshift hotels, restaurants, hairdressers and whorehouses, where truckers can indulge in lethal doses of illicit carnal pleasure.

'I had reached my destination and there in front of me was my new future,' says Kennedy. 'It was easy to pass the border posts because there were so many people and so much movement. You mustn't walk too fast. You walk and wait, walk and wait. Lots of people were passing with bags because they wanted to sell something or buy something in South Africa. I joined them. There were lots of trucks. You hid behind the trucks waiting to pass. There were truck drivers eating and cooking. I spoke to them for a while and walked on. I was through!'

Kennedy walked the ten kilometres or so from the bridge to the bustling border town of Messina (now Musina), where he asked for the road to Johannesburg. After being told it was another 500 kilometres, he decided to stay for a day or two and started begging. 'There were lots of white people,' he says. 'I told them, "Please, I am short of money and can you give me a five or ten rand?" I told them I was from Somalia. One old man stopped and spoke to me and gave me R50. I now had R160. I slept on the streets of Musina for one night and took the bus to Johannesburg the next day. I had never seen roads like that. I asked myself how can a human being build these things? Everything around me was unreal. I hadn't known that these things existed. Remember that I didn't know television. For me, a television and a computer were the same thing. And I didn't know or understand either of the two.'

* * *

It was evening on 11 June 1998 when the bus dropped Kennedy somewhere in Africa's rattiest, crankiest and grumpiest suburb: Hillbrow. As it was midwinter on the Highveld, temperatures had plummeted towards zero. Kennedy says he's never felt cold like that, not even in the Virungas. He had a thin sweater and nothing else. Many of the passengers booked into a nearby hotel, while the others dissipated into the concrete jungle.

He wandered around Hillbrow, gazing in near bewilderment at the races, nations, colours, clans and tribes from every corner of the globe that fused into the suburb's streets and flatlands. He loitered for a while at Fontana, a famous all-night takeaway joint slap bang in the middle of the suburb of sin and famous for its early morning clientele of hookers, pimps, drug pushers, clubbers, insomniacs and ambulance men. He salivated at the smell of fresh bread and roasting chickens before heading further down Kotze Street.

'I was happy,' he remembers. 'I felt as though I was in New York. I wasn't scared, because then I didn't know about crime in Hillbrow. I knew I would have to sleep outside and it was very, very cold. I found a wall and just sat against it. I didn't sleep because I was worried. What was I going to do in the morning?'

37

Slumdog

Among South Africans, Hillbrow is renowned for three things: immigrants, drugs and violent crime. It is easily the most feared neighbourhood in the country – the most insecure suburb in an insecure city. In this epicentre of drug dealing, addicts dither in fuzzy chemical clouds in creep-joints like the Park Lane and Dorchester hotels – named decades ago for their posh London counterparts. Sex workers scrounge the streets in the hope of enticing death-defying customers to secure their next hit of head candy. In the shadows of these wasted wretches lurk their slave masters: two-legged hyenas that continue to import waves of vice and violence.

Hillbrow is Johannesburg's oldest suburb. On one side of the late nineteenth century, mine-camp pioneers dug into the earth and piled pale dumps of yellow soil; on the other, those who prospered fled the dust and grime and found sanctuary on a rocky ridge a mile away. And there you have it: the first suburb, built on the brow of a hill. Half a century later, the rich had expanded north beyond Parktown, Forest Town, Westcliff and Houghton. A need arose for mass lodging close to the centre of the city and before long mass-produced high-rises crusted the crest.

In the 1970s and 1980s, Hillbrow's nonconformist credo was a magnet for European immigrants, the young (mostly English), the bohemian, the footloose, the arty, dropouts, intellectuals, pale-skinned *tsotsis* and mixed couples, who bled into its concrete lairs. It was multiracial long before the ending of apartheid and, in an abnormal society, it was surprisingly normal.

In the late eighties and early nineties, Hillbrow became the Harlem of Johannesburg. Blacks, condemned by apartheid to eke out a living in far-flung townships, moved closer to the centre of town and settled in suburbs such as Hillbrow. Most of the whites left, leaving behind the elderly, the addicts and the unemployed. Brits and continental Europeans feared black rule. They closed Café Zurich and Café de Paris and scuttled back to their motherlands.

When South Africa opened its borders in the mid-nineties, an influx of African immigrants and refugees pounced on Hillbrow. Today it is a truly African metropolis, infused with the rhythms, smells and sounds of the continent. Its residents are often temporary and on the move; they are waiting for that big break to get the hell out of what many would describe as a multi-storeyed slum.

Some of the buildings are either owned by absentee landlords or have been 'hijacked' by ruthless slumlords. They are dank and dingy concrete shells unfit for human habitation, teetering on the brink of collapse. They are without water or electricity and the lift shafts are filled with rotting garbage. Their alleyways reek of piss and are littered with used syringes and condoms.

According to the 1999 population census, 97 000 people live in this one square kilometre of flatland, although the figure is probably twice that if immigrants – most of them unregistered – are taken into account. In 1999, Hillbrow had 205 murders, 353 cases of reported rape, 1 700 robberies, 1 300 assaults and more than 800 burglaries. Between 1990 and 2001, a staggering 59 000 crimes were recorded in the suburb. It's safe to assume that many more crimes went unreported. Immigrants – especially those without a Section 21 (an Immigrations Act document that entitles an immigrant to stay temporarily in South Africa) – don't dare to call the men in blue when they are in trouble. The crime will probably never be investigated anyway and the last thing an illegal wants to do is draw attention to him- or herself.

* * *

It was somewhere in Johannesburg's concrete heart that Kennedy confronted his first day in South Africa. 'I got up. I didn't know where I was. I started walking. I heard lots of foreign languages. I heard French, Swahili, other African languages. I didn't hear any Kinyarwanda. Congolese were all over, but there were not many Rwandans in Hillbrow. Even now, there are only 2 000 Rwandans living in South Africa. And you seldom find them in Hillbrow. They live in Cape Town, Durban and Pretoria.'

With the very last coins in his pocket, Kennedy phoned the number that Hassan had given him in Lilongwe in the hope that the Tanzanian might give him a place to sleep. The number was disconnected. He wandered around Hillbrow, gaping at the tiered landscape towering around him and contemplating his predicament.

'I was back in the jungle, another kind of jungle,' Kennedy tells me. 'It was like taking someone from the city and throwing him in the Virungas.

He can easily die in a place like that. Where does one start? I stopped at Shoprite Checkers and looked at people buying things. I waited outside and asked them if I could carry their bags. Some looked at me very funnily. Others gave me a little coin. It was enough to buy half a loaf of bread and Kool-Aid cold drink. I slept on the pavement again that night. What was I going to do?'

The next day, he walked from shop to shop in Hillbrow hoping to find a paid security or doorman job. Most shopkeepers waved him away; others asked him for his identity book or refugee papers. He had neither. All he had was his matric certificate, still securely strapped to his body. After a few days of no success, he again attempted to carry supermarket bags.

'Sometimes I got two or three rand and then I ate food sold on the streets by some Nigerians. It's called *iguse*. It is a mixture of cow hoofs, fish and green vegetables. It was terrible, but it was cheap and nutritious. You eat it with pap, but their pap. It is very soft. You could live on that. So even if I got just a little money every day, I could live.'

There's a general perception among local Hillbrowans that the invading foreigners are responsible for the area's decay. They are quick to say that everything was just fine until the West African *brudders* with their pointy shoes and slippery tongues arrived in their droves and stole their women and chemically enslaved their children. Others blame the Ethiopian clothes sellers, the Zimbabwean security guards, the Pakistani and Somali shopkeepers, the Zambian vegetable vendors, the Congolese car guards, and so on and so on.

Xenophobia in Hillbrow is rife.

It wasn't long before Kennedy was confronted with the dreaded *makwerekwere* – local slang for 'foreigner'. The word originates from *kwere kwere*, a sound that locals say the inarticulate foreign tongue makes. One day when he asked to carry someone's bags, Kennedy heard a 'Hey *makwerekwere!*' followed by something in a language he didn't understand. At first he thought it was someone's name, but soon realised that people like him were being blamed for turning Hillbrow into Hellbrow.

* * *

Kennedy befriended a band of glue-sniffing street children, the younger ones nothing but grimy urchins with snotty noses, the ghosts of lost childhoods in their foggy eyes. The oldest, alpha male and leader of the pack, was not even sixteen, having claimed his position at the top of the chain simply because he had lived long enough to earn it.

'They watched me carrying things and struggling to survive, so they saw me as one of them,' Kennedy remembers. 'The leader was very, very naughty and his name was Mofokeng. He was about fourteen and he controlled everything. They were four boys and they all had knives. They were fighting with one another. It was good that I had nothing because there was nothing anyone could rob. They all came from townships and they came to town to look for something to eat. They had no schooling and lived from crime. They would move in a crowd and when you had something in your pocket they wanted, they took it. They loved cellphones. And they were successful! They sold the stuff and used the money for glue and *ganja* [dagga]. They were high all the time.'

Inhaling fumes from glue-soaked rags and glue-filled plastic bags and bottles is a daily ritual for street children. It makes the nights a little less frigid and an empty stomach a little less insistent. Glue is said to be stronger than marijuana and cocaine, leaving many children all but oblivious to the world around them. But the glue that makes life more bearable also cuts fragile lives short. The lungs of habitual users become scarred and begin to fill with fluid. The fumes also irreversibly damage the brain and kidneys. A chronic wet cough precedes a slow death from pneumonia.

Although Kennedy was ten years older than the oldest, they nevertheless accepted him as one of their own and allowed him to cuddle up with them under a bridge in Harrow Street near the fifty-four-storey Ponte building. 'The glue made them mad. It made them sick and they were coughing a lot. They fought among themselves for the boxes or old blankets. I couldn't take that glue. I never even thought about it. I had an old blanket that I picked up. We took some boxes and lay down on them. When you lie close together, you get warm. And we'd make fire with sticks. I didn't sleep a lot because I was worried. How am I going to live like this and how will I get out of here? I was beginning to regret that I had left Rwanda.'

Kennedy was dirty, but there was a tap in a nearby park where he would wash himself every morning with icy-cold water. He would then walk down to a taxi rank or supermarket where he tried to carry things in order to earn some money. One afternoon, on his way back to the bridge, he passed a line of street vendors. A young foreigner, no older than twenty, was selling cigarettes, sweets and biscuits. A group of men walking past grabbed his cigarettes. He jumped up to protest and a struggle ensued. One of the bandits pulled out a gun, put it against the vendor's head and pulled the trigger. The vendor fell down dead and the killers strolled away. Nobody did anything. Kennedy's feet were splattered with blood.

'There was blood everywhere. Everyone was running. I also ran. When I told the street kids the story that night they laughed. "It is happening everywhere and so what," they said. I felt as though I'd escaped war and now I was back in war. You heard guns shooting every night. It seemed as though everyone had a gun. You saw people being robbed in the middle of the day. I was also robbed: at ten in the morning in Hillbrow.'

Three guys, armed with knives, cornered Kennedy and demanded money and his cellphone. When he said he had neither, they ordered him to take off his shoes and his waistband. They walked away, leaving him with bare feet in the cold.

A month or two after Kennedy arrived in Hillbrow, he fell sick. With a high fever, stomach pain and severe headaches, he stayed on his box with his frayed blanket over him for almost a week. He then realised that if he did not get medical help, he might die. He made his way to the Hillbrow hospital's casualty ward and asked to see a doctor, who diagnosed typhoid. He had obviously contracted the illness from the unhygienic conditions in which he was living. He was given an array of pills and sent back 'home' to recuperate.

* * *

By December 1998, Kennedy had been living on the streets for six months. It was the Muslim fasting month of Ramadan, the ninth month of the Islamic calendar, in which Muslims must refrain from eating, drinking, smoking and sex during daylight and teach one another about patience, spirituality and submissiveness to Allah.

While in Lilongwe, Hassan had urged Kennedy to embrace Islam because of the fellowship and benevolence the religion affords its disciples. Hassan was a living example of this generosity, and with that in mind Kennedy ventured to the mosque in neighbouring Berea. He knew that during Ramadan Muslims prepared after-dusk feasts to break the fast. Hassan had a brother in Canada with the name Nurudin, and that was the

Muslim name Kennedy adopted when he went to the mosque for the first time. It should actually be *Nuruddin*, which means 'brightness of the faith'.

'There were many Muslims in Uganda where I was brought up and I knew they shared, and that during Ramadan after evening prayers they put out food so that people could eat. So I went to the mosque in Berea. There was rice, bread, soup, meat and chicken. It was fantastic! I was so hungry!'

Kennedy didn't know how to pray but, summoning his courage, he entered the mosque, fell on his knees and took his cues from his 'fellow' believers. 'So when they said "*Barakallah*" [May the blessings of Allah be upon you] or "*La ilaha illallah*" [There is no lord worthy of worship except Allah] I just followed them,' Kennedy tells me. 'They gave me a gown, that white one. I wore that, even on the streets. I ate with them. At six, after prayers, the food came out and we ate. I was still a Catholic and had my rosary, but of course I didn't have it with me. Some days I spent the whole day at the mosque.'

One of his newly acquired Muslim friends suggested that Kennedy report to a Home Affairs office in order to become 'legal' and acquire refugee status. The man accompanied Kennedy, who then had no choice but to write his Muslim name on the applications as well. And that is why Nurudin now appears on all his documents.

Kennedy continued to live as a slumdog under the bridge in Harrow Street, scrounging a living from carrying bags, until one day someone tapped him on his shoulder and asked: 'Are you Rwandan?'

38

Homeboys

Roger Kidigi is a scrawny and fidgety fellow with wide eyes and a perpetual snigger. Claiming several nationalities, he potters in the shadowy business of imports-exports, some of his commodities, I suspect, illegal arrivals from across the continent. He has lost his Congolese passport, the visa in his Burundian one is no longer valid, and his Rwandan refugee status has recently expired. He was once a taxi owner who boasted a booming saloon and drove a fast car. Then he accidentally impregnated a Congolese woman and his Somali wife kicked him out. His situation is now dire, but he has plans to launch a new business. Do I want to invest in a worthwhile cause? In the meantime, he orders a doggy bag for his half-eaten steak and solicits a packet of cigarettes.

Kennedy speaks admiringly of Roger as a Good Samaritan with a heart of gold who salvaged him from his hole under the bridge in Harrow Street and afforded him his first soft bed in a very long time. They met in early 1999, when Roger was on his way to the post office in Hillbrow.

'Kennedy stood in the street talking to other people,' recalls Roger. 'When I passed, I heard him speaking Swahili. I looked at him and knew that he was a homeboy. I stopped and greeted him. He said he was from Rwanda and that he was sleeping under a bridge. He had a street face. He was thin and looked like someone who was hungry.'

'Roger said he was a Tutsi from Burundi,' Kennedy tells me. 'I said I was from Rwanda. He said I looked like a street boy. I said, "My brother, you have no idea how happy I am to meet someone from home because I haven't eaten for a long time and I am really suffering."'

'Before he was even finished I said to him, "My brother, let us go", and we went to my flat,' says Roger. 'My Somali wife was very happy to see him because Kennedy was wearing that white gown and she had that black cloth over her head. They greeted in Arabic and she cooked him macaroni and cheese.'

Kennedy chimes in. 'He was a businessman, selling cigarettes. Not on the street, but big time. There were lots of deals. There were already four other Rwandans living in his flat with him. They were all selling his cigarettes on the street to pay the rent. He gave me a mattress and a blanket and I was happy.'

'My wife called him Nurudin but I called him Kennedy,' remembers Roger. 'I asked him, "Why are you wearing this white thing?" And he said, "It is my religion." My wife liked it and made him breakfast every morning. He used to pray like a real Muslim, on his knees. He didn't touch beer either. It lasted a couple of months until he got a job. Then he wasn't a Muslim any longer; then that gown was gone.'

* * *

Kennedy entrusted Roger with the plastic bag containing his matric certificate and Paul Kagame's demobilisation letter.

'Why do you need these things?' his friend wanted to know.

'I want to study,' replied Kennedy.

'No, that's not going to work,' said Roger. 'We must first find you a job.'

'I could see that this man was smart, very smart,' Roger tells me. 'He was different from the other guys who stayed with me. He would wake up, pray, start cleaning and make tea. He was looking for a job every day, but it wasn't easy. I could see that he was going to be someone one day, but he needed direction.'

'At the time, I didn't think life would ever get better,' recalls Kennedy. 'I couldn't even buy a shirt or pay rent or buy food. I saw other refugees who had come years before me and they were all in a terrible state. So was this how I was going to live forever? But then Roger said he had a plan. He gave me a few hundred rand and told me to go downtown and do a security course. I did a Grade E course. It was the lowest grade. It takes a week and you get a certificate with which you can be a guard at a gate. You cannot carry a gun or anything like that. You just open a gate.'

It took several months before a small security company hired Kennedy. They dispatched him to Fourways on Johannesburg's north-western edge to man the access gate to a security estate. His salary was R700 a month and he got a uniform. He worked from 6 p.m. to 6 a.m. with no overtime and had maybe one day off a week. He used that day to wash his uniform, clean the flat and catch up on missed sleep.

Kennedy's rent was R250 a month and he spent R300 a month on transport. He then still had to eat and buy essentials. He had no money for clothes, so he wore his uniform every day. All he brooded about was studying. By then he had opted for law because lots of African leaders and prominent figures were lawyers. He decided to save R50 a month to put towards his studies.

On one of his days off, he travelled to the University of South Africa (UNISA) in Pretoria to enquire about entry requirements, fees and courses. His matric qualification was acceptable, but when he enquired about study fees, he got the shock of his life.

'A law degree had fifty-six modules and with the money I was saving I could do two modules a year. It would take me almost thirty years to complete a degree. I would be sixty years old! Was I going to stand at that boom for the next thirty years? Was this the plan God had for me?'

* * *

By June 2000, Kennedy had saved R700. He registered for a law degree and two modules, 'Introduction to Law' and 'Law of Persons'. He couldn't afford any textbooks, but returned to Hillbrow with a bag full of study material.

'I couldn't believe it! When I got home, he was sitting there with all these papers,' remembers Roger. 'I said we should go and celebrate but he said no, he had work to do. I was very proud of him, but I never thought he would become a lawyer.'

'My flatmates thought I was wasting my time, but I was determined,' says Kennedy. 'They said, why are you doing this, are you crazy? Are you ever going to finish? Why don't you do other things and make money? I said you just wait and see.'

Towards the end of that year, Roger and his wife bade Hillbrow farewell. He had just been robbed for the third time and decided to open a business in Cape Town. Kennedy and two friends, Hassan and Jacques, moved into a bachelor pad in Hillbrow. The one cut hair on the streets and the other sold sweets and cigarettes at the taxi rank. Between them, they had a carpet that Roger had given them when he left, three blankets, three cups, three plates and a teapot. Their water and electricity were cut off, but they made illegal connections and fetched water in buckets. They mostly ate porridge or bread and, if they could afford it, vegetables.

It was difficult for Kennedy to concentrate in the flat, which meant he had to study at work. It was quiet after ten or eleven and he sat in the guards' hut with his study material. They were not allowed to read on duty and he would have been fired if he had been caught.

Kennedy did not just pass both modules, he got 84 per cent for 'Introduction to Law'. He says he already felt like a lawyer and prayed for a miracle to get out of Hillbrow and earn more money to enable him to take more modules.

That miracle came in the form of a wiry and bespectacled Tutsi who could have been a caricature from a Hutu Power manual. This guy, Kennedy says, was the other Samaritan and homeboy who changed his life.

* * *

Fundi Felix is a refugee turned graduate. He also grew up in exile in Uganda, but the UN afforded him a bursary to study in Canada. After the genocide, he became a diplomat and was the first secretary at the Rwandan embassy in Pretoria.

Kennedy met Fundi in April 2001, when he attended a memorial service for the seventh anniversary of the genocide. The two got talking and Kennedy pleaded with Fundi for a security job at the embassy.

In the meantime, Fundi recruited Kennedy as an intelligence mole to gather information on Hutu extremists and genocidaires hiding in South Africa. The remnants of Hutu Power were using the country as a base to plot the overthrow of the Kagame government. Although Kennedy had left Rwanda disillusioned, he remained a supporter of the Tutsi regime.

After the mass killings in 1994, the genocidaires and former FAR soldiers and officers regrouped as the Armée pour la Libération du Rwanda (ALiR; Army for the Liberation of Rwanda) and set up bases across eastern Congo. ALiR killed thousands of civilians, drove peasant farmers from their land, and kidnapped and dragged young men across the border and forced them into military service.

Kennedy embarked on an intelligence mission to expose ALiR agents. He befriended a woman by the name of Chantelle whose father was Hutu and her mother Tutsi. She was no supporter of Hutu Power, but had contact with a band of extremists skulking in Hillbrow and the surrounding flatlands. She told Kennedy that a former FAR lieutenant by the name of Gratien Gatarayiha was a core member of ALiR. He provided extremists with false passports and regularly travelled between Johannesburg and Brussels in Belgium to secure funds for the Congo war effort. She also fingered a Rwandan by the name of Paul Habimana as the head of Hutu

Power in South Africa. He ran a refugee agency in Pretoria that was nothing but a front for ALiR to recruit young Rwandans for the war.

Throughout the year, Kennedy passed information to Fundi. Gatarayiha and Habimana suspected Chantelle of snitching on them. They interrogated her: 'Where's your *inyenzi* friend that Kagame sent to kill us?' She hastily left the country.

The extremists were looking for Kennedy and it was time to get the hell out of Hillbrow. At the end of 2001, he received a phone call from Fundi.

'When he said the embassy needed a guard my heart jumped. He offered me R2 000 a month, which was three times what I then earned. They also gave me a boy's quarter at the back of the embassy. It was small but it had a toilet. It had no bed but I bought a thin mattress. Best of all was that the embassy was very close to the University of Pretoria. This was a dream come true.'

39

Goodbye, Rwanda

As Paul Kagame indulged in his new passion for tennis (he said in interviews he wouldn't mind swapping places with Roger Federer) at Kigali's swanky Cercle Sportif, an equally lanky man skulking behind mirrored sunglasses overlooked his every forehand, backhand and volley. It was spook Emile Rutagengwa who, five years earlier, had been one of 600 rebel soldiers stationed in Kigali just prior to the genocide and my bodyguard at the parish of Nyarubuye. After the genocide, Emile was promoted to captain and put in charge of VIP protection in the presidency.

As Kagame's stature grew and he was compared in the United States to another lanky and visionary warrior – Abraham Lincoln – dignitaries such as Bill Clinton and Nelson Mandela descended on Kigali to pay homage to the Great Lakes' new strongman. Emile lurked in the background, his hand caressing the bulge in his jacket.

Emile had a secure and promising future in Kagame's armed forces, and he had an impeccable record. He had known Kagame since the early days of the RPA's civil war against Habyarimana and his personal interface with the leader was jealously revered by fellow officers. 'We spoke regularly,' recalls Emile. 'We knew each other from the bush, where we played volleyball together. We were in the same team but I was much better than him. He was not a nice person and wasn't friendly. He was stubborn and disturbed. I remember him beating some commanders. Imagine: beating them! He was like a snake; a child. He was not liked. Everybody feared him.'

* * *

Five years after the genocide, Rwanda had, on the face of it, risen from the ashes. The economy was booming, there was a constant supply of water and electricity, the roads were sealed and police and officials didn't demand bribes. However, the normality on the streets belied Kagame's darkest secret: his stripping of a huge swathe of eastern Congo of everything worth stealing. It was, in Kagame's defence, not just Rwanda doing the looting, but also its ally across the border in Uganda and bands of rebels aligned to both regimes. Their itch was for diamonds, gold and especially coltan, a metal that enables the technological world to ring and bling. Columbite-tantalite – coltan for short – is contained in mobile phones, laptops and PlayStations, and 80 per cent of the world's supply sits beneath the Congo.

In 1999, Kagame invaded Congo for the second time, ostensibly to hunt down Hutu extremists and the remnants of FAR. The UN later discovered that the Rwandan troops did not head for the areas where the genocidaires were hiding, but for the coltan, gold and diamond mines. They enslaved locals to dig for them and teamed up with former enemies to loot the country. They armed, funded and deployed pet rebels who plundered, killed and raped. The UN found that the Congo was being ravaged by 'armies of business' commanded by men who 'carefully planned the re-drawing of the regional map to redistribute wealth'. Kagame and his allies occupied a third of the country. Rwanda – without a gemstone ever having been found on its soil – became an exporter of diamonds.

The scramble for the Congo degenerated into Africa's world war and the deadliest conflict since Hitler's blitz across Europe. Rwanda, Uganda, Zimbabwe, Burundi, Namibia and Angola turned the country into the Democratic Graveyard of Congo. Mass graves littered the countryside and bodies drifted down chocolaty rivers. Life expectancy plummeted and more than 60 per cent of children were undernourished. Cities regressed into broken shack-settlements and the countryside into a jungle-like wasteland.

* * *

I interviewed Kagame in Kigali in 1999. I was at the time a grudging fan, the images of genocide still fresh in my mind and my judgement beguiled by his achievement of bringing security to his country. I had spoken to him for the first time during the height of the genocide, when I was part of a small group of journalists accompanying an RPA platoon. We had just crossed the Akanyaru River in southern Rwanda when a gangly soldier with a swift loping step arrived on the scene, an AK slung across his bony shoulders. I don't remember him wearing any epaulettes or rank, and nobody was sure who he was until officers told us it was Kagame. His stern, gaunt face looked barely older than those of his troops and a set of old-fashioned rimmed spectacles covered most of it. He hardly seemed the strongman he later proved to be.

A few years on and the green uniform had made way for a grey suit and a statesman-like demeanour. His erstwhile mousiness and shyness had bloomed into poise and confidence. The steely and piercing eyes, however, remained unmoved and stabbed into me. Like many of his interviews, it started with him asking me what I thought of his country.

He spoke eagerly and passionately about genocide, reconciliation and his country going forward. Towards the end of the interview, I dared to ask him about allegations against his forces in the Congo. His expression turned into a führer's taunt. He sneered. 'It's a lie, nothing but lies, bloody lies, more lies, all lies, blatant lies, don't tell me you believe these lies, why all these lies?' It was the same reaction I'd seen from other despots and warlords I'd interviewed, such as Eritrean president Isaias Afewerki (presiding over one of the most repressive dictatorships in the world and the worst place on the planet to be a journalist) and Sierra Leonean rebel leader Foday 'One Man One Hand' Sankoh (the trademark of his murderous campaign was the amputation of hands and feet). When confronted with their nefarious actions they sneered, sniggered and smirked.

* * *

It was against the background of Kagame's exploits in the Congo that Emile was called to IS headquarters in Kigali and told to prepare for a tour of that country.

'I knew it was one of two things: I was either going to the Congo to kill and do terrible things or they were sending me there to kill me,' he tells me. 'That's how they work; as soon as you know too much, you disappear. I had to save myself. I was given two weeks to prepare for the mission. I decided to escape.'

A week later, Emile deserted. He skipped the border without a passport and made his way to Nairobi. He bought a false Rwandan passport and an air ticket and jetted into Johannesburg with five thousand US dollars in his pocket. Convinced that Rwandan intelligence would hunt him down, he rented a hideout in a southern Johannesburg suburb and went to ground. He assumed the name in his false passport: Christian.

'I had no friends, no girlfriend, nothing. Sometimes I would sleep for three days. I was very depressed because I had no future. If I wanted to drink, I went to the township because there are no Rwandans there. For eleven years I've been living like this. I still don't trust anyone.'

Emile eventually befriended a few Rwandan Tutsis and heard that an old friend by the name of Kennedy Gihana was living in Hillbrow. He obtained an address and knocked on the door.

'Kennedy couldn't believe who was standing in front of him,' Emile remembers. 'I told him to call me Christian and never to say I was in the army. I was surprised how he was living. He was sharing with many others and there was nothing. No food, just tea. He said he was studying to be a lawyer. I thought, oh my God, is this man dreaming or what?'

* * *

At Aceper Secondary School in the southern Rwandan town of Gikongoro, Xavier Ngabo slipped into a white shirt and short, dark trousers. In 2001, nine years after interrupting his education in the Congo to join Kagame's rebel army, Xavier finally got permission to go back to school. He was almost thirty years old.

'I sometimes felt that in liberating my country, I had imprisoned myself,' says Xavier. 'But now I was back in school. I was shy and didn't tell the other children what had happened to my family. I didn't want them to feel sorry for me. Nobody knew I was a soldier because I didn't want to scare them. I told everyone I was from Congo and had come back to Rwanda. I tried to be just a schoolboy, but I was older than some of my teachers. Although I was different, everyone wanted to be my friend. Even young ladies came to me for help!'

Xavier soon realised that he was just one of a multitude of pupils that had lost family in the mass killings. Gikongoro was at the heart of the genocide, and not far from the town is terraced Murambi Hill, as lovely as any other in Rwanda and covered with matted green grass. A sense of serenity belies the horror that lurks in a half-built school on the hill. Frozen in time, the rooms are filled with desiccated and lime-covered corpses with gnarled hands and twisted feet. Outside there are mass graves, hastily dug and covered by a bulldozer to hide evidence of the massacre. Murambi is now a memorial to the 45 000 Tutsis that were murdered there in the space of three days.

'I eventually told my friends that I was also a survivor and I was chosen to be the leader of the Survivors' Club,' says Xavier. 'We were like family and we were very close. I wrote a song for survivors that I sang with a small drum.

Have hope ...
that it will never happen again.
Stay full of hope ...
that it will never happen again.
We will never forget our brothers ...
who died in Nyarubuye, Bisesero, Bugesera, Bigogwe, Mukamira,
  Murambi, Gisose.
It will never happen again ...'

While he was at school, the army demobilised Xavier. Most Rwandan troops had withdrawn from the Congo (their domesticated rebels continue the looting) and Kagame discharged his older soldiers. Xavier received a meagre payout, was thanked for his patriotic contribution and was left to fend for himself.

'I saved my country, but enough was enough. I was very happy to leave. I wanted to lead a normal life. I wanted to get married in a church and love my wife and have children with her. God made me survive so that I could have a family. I wanted to plant that eucalyptus tree again. But how was I going to give a family a good life?'

Xavier passed matric with five distinctions. He wanted to go to university and study to be a teacher, but couldn't find a bursary. He took a job as a low-paid French tutor in Ruhengeri, but realised that he would never make enough money to sponsor his university studies or feed a family. It was in the shadows of the Virungas that he was introduced to his neighbour's cousin with whom he fell in love.

'Her name was Josephine and she was still in school, doing her matric. I told her that I loved her and she said she loved me too. I said to her, "I want to marry you, but we can't make that decision now because I must get an education so that I can look after you." She said she wanted to go to university first. Her parents had some money. It was then that I decided to leave the country and find an education somewhere else.'

* * *

Xavier made one last attempt to find the bones of his parents and afford them a decent burial. In the early 2000s, Rwanda announced the reintroduction of the ancient *gacaca* custom. It was a brave yet flawed effort to expedite justice to those who had participated in the mass killings. Years after the genocide, tens of thousands of genocide accused and convicted were still incarcerated in horrific conditions around the country.

Remember the story of Kennedy's grandfather meting out justice as a chief and elder beneath the trees of his village near Gikongoro? This was based on exactly the same principle, and across the country both convicted and accused were hauled before community courts to plead for mercy and be sentenced by elders. *Gacaca* excluded the worst perpetrators of genocide, who were dealt with by the Rwandan courts.

Xavier approached *gacaca* and requested a hearing in Mukamira for both his father and mother in order to find their bones. This was one of *gacaca*'s very first hearings and most people were suspicious of the government's true intentions. His mother's hearing took place first and *gacaca* ordered Marciano, the Hutu neighbour who had sheltered her for a day before the killers dragged her away, to appear before the elders. They asked Marciano to recall Beatrice Ndebereho's last day. She said she couldn't remember anything. Xavier confronted her with her recollection of a few years earlier. 'It's a lie,' responded Marciano. 'I never told you anything.'

Boniface, Fati, Jean-Paul and the others who killed Xavier's father were also hauled in front of *gacaca*. The elders could lessen sentences of the convicted if they confessed and contributed towards reconciliation, such as by helping a relative to find the deceased's bones. One by one, they stood up, shook their heads and denied their complicity in the death of Edward Mushatsi. When Xavier addressed *gacaca*, he pointed at the executioners and promised them that he'd be back one day to give his father a proper burial.

A few weeks later, Xavier boarded a bus headed for Kenya, where he stayed a few days before travelling down to South Africa. It took him a week to reach Johannesburg.

40

Student no. 22026208

The University of Pretoria rekindles nightmarish memories of a chauvinist institution entrenched in the racist dogma of the apartheid government and the Dutch Reformed Church – branded 'the National Party in prayer'. When I entered the university's lair in the late seventies as a seventeen-year-old to immerse myself in anything that was easy to pass, it was an all-white institution. A blind student had a black teenager who escorted and assisted him around campus. Nobody asked why the boy wasn't in school. Instead, students objected to his presence in the lecture rooms. He couldn't use the student toilets because he wasn't a student. One of my anthropology lecturers was a right-wing nutter who was later convicted for planting bombs. A history professor was tarred and feathered by the fascist Afrikaner Weerstandsbeweging (Afrikaner Resistance Movement) for being too *verlig* – liberal. A National Party cabinet minister was the university's chancellor and the council bestowed an honorary doctorate on the arch-conservative former prime minister John Vorster. The institution was a breeding ground for Afrikaner nationalism and, instead of enlightening and educating its freshmen, it stultified and discouraged open and free-thinking debate.

Since then, the university has changed immeasurably and, although the campus still doesn't reflect the South African racial landscape, it proudly occupies a place among the country's finest academic institutions. When Kennedy set foot on its manicured lawns at the beginning of 2002, the university was bilingual and multiracial, and a troop of students from across the continent occupied seats in the lecture rooms. Kennedy vowed that this was where he would commence his studies and obtain his LLB degree.

'I wanted to study at that university. It was too beautiful,' says Kennedy. He ventured into the administration building to enquire about study requirements and class fees. 'Just registration cost R2500! And then they wanted much more for a single module. It could easily cost R30 000 for a year's study and then you still had to buy textbooks. I had R300 in my pocket that I had saved from the previous year. I got my first salary at the embassy at the end of January so I had R2300. I wasn't eating.'

Exorbitant class fees were only the beginning of Kennedy's predicament. A quick glance at the websites of South African universities – and
Pretoria is no exception – brings home the vast requirements immigrants
have to comply with in order to study. (Students studying at distance
universities – like UNISA – are exempt from these requirements.) They
need a passport and a study permit, which they can only apply for once
they have paid an administrative fee, confirmation of a medical aid scheme,
an admission letter from the university, proof of funds to cover tuition fees
and living costs, a police clearance certificate and prearranged accommodation. The admission letter must attest to the fact that the immigrant is
not taking the place of a local and that a medical and radiological report
have been submitted by the student. If students want to extend their study
permits, they must pay a repatriation deposit. Most immigrants – Kennedy
included – need a yellow-fever certificate and a return air ticket to their
country of origin.

Refugees and foreigners with permanent residence are exempt from
most of these requirements. In 2002, Kennedy was still an asylum seeker
(he only got refugee status at the end of 2003) and therefore had to meet
all the above conditions. He didn't comply with any of them.

Fundi advised Kennedy to continue studying at UNISA, but he was
adamant that he wanted to attend classes, mix with fellow students and
interact with lecturers. Fundi wrote a letter to Kigali requesting a bursary
for Kennedy. He was turned down. The ambassador to South Africa at the
time was Colonel Joseph Karemera, an RPF veteran and a medical doctor.
A former minister of education, he wielded enormous influence in the
country. Kennedy made an appointment and two weeks later was taken
to his office.

'Don't I know you?' Karemera, a tallish, handsome man with a square
jaw, enquired.

'You do indeed, sir,' replied Kennedy. 'I was a rebel soldier in Byumba
when you were the head of the medical services. I think you even treated
me for a minor wound.'

'Oh yes, and what are you doing here?'

'I am in South Africa to study, sir. I want to be a lawyer. That is why I
beg your attention, sir. I need your kind assistance to enable me to continue my law studies. Do you think, sir, that the embassy or the government
of Rwanda might assist me?'

Karemera shook his head. 'I am sorry but that will not be possible. We don't have funds for such things.'

That would be the last time for almost two years that Kennedy would speak to Karemera, although he saw him every day as he was chauffeured in and out of the embassy in his black Mercedes-Benz. The ambassador now and then waved at him.

* * *

Kennedy walked into the university's administration building smartly dressed in long trousers, an office shirt, a tie that his previous employer had given him as a farewell present and a pair of borrowed black shoes. He was trying to resemble a diplomat. A white clerk took his application form. Kennedy has a remarkable ability to instantly befriend people with his open face and cheery and genial manner. Babbling incessantly, he sprinkled a smattering of diplomatic jargon in the conversation. The clerk said he also planned to study law part-time and the two chatted about the perils of extramural studies and a future in the legal profession.

'Passport?' the clerk demanded.

Kennedy pulled two letters from an envelope and handed one to the clerk. It was written on an official letterhead of the Rwandan embassy in Pretoria, had an official government stamp and was signed by the first counsel to the ambassador. The letter was addressed to the registrar of the university and stated that Kennedy Gihana was an accredited attaché at the embassy, but that he had recently lost his passport and was awaiting a new diplomatic travel document from Kigali.

'I knew that diplomatic staff were exempt from all those requirements,' Kennedy tells me. 'I therefore had to become a diplomat. That was my only chance of studying at that university.'

The clerk glanced through the letter, excused himself and disappeared into an office. Kennedy held his breath and looked at his mobile phone. He expected it to ring at any moment because the number for the first counsel on the letter was his own. The previous day, Kennedy had waited for embassy staff to go on lunch. He had sneaked into the receptionist's office, taken two embassy letterheads, slipped them into the printer and typed the letters on her computer. He had found the stamp in her drawer. He knew that if his subterfuge was discovered, he would be back on the streets.

The clerk returned, smiled, nodded his head and said the letter was acceptable but that the university would later need a copy of his diplomatic passport.

'Proof of income, please?'

Kennedy handed the clerk the second letter, also signed by the first counsel and graced with a stamp. It stated that Kennedy earned R8 000 a month as a diplomat. The clerk again nodded his head and added the letter to the pile of documents.

Kennedy ventured to the law faculty, where another clerk studied his matric certificate and the modules he had passed at UNISA. He said the faculty would credit him for the modules but that he had to pass another six in the first semester. No problem, Kennedy promised with a smile. In reality he was overwhelmed by anxiety and apprehension, not just because of the daunting academic burden ahead of him, but also because of the financial implications of paying for it all.

Back at administration, the clerk asked: 'And how are you going to pay?'

Kennedy took a roll of banknotes out of his pocket and counted out R2 500 for registration fees. The clerk was satisfied but wanted to know how he planned to settle the bill for his modules.

'I'll pay the university R2 000 a month,' he said. That was his whole salary.

The clerk made a note and confirmed: 'You are registered. Good luck.'

Kennedy rushed back to the embassy and collapsed onto his mattress on the floor. He cried, but this time because he was beside himself with happiness.

* * *

I inevitably compare Kennedy's tenacity with my own delinquency and slackness as a student at the University of Pretoria. He reminds me of how I staggered (sometimes literally) from *jol* (party) to *jol* on campus without a trouble in the world. My priorities were to get a girlfriend, persuade Daddy to replace my Corolla and get Mommy to furnish my paid-for apartment in Church Street overlooking the Union Buildings. Cracking it academically was the last thing on my mind and I had little interest in my studies. My fellow students were all white and mostly privileged, and oblivious to the world around them. I had five subjects in my first year that probably amounted to ten modules. I passed three by the skin of my teeth.

'I passed all six modules in the first semester with flying colours,' says Kennedy. 'I didn't get distinctions but my marks were high. I registered for more modules.'

'How did you manage to attend classes if you had to work?' I ask him.

'The embassy was less than a kilometre from the university. I was running the whole day, from the one to the other, all day long! I had four to five classes a day and missed some of them.'

Kennedy rallied behind him a support team at the embassy. Fundi covered for him when the ambassador and other diplomats wanted to know where their security guard was. 'I've sent him on errands,' Fundi would explain. A Malawian gardener stood in as security guard and opened the gate when Kennedy was in class.

'I got a cheque at the end of every month. The next day I paid that cheque into my university account. I had not a cent left. I had no books, nothing. Each professor gave us a list of textbooks to buy, but I borrowed books from other students and at lunchtime I sneaked into the embassy and made photocopies. I wasn't allowed into the office but I had to do it.'

'How would you describe your life then?'

'I had three shirts and three jeans, a pair of shorts and one pair of shoes and that was it. My best friend was Sabelo and he was from Swaziland. His parents sent him money. He bought me beer and burgers. I was a student and I was nearly thirty years old but I seldom went out with my friends. If I had R20, I paid it into my university account.'

* * *

I initially had a picture of Kennedy as a reserved and withdrawn student who kept to himself and worked far too hard to have any fun. That was until I met Sabelo Khumalo at a weekend retreat in the woods outside the Swaziland capital of Mbabane. Sabelo – his brother was a Bafana Bafana soccer player – had been Kennedy's closest university friend.

On our way to Swaziland, Kennedy says, 'There is something I want you to know. Even though Sabelo and I were like brothers, he knew nothing about my past.'

'Did he know what you were going through as a student?'

'No, never.'

'Why didn't you tell even your best friend?'

'I didn't want him or anyone to feel sorry for me. I always looked happy but I wasn't really happy because I had nothing and no one. Life was hard. Sometimes I cried without tears.'

After the three of us have settled with red wine and brandy in front of a crackling log fire, a chilly wind sweeping through the pines outside, Sabelo says, 'Kennedy was always laughing and talking to everyone. I never saw any student with so many friends.'

Sabelo, nine years younger than Kennedy and a member of an affluent Swaziland family, says they became friends on day one and were inseparable for the next four years. As he puts it: 'We clicked and our blood mixed. We were brothers.'

The foreign law students on campus forged a friendship circle. Kennedy was the only Rwandan, but among his chinas were the son of Tanzania's education minister, a grandson of former Malawian dictator Hastings Banda and the son of an esteemed Ugandan lawyer. It was because the others were so privileged that Kennedy withheld his true circumstances from them. He pretended to be one of them.

The group bestowed a pet name on Kennedy: *Mweshimia*, which is Swahili for 'honourable'. 'He was serious about his studies and determined to succeed,' says Sabelo. 'We called him *Mweshimia* because he was older and we respected him. He was much wiser than us.'

Kennedy and Sabelo recollect their student days, and for the next hour squalls of laughter, accompanied by the odd back-slapping and the clinking of glasses, echo round the bar.

'Do you remember that Toyota you bumped?' Sabelo wants to know.

Kennedy just about convulses with merriment. 'I was in such big shit!' he exclaims. A Rwandan university friend was going on a prolonged holiday and had been looking for a place to store his car. Kennedy invited him to park his aged Toyota at the back of the embassy, where he would keep an eye on it. The friend made the mistake of entrusting Kennedy with the keys. Kennedy waited until five for the staff to go home, then got behind the wheel and turned the ignition key. After the engine had roared to life, he grinded the gearstick into reverse and manoeuvred the car out of the parking bay. He opened the gate, thrust the car into first gear and sped off in high revs in the direction of his friends.

'I'd hardly ever been in a car, never mind driven one!' Kennedy chuckles.

'I didn't know on which side to drive and just followed the other cars. I didn't know what the road signs stood for.'

'The next thing he arrived with this car to pick us up,' remembers Sabelo. 'He didn't say where he got it from but it didn't matter. We jumped in and off we went bar-hopping!'

At three the next morning, the police pulled them over. Kennedy was by then slumped in the back seat. 'That was when I knew he was going to become a good lawyer,' says Sabelo. 'He got out of the car and spoke to the police. He first convinced them that he wasn't drunk. Then he told them we were foreign students and very poor and they were not going to get anything from us. He persuaded them to let us go. They said Kennedy was the only sober one among us and should drive us back to the residence.'

The nightly sojourns with the Toyota ended in calamity when Kennedy skipped a four-way stop and bumped into another car. 'The driver of the other car sued me, but I wrote him a letter saying, "I'm very sorry for your damage but I'm a refugee and unfortunately I cannot pay you." I tried to put the car together with wire, but it looked bad. The engine was okay but the car looked like shit. My friend was fuming when he got back. I said I'd pay him back, but of course I never did. But today we're still friends. He has forgiven me.'

Hours into our conversation, I ask Sabelo where he thought Kennedy came from and under what circumstances he had been studying.

'He told me he grew up in Uganda but went back to Rwanda,' Sabelo tells me. 'He said he worked for the Rwandan government and was a diplomat. He had been chosen as the most promising student and sent as the second attaché to South Africa. He was studying with a government bursary.'

'So you thought he was a diplomat?'

'Yes, that's what he told all of us. We believed him because he spoke like one.'

'Did you know he was a soldier in the genocide?'

'Not a thing. He never told me anything.'

'Did he tell you he walked to South Africa?'

'With what? By foot?'

'Yes.'

'You must be joking! I thought he was a just a normal boy like us.'

'Didn't you suspect anything was wrong?'

'He was always talking with a clerk in administration about payments and was promising him this amount and that amount. When I asked him what the problem was, he said the embassy was late in paying his fees, but that it had been sorted out.'

'Anything else that was wrong?'

'He had little money. He said they didn't pay him much as a diplomat because of this big bursary he had. But then he always borrowed my text-books to make copies.'

'Do you know he was actually the embassy's security guard and stayed in a little room at the back?'

Sabelo's mouth falls open and he glances at Kennedy, who is staring into the fire, nodding his head from time to time. 'My God!' Sabelo exclaims. 'I knew he was staying at the embassy, but I thought as a diplomat he had a flat. But he never wanted to take me there.'

'So you never thought anything was wrong?'

'I always knew there was more to this man than what he was telling me. One of the secretaries in the law department told me I should look after him because he was suffering. But I couldn't see it.'

'So why didn't you ask?'

'It is not in our culture to fish around and probe people. If someone tells you, he tells you. If he doesn't, it means the time is not ripe. You have to accept that.'

41

Esperance

As Kennedy plotted his registration for the 2003 academic year, a slender and graceful woman by the name of Esperance Kagubare took up the post of educational attaché at the Rwandan embassy. Her window faced the entrance and she watched the rangy guard opening and closing the gate and signing visitors into the embassy every day. 'He's studying law at the university so sometimes he's not here. We're all trying to help him,' Fundi had told her.

A day or two later Fundi introduced Esperance to Kennedy and they started talking. She explained that she was a Tutsi from the Abajiji clan and had been born and raised in the Congo. Kennedy proudly told her that he was an Abanyiginya who grew up in Uganda, and that he wanted to become a lawyer. Esperance, herself a graduate who spoke five languages, and Kennedy forged a friendship that in the following two years would not just keep Kennedy alive but inspire him in the face of incredible adversity to persevere with his studies.

Kennedy calls Esperance his mother, guardian, feeder, inspiration and protector, and mentions her in the same breath as Grandmother Kamabera, who, many years earlier, showered him with love on the pastures of Uganda and nurtured him into a healthy young man. Esperance played a critical role in helping Kennedy fulfil his dream and to this day he speaks of her with great reverence.

Esperance remembers seeing Kennedy at the gate, but the next moment he was speeding off in the direction of the university. She slipped into his room and found nothing more than a few eggs, a mattress and scant items of clothing. She asked him what he ate.

'Those eggs and now and then I buy a piece of chicken,' he replied.

'No,' she said, 'that is not good enough. Those foods are high in cholesterol. You need to eat healthily so that your body is strong and your brain sharp. From now on, I'll feed you.' She provided him with beans, rice and oil, and necessities like soap and toothpaste.

'I didn't ask. I just gave,' says Esperance. 'There was a big hunger, both to learn and to eat. He never asked me for anything but I told him I will provide the food, you just study. My salary was not big, but this man needed help. I come from a family of graduates, but have never seen such a hunger for knowledge. I had no doubt that he would succeed. He was hard-working, motivated, focused and talented. What more do you need?'

* * *

Esperance grew up the daughter of a Rwandan veterinary surgeon who lived and worked in Zaire. Three of Esperance's siblings died early, but the remaining five all acquired a university education. Two of her brothers are doctors; one practises in South Africa, while the other is a research fellow at the esteemed Johns Hopkins University in the United States.

Her upbringing was carefree and idyllic. Esperance never saw Rwanda as a child (after the 1959 Hutu uprising, the family couldn't go back), but her father raised his children in true Tutsi tradition by showering them with tales of the place where God rests his head at night, from the esteemed reign of the *mwami* to the *intore* dancers stamping their feet. They only spoke Kinyarwanda, and the local tongue of Lingala was banned in the house.

When Esperance went to the University of Lubumbashi to study languages, her father decided that he needed a new career. He enrolled at the same university and outshone his daughter. He became a school headmaster before going to work for a European mining giant on the copper fields of south-eastern Zaire.

Esperance moved to Kinshasa, then a throbbing metropolis bursting with life, music oozing from every haunt and hollow in the capital. She worked at a travel agency, got married and had two children. An uprising in Kinshasa in the early nineties forced her and her children back to Lubumbashi, where her parents lived. Esperance later went to Swaziland, where her brother had been a doctor. When Zaire descended into chaos in the early nineties, her parents abandoned their 600-hectare farm and also moved to Swaziland, where Esperance had been teaching French.

Her parents went back to Rwanda after the genocide and her father worked in Parliament. Esperance eventually came to South Africa and found a job at the Rwandan embassy.

* * *

After attending classes for a few weeks, the deadline for re-registration loomed. Kennedy once more donned his formal trousers, shirt and tie and ventured into the administration building – again armed with official embassy letters (which Esperance didn't know about). When he got to the registration clerk, he merrily chattered as though he had no concern in the world. The clerk told him his account was blocked due to his arrears. He flaunted the letters, claiming his salary as attaché had been greatly increased and that his account would be fully settled within six months. The university tentatively allowed him to register.

Kennedy has never officially received any results or marks. When a university account is in arrears, the authorities don't release the results but merely inform the student whether he or she has passed or not. They grudgingly allow students who meet their academic requirements to continue with their studies, as a graduate affords them their best opportunity to eventually recover their bad debt.

And so Kennedy played a cat-and-mouse game with the administration. His solution was to befriend the faculty secretary at the law department.

'When they block your account, your results are also blocked,' he says. 'You only hear if you've passed or not. When you register the next year, they temporarily unblock your account, but just for a few hours. That's when I ran to the secretaries and begged them to access my record before it got blocked again because it was in the red.'

* * *

To this day Kennedy and Esperance share a special attachment that was brought about by a devastating event that took place at the embassy at the end of 2003. It forged an unbreakable bond, and when the three of us meet during the writing of this book to relive that moment, they greet with a long and warm embrace and push their cheeks tightly together.

It started with Fundi informing Kennedy halfway through the year that he was leaving because he had been transferred to Kampala. In his place arrived a diplomat by the name of Abel, another Tutsi who grew up in exile in Uganda. Before Fundi departed, he briefed Abel about Kennedy's studies. Shortly afterwards, Abel asked Kennedy what he was actually doing at the embassy.

'This guy didn't like me,' says Kennedy. 'He was also a soldier and an officer, but he came from yesteryear and didn't fight in the genocide. But he had connections so he went to university and became a diplomat and now he was my boss. He was jealous because I had to take his wife to the university to register but they didn't accept her school qualifications and she was turned away. From then on I knew there would be problems. This man was going to make life difficult for me.'

After Fundi's departure, Kennedy felt Abel's growing animosity. The diplomat sent him on personal errands that made it impossible for him to attend all his classes. Soon afterwards, the embassy got another diplomat by the name of Festus. He was in charge of administration and as such was Kennedy's boss.

'He was a Hutu. He ran to Congo after the genocide but they brought him back and he became a diplomat. He didn't even know that I was studying and he didn't care. Tutsis have secrets that Hutus don't know about. We have our own things and they have their own things. I knew that he didn't trust me and I didn't trust him.'

In October, the embassy announced that it was moving to new, larger premises in Arcadia, further from the university but still within running distance. At the back of the embassy were three rooms, one for the gardener and one for Kennedy – or so he thought.

October is jacaranda month in Pretoria. Sixty-thousand trees cloak the capital in a glowing purple haze, turning the boulevards of its upmarket eastern suburbs into carpets of mauve, lavender and violet. The blossoming jacarandas spell the onset of year-end exams and students eagerly walk under the trees because legend holds that every flower that drops on your head is a sign of a subject you'll pass. Hundreds of flowers must have dropped on Kennedy's head during his daily sojourns to and from the embassy because he passed all his modules.

'I was making unbelievable progress,' he recalls. 'My account was in arrears but that was next year's worry. Esperance was feeding me and I was healthy and fit from running to and from the university. I had my friends and it was the happiest I had been for a very long time. The future looked bright.'

Life looked even rosier when Kennedy finally received notice that Home Affairs had approved his application for refugee status. He had first applied in 1998 and the process was supposed to have taken three months. Instead, it took the department five years to determine his status. Refugees get an ID book, have almost the same rights as citizens and can, among other things, work and study. Kennedy's newly acquired status meant that he didn't need a study visa or need to pretend to be a diplomat in order to get access to the university's halls of learning. The only issue now was money.

* * *

As Kennedy opened the gate for Festus on the afternoon of 14 December 2003, the diplomat rolled down his window and said he had a message for Kennedy but that he would give it to him the next day. Kennedy didn't think anything of it. The next morning, both Karemera and Abel left for their annual December holidays. Later in the afternoon, Festus handed a letter to Kennedy saying, 'I am sorry, but it is not good news.'

Kennedy opened the letter. It was typed in English on an official letterhead. He slowly read the contents. It said the embassy was relocating to another premises and had retained the services of a professional security company. Kennedy's employ was no longer needed and his last day at the embassy would be 31 December. Karemera had signed the letter.

'My world collapsed,' remembers Kennedy. 'Everything I had achieved and everything I had struggled for turned into ash. Without that job I couldn't continue at the university. My life was ending.'

He stumbled back to his room, fell down on his mattress and cried. When he had regained some composure, he phoned Esperance.

'I had just come home when he called,' Esperance tells me. 'He was crying. He said he had lost the job. He must be out of the embassy by the end of the month.'

'What made it worse was that they waited for everyone to go on holiday before they gave me the letter,' says Kennedy.

'I said to him, "Don't do anything until we have talked. Tomorrow morning, come to me,"' remembers Esperance. 'He was still crying the following morning, but I assured him that he would eventually be a lawyer. I told him to be strong because it was not the end of the world. But he thought it was.'

Kennedy's life is speckled with traumatic and painful episodes that have moulded him into the human being he is today. Three events continue to haunt him: the killing of the mother and her baby in April 1994; the young woman and her compatriots that were seized, tortured and dispatched to an excruciating death later in the same year; and his dismissal by the Rwandan embassy.

The events of December 2003 surface continuously throughout the days and weeks and months of our interviews and conversations. Every time, it brings Kennedy to tears. In contrast, we discuss the executions he was involved in as a soldier only once and relatively briefly. There is at the onset of death an immensely personal relationship between the executioner and his victim that is almost impossible for a third party to fathom or describe in words.

When it comes to Kennedy's truly darker deeds, I seldom prompt him to reveal more than what he wants to impart. The less said and explained about the act of terminating life is often more telling than a rambling and incoherent justification of an unjustifiable act.

The letter signed by Karemera was the ultimate betrayal in Kennedy's life. Even though he left Rwanda disillusioned, he was always 'one of them'; a Tutsi boy who liberated his country and spilt blood for his tribe, his clan, his grandparents, his comrades and his president. A summer's day in December 2003 shattered that illusion and reiterated the reality that Kennedy Alfred Nurudin Gihana stood as exposed and naked at the gate of the Rwandan embassy in Marais Street, Pretoria, as the day he was brought into this world under blue canvas in a refugee camp in Burundi.

'I was bitter and sad. How could Karemera do this to me? We were both freedom fighters and I trusted him. He was my comrade. We were in the same camp during the war. We loved each other and I would have died for him. Now he had left me dying. He knew I was a Tutsi boy who had given my life so that he could be ambassador. How could a powerful man like that bury me in a foreign nation?'

'All he wanted to do was sit in his room,' says Esperance of Kennedy. 'I said he must come and have Christmas with me and the children. There were other friends as well, but Kennedy was very quiet.'

'I don't remember that Christmas,' says Kennedy. 'I was thinking of killing myself.'

* * *

Karemera returned from his holiday just before New Year and a few days before Kennedy had to vacate his room. Kennedy walked into the embassy and managed to see Karemera. 'I asked him, "Sir, can you help me? You know that I have taken your cheque every month to the university. I have not saved a single cent. You have been my father and now you have thrown me out." He said it was a decision of the diplomats and he couldn't do anything. I asked him, "Sir, can you give me accommodation? There are three rooms at the back of the embassy and only one will be occupied." He said, "Sorry, but you are no longer in our employ. I cannot help you." I asked him for a room at his mansion, where there were also outside rooms where only his driver stayed. He said, "Sorry, but I cannot do that." I stood up and said, "Thank you, sir, and goodbye, sir." That was the last time I saw him.'

Kennedy says he has always dreamt of bumping into Karemera, just to shake his hand and greet him as an intellectual and academic equal. I doubt whether he will. Karemera returned to Rwanda in the mid-2000s, but never regained his former glory as a political heavyweight and was condemned to live out his life in relative obscurity in the Rwandan senate. Newspapers reported that he was linked to an opposition party that wanted to unseat Kagame. In the Rwanda of today, dissent can be lethal. Karemera fell sick and newspapers say he is ailing and terminally ill. Rumours abound in and outside the capital that he was poisoned. A dissident newspaper remarked: 'Once given Kagame's water, no doctor can find out the cause of death or frailness.'

* * *

Kennedy collected his last pay cheque, gathered his meagre belongings and took them to Esperance's one-bedroomed flat in Sunnyside that she shared with her two daughters. There was no place for him to sleep, but she told him that she expected him every day for lunch or dinner.

She said to her children, 'When Kennedy is here, don't ask him if he wants food, because he is proud and would say no thank you. Just feed him.'

With only a blanket, Kennedy headed for Magnolia Park, a charming stretch of lawn and gardens adorned with wide circular ponds and spurting fountains. It is a stone's throw from the university and the revered and feared amphitheatre of Blue Bulls rugby, Loftus Versfeld. As a boy, I often played in the shallow ponds at Magnolia and headed to Loftus every Saturday with my father.

There was a restaurant in the park where the homeless gathered at night to sleep on the veranda. Kennedy threw his blanket in a corner and plonked himself down on the ground. He was back where he had been five years earlier, except this time as a parkdog.

42

Parkdog

Life in a park and survival in a refugee camp are almost one and the same thing: the lodgers are swamped by emotions of futility and lethargy, their lives in limbo. At least those clapped in the chains of dependency in a camp have been processed and labelled and are entitled to handouts from do-gooders. Parkdogs are scorned. They hamper attempts by ratepayers to rid the city's green spots of undesirables. They scare little boys who hit or kick balls into the bushes where they sleep. They peer for hours into a void and their sole obsession is to be the first to lay their squalid paws on a discarded box of KFC in the hope that it still contains a plastic tub of coleslaw or a half-eaten drumstick.

Morning after morning, Kennedy positioned himself on a bench and stared across the beds of clivias and hydrangeas at children gambolling about on Magnolia's tended lawns. It was almost the end of the school holidays and he was contemplating his dire future.

I ask him during our interviews if he ever contemplated turning to crime during times like this.

'I was not brought up in that way,' he replies. 'In Tutsi culture, it is a terrible thing if you hear that so-and-so from this or that family has stolen something. It never crossed my mind. We are proud of ourselves, us Tutsis. No matter the circumstances, you don't do it. If you steal today, what are you going to do tomorrow? Steal again? So are you going to steal your entire life, year after year? No one can live like that.'

'So how were you going to live?'

'It was while I was sitting in the park that I decided I'd show them. I would not give Karemera the satisfaction of knowing that I was eating from the streets. I had been thinking of killing myself, but was now thinking of ways to continue studying.'

Kennedy had his last pay cheque of R2 500 in his pocket, but his university debt had in the meantime bloated to R25 000. Unless he found money to settle at least part of his debt, the university authorities would probably not even allow him to re-register. On the face of it, his student days were over.

'No, no, no, I couldn't accept that. There had to be a way forward. I'd managed to do half my law degree by being a lowly security guard. I'm a religious man and God was not just going to leave me to die alone and cold in a foreign place.'

When Kennedy told his park chums that he had been working at an embassy but that the big boss boy had chased him out, they glanced incredulously at him. He added that he was studying law and was going to become an attorney. Parkdogs don't waste energy unnecessarily and their eyes didn't even shift. He decided that he had nothing more to say to them and toiled the kilometre to where Esperance lived to have his daily meal.

'The man wasn't talking,' says Esperance. 'I said positive things to lift his spirits but he didn't answer me. He was as thin as a reed and his mood was black. I was very worried about him.'

Esperance came up with an idea to approach wealthy Rwandans living in South Africa to contribute towards Kennedy's study fees. They compiled a list and Esperance made telephone calls to a Congolese lawyer in Johannesburg, a Rwandan chemist at the University of the Witwatersrand and a former adviser to Kagame who had fled Kigali and found sanctuary in South Africa. They all pledged their support. It was not nearly enough to clear Kennedy's debt, but at least enough to maybe persuade the university to allow him to register for another year.

* * *

The university's Merensky Library opened around 20 January. Although classes hadn't started yet, it at least gave Kennedy something to do during the day – and a place to sleep.

'I still had my student card from the previous year and everybody in the library knew me. I didn't tell anyone what had happened. I pretended to be happy and laughed and joked, but my inside was burning. How was I going to register and how was I going to pay the university account? And how was I going to live?'

Every night after dinner at Esperance's, Kennedy tramped to the library, gathered a few books and took a seat as far away from staff as he could. The library has a study centre that can house more than a thousand students and is open twenty-four hours a day, seven days a week. Kennedy sat in the centre and slept. He rested his head on his folded arms and was fast asleep within minutes. He sometimes put three chairs together and lay down. He washed himself every morning in the bathroom.

Kennedy's friends didn't notice anything peculiar in his behaviour. Sabelo says when he returned from holiday, Kennedy laughed and joked as though he didn't have a worry in the world. He didn't tell anyone that he had lost his job.

'If I think back now, he didn't want to go out and was spending lots of time in the library,' Sabelo tells me. 'He looked tired but I thought he was just working hard. If only I had known. I should have seen it.'

'I didn't want those guys to know,' says Kennedy. 'I was ashamed of myself. I tried to look happy and pretended that I was still working at the embassy. My friends now and then bought me a beer, but afterwards I had to go back to the library to study and sleep. I didn't know for how long I would be able to do this. I was like a ghost.'

By the time lectures commenced, Kennedy had not yet registered. Registration only closed towards the beginning of April and he was waiting for the pledges from his benefactors to come in. Tired and often with an empty stomach, Kennedy attended most of his lectures but had difficulty concentrating. He had also lost the use of the embassy's photocopy machine that had enabled him to copy textbooks.

* * *

On the eve of the closure of registration, Esperance phoned Kennedy's Rwandan benefactors. She initially raised only R1 000, a drop in Kennedy's ballooning bucket of debt.

'At nine the night before registration closed, I phoned people. I said if Kennedy doesn't have more money tomorrow, he is not studying. I didn't have a cent myself but borrowed a hundred dollars from the embassy's small cash, which I repaid at month-end. My friend had a hundred dollars that she was sending to her son but I begged her to give it to Kennedy. She said, "If Esperance says there's someone who needs it more than my son, it must be urgent. My son won't starve."'

Kennedy walked into the dreaded administration building five minutes before registration closed. In his pocket was his new refugee ID book, R2 500 in cash and his December pay cheque that he had guarded with the same vigilance as his matric certificate. Earlier that morning, he had gone to Esperance's flat, dressed in his nice pants and good shirt, and knotted the security company's tie around his neck.

The clerk glanced at his computer screen and shook his head. 'Your account is locked. You have to settle your bill.'

'That will be no problem,' Kennedy blustered. 'I am getting a new job soon and I'll settle my whole account before the middle of the year.'

The clerk shook his head again. Kennedy persisted. 'I have some money that I can put down towards paying off that account.'

'It's not enough,' said the clerk.

'Can I speak to your superior?' Kennedy asked. He blustered, begged and pleaded his way up the administrative ladder until he strode into the office of some pen-pusher who had the authority to say yea or nay. He continued to drivel about the rosy outlook of his financial affairs.

'It can't go on like this, Mr Gihana. I can't register you,' said the registrar.

'I beg you, sir. I've been working very hard, sir. Just look at my good marks. I promise I'll settle that whole bill very soon, sir.'

The registrar mulled over the predicament of the student eyeballing him across his gleaming desk. The young man didn't qualify to continue studying, but his marks were exemplary.

'This the last time, Mr Gihana,' he announced. 'You have to settle that account very, very soon.' He paused for a moment before adding: 'I'll register you.'

'Once you're registered,' says Kennedy, 'it's like being registered for life, or at least for that year. Your account grows but they can't prevent you from writing exams. When I got outside, I jumped! Very high!'

Jobless, homeless, family-less, moneyless, foodless and country-less, Kennedy didn't even contemplate where the money to pay for the twelve modules he had registered for was going to come from.

'That was a very, very big step in getting closer to my degree,' he tells me.

* * *

Kennedy was falling apart. Nights and weeks of insufficient sleep had forced his eyeballs back in their sockets. He was skin and bone and worn out to the point where he hallucinated in the library and was tormented by nightmares. He was often too busy reading textbooks and trying to pass his first-semester exams to walk the kilometre to Esperance's flat for his daily meal. He continued, however, to brag and boast about his job at the embassy and pretended to not have a worry in the world.

'What did you think of the privileged white students studying with you?' I ask Kennedy.

'Nothing. I was just not lucky enough to be privileged as well. I wished I also had a family that could help me. I had lots of white friends. When one graduated, his father gave him the keys of his house in Centurion. But my black friends were also privileged and had rich fathers. But when we wrote exams, we were all equal. The difference was that they only had to worry about their results. I worried about what I was going to eat and where I was going to sleep.'

Kennedy failed two of his modules and passed the rest on the skin of his arse. He was a far cry from the exemplary student he had been a year before.

'Every time I saw him, he looked worse,' says Esperance. 'He was getting thinner and thinner. I said to him, "Son, you are going down. Very fast. Look at you!" But he didn't listen. He was driven by a very big force. I had no control over him.'

43

Kennedy Gihana, LLB

What follows is a real-life drama that almost eclipses the fable of eighteen-year-old Mumbai ghetto-dweller Jamal Malik in the blockbuster movie *Slumdog Millionaire*. Jamal was one question away from winning twenty million rupees in an Indian game show. Of course he got it right and, in true Hollywood style, love championed and everybody lived happily ever after. Only in the movies, right?

Well, here's another script, but this one is real. A destitute African outcast escapes the conflicts and upheavals of the Great Lakes and reaches foreign shores. He lives on the streets, but has a dream of becoming someone some day. Don't we all? He pursues his vision, and without money, a bursary or a sponsor, he enrols for a law degree at a leading university. He connives and lies his way through registration and then excels academically.

But two years down the line his dream is shattered. He has exhausted his ploys to circumvent the financial constraints of his endeavour. He has nothing to eat and nowhere to sleep. In short: he's down and out. With nothing to lose and with his pride in his shoes, he ventures to the university's international student office and asks for help.

This is the moment the story becomes a fairytale; when fairies, elves and goblins chase trolls, witches and wolves into dark woods and condemn them to live out their lives in foggy, cold swamps; when a white duck appears to ferry Hansel and Gretel across the impassable river that is blocking their journey back home. This is the moment that changes Kennedy's life forever.

* * *

International student adviser Laura Pienaar was in her office when her boss summoned her.

'I have a man with me who is crying,' he said. 'He walked into my office and said he can't cope any longer. I told him we cannot help him. He is now asking for you.'

Laura recognised the man as Kennedy Gihana, a Rwandan student she had seen and spoken to a few times before. He was sitting with his head in his hands and was sobbing.

'This is the end of the road,' Kennedy said to her. 'I cannot go on. This is where it ends.'

Laura was convinced that Kennedy was close to suicide. She didn't know what to do because the International Student Affairs Office didn't have money or a fund to help him. She listened to and counselled him, and gave him R200 to buy food. She promised to see what she could do and told him to come back in a few days' time.

'I phoned around, but nobody could do anything. I eventually phoned the dean of the law faculty,' Laura tells me. 'His words to me were that he didn't want to lose this student. He said he was going to see what he could do.'

* * *

A few days later, the dean of the law faculty, Professor Duard Kleyn, summoned Kennedy to his office. 'I thought he was going to say, "Sorry about your situation, but I can't help,"' recalls Kennedy. 'By then I had given up hope.'

The professor had lunch ready when Kennedy arrived. He then called one or two staff members and announced: 'Welcome to the law faculty, Mr Gihana. I am appointing you as an assistant in the dean's office.'

Kennedy can't remember what he felt or what went through his mind. 'I just cried. Professor Kleyn changed my life. He resurrected me from the grave. He saved my life.'

Kennedy received a letter of appointment, a salary, daily lunch and unlimited access to the law library. And that was not the end of his good fortune. The next day, he was shown a room at Tuksdorp, a vast complex of residences for international and postgraduate students ('Tuks' is the epithet of the university and *dorp* is the Afrikaans for 'town'). As Tuksdorp was full, Kennedy was given a small room at the back of a house. There wasn't much more than a bed and a mattress, but it didn't matter; he had a place to sleep. He was issued with a meal card to eat at the hostel.

When Kennedy wasn't attending lectures, he worked in the law department. His salary of R1 800 a month was paid directly into his university account. The department gave him R500 cash for the first few months in order to buy necessities such as clothes, toiletries and shoes.

Kennedy says best of all was that the administration could never again deny him registration, because he was now a staff member. He was entitled to study irrespective of his debt.

When Sabelo saw Kennedy again, he was grinning from ear to ear. 'Guys,' Kennedy informed his cronies, 'I am now a staff member of the law faculty.'

'What about your diplomatic job at the embassy?' Sabelo wanted to know.

'This is much better,' said Kennedy, adding that he had resigned.

* * *

'I was getting strong and doing unbelievably well,' says Kennedy. 'I even got some distinctions in the second semester. I wasn't going to disappoint Professor Kleyn and the only way I could thank him was to make him proud of me academically.'

Once again a team of do-gooders rallied behind Kennedy. The dean's secretary slipped a few banknotes into his hand every Friday, while her husband donated a jacket and a pair of jeans. A faculty secretary – a long-time confidante who had for some time been slipping Kennedy his results – took him shopping every Saturday in order to buy basic food-stuffs. Although Kennedy had a meal card, he had been told that the bill would be added to his nightmarish university account, and so he preferred to eat in his room until Sabelo gave him his own card to use.

'My confidence was back. In fact, my friends had new respect for me because I was employed by the university. I even went out with them for a drink or two. I still didn't have money to buy books, but I made copies in the dean's office.'

Because of the disaster earlier in the year, Kennedy failed two modules at the end of 2004. The faculty secretary once again sneaked him his results. If he wanted to complete his LLB degree in the minimum of four years, he would have to register for an almighty thirteen modules in his final year – a load so demanding that he had to get special permission to do so.

As Sabelo and the others embarked on their annual holiday, Kennedy asked permission to stay in Tuksdorp. He was preparing for the next academic year.

* * *

Registration 2005 was a mixture of glee and triumph. Kennedy strolled into the administration building, plonked himself down in front of the clerk and, before the latter even had an opportunity to call up his account, Kennedy presented him with his staff member card.

'Do you know how much money you owe, Mr Gihana?'

'I am aware that I owe you a lot,' he responded. 'I assure you that you will eventually get your money. But for now you can just register me. I'm a member of the law faculty.'

Kennedy worked day and night. He wrote his final exams and received a letter from the university in December saying that he had failed criminal law and therefore could not graduate. He hadn't been granted a supplementary exam either. He applied to the dean for special permission to write a supplementary, which was granted.

He stayed in the residence for the whole of December to prepare himself to jump this final hurdle. He wrote his supplementary on 20 January 2006 and a few days later one of the secretaries called him. 'Son,' she announced, 'you've made it. You've passed.'

'I cried, but this time out of joy,' Kennedy recalls. 'I wished I had a family I could share it with. There was only Esperance, because my friends had gone back to their families and their countries. She also cried. My suffering had come to an end.'

* * *

'What did it feel like when you finally stood there in your gown and received your degree?' I ask.

Kennedy scratches in a white envelope for a DVD. We are sitting in his lounge in his second-floor apartment in Pretoria's western suburbs, an area generally regarded as a stamping ground for the lower middle class and the poor.

Kennedy rents in a complex of two- and three-storey blocks on a hill overlooking Pretoria's steelworks. The complex previously housed steelworkers, but has since been sold on. His flat is simply but comfortably furnished, the dominant feature an enormous flat-screen television set. Mementoes from Rwanda that Kennedy and Goreth gathered when they got married at the end of 2010 and brought back to South Africa are scattered around the place.

Goreth, who is plying me with milky tea, is as reserved and introverted as always and doesn't say much. She is still mastering English and is in her matric year. She wants to study nutrition and Kennedy is enquiring from various universities about their academic requirements and fees. The commencement of her higher education will, however, have to wait for a year or two. She's pregnant and is going to be a mother first.

With the DVD in the player, Kennedy commences a running commentary. 'That is Professor Kleyn over there,' he excitedly exclaims. He names virtually every student that steps onto the podium to receive his or her *Legum Baccalaureus*. After what seems like hours, the name of Kennedy Alfred Nurudin Gihana is called out. Draped in a red and black gown, he shakes the chancellor's hand and turns around in order for the cloth to be draped around his neck. He is presented with a white envelope.

Kennedy pauses the video. I look at him. He shakes his head. 'Do you see that envelope in my hand?' he asks.

'Yes?'

'My degree certificate was supposed to have been in there. But it was empty. It only had my account of how much money I owed.'

'Why?'

'That's what they do. You don't get your certificate until you've paid your study debt. They just give you an empty envelope.'

'That's not fair!'

'No, it's not. And do you know how many we were when we started our law degree in 2002?'

'How many?'

'Almost 800. But do you know how many finished?'

'No, how many?'

'We were 157.'

44

Jennifer and Goreth

I can't remember where we were – at my home in Johannesburg, at the Mediterranean café in Pretoria where we often sat and drank copious amounts of wine or on our junket to East Africa – but we were at the point in the story where Kennedy had received his LLB degree and was about to commence his two-year attorney articles at one of the oldest law firms in the Jacaranda City. I had by then recorded many hours of interviews and had scribbled notes in a stack of notepads. I expected us to start winding up his story; his life was approaching 'normal' and the years of destitution and uncertainty were behind him. How wrong I was. An era of unrelenting hardship might have been over, but we would continue talking for many more hours and days to come.

Kennedy says when he started his articles he was looking forward to being just an average guy with a good job and money to spend. 'People were talking about things like holidays and staying in hotels. I've never even been to places like Durban and Cape Town, and have never stayed at a good hotel for a weekend to enjoy the sun. But I earned only R3 300 as a clerk and had to buy clothes. I stayed in a small flat in Sunnyside with another guy. Candidate attorneys are nothing but servants. You run around looking for files and submitting applications and things like that. But I served them with my full heart. I never missed a day's work.'

'And how were you treated?' I ask.

'Ha, my friend!' he exclaims. 'Sometimes I think I will always be a foreigner in this country. One day I was in the court building drawing case files when this woman said, "What are you doing here? You are a foreigner." I told her I was going to be an attorney soon. She continued, "But there are universities in your homeland. Why didn't you study there? You guys come here to take our jobs and our women." She said this in front of other candidate attorneys and they all laughed. I reported her to the court manager, who took it to the chief magistrate, who called her in. Everybody knew about this. They respected me after that.'

'So what did you do when you were not working?'

'I would go to a bar and have one beer and go home. I was worried about the university account that was in my envelope instead of my degree certificate. I lay awake at night thinking about the interest pushing it up and up. I knew they were going to come for me at some point. I just asked God to help me.'

'And a girlfriend, did you at least have a girlfriend?' I ask. I know he hates these questions.

He waves his hand and clicks his tongue. 'Now why should I have entered into that? They just want money, and I had no money to waste. I had R500 left; where's money for a girlfriend?'

But Kennedy was thirty-five years old and increasingly desperate to re-establish the family he had left behind on the savannahs of south-eastern Uganda. Alone and companionless, he yearned to be part of a household and have his own flesh and blood. In short, he was looking for a wife, but not just anyone. She had to be a Tutsi and, as he called it, a 'home girl'.

His opportunity came when he met a Rwandan woman by the name of Jennifer Rwamugire in 2006. She was only a few years younger than Kennedy and married, but back home she had several sisters.

* * *

Jennifer had come to South Africa in early 2006 after receiving a bursary to study for a nursing degree at the Tshwane University of Technology in Pretoria. Kennedy met her shortly after she arrived, when he went to Esperance one evening for dinner. The two became close friends and Jennifer attended his graduation ceremony.

'He showed me how the taxis work, helped me with my registration and walked with me at night because I was scared,' recalls Jennifer. 'But he was a secretive man. He didn't even tell me he had walked to South Africa. Later on he told me about his grandparents, but started crying and said he wished he had buried them.'

Jennifer is a member of an esteemed Tutsi family. The daughter of a businessman and a teacher, she is the eldest of ten children. Her parents also went into exile in Uganda following the Hutu Power surge of the late 1950s. Her father was an organiser for the burgeoning RPF in the late eighties, and several of Jennifer's brothers and cousins fought in the civil war. One was a major and the other a colonel who became a war hero, but subsequently died. The family returned to Rwanda after the genocide.

From an early age, Jennifer wanted to be a nurse. She trained in Uganda, and then, in 1997, started working in Rwanda's Kanombe Military Hospital in Kigali, mostly taking care of the war casualties of Kagame's looting campaigns in the Congo. She saw the devastation of war on a daily basis: soldiers dying of festering wounds, bodies without arms or legs, and boys paralysed as a result of bullets piercing their spines. She worked at Kanombe until she came to South Africa. She has two children, one of whom is at university in Uganda.

Jennifer told Kennedy she was going home for Christmas and invited him to accompany her. He borrowed money from the law firm where he was doing his articles and bought an air ticket.

* * *

It was Kennedy's first aeroplane trip and the first time he had been back to Rwanda since crossing the border into Tanzania in January 1998. He was picked up at the airport by an old army buddy who he stayed with for a few days. Jennifer invited Kennedy to spend Christmas with her family on their farm in eastern Rwanda. That was where he fixed his gaze on her adorable sister, Goreth, at the time nineteen and still in school.

Goreth was a coy girl with wide, skittish eyes that probably reminded Kennedy of a healthy Ankole calf. She peeked at him and lowered her eyes. Kennedy gawped starry-eyed at her, not sure what to say or do. There and then he decided that she was going to be his wife and the mother of his children. A few days later, he approached Jennifer, thirteen years older than Goreth and three years younger than himself.

'I want to marry your sister,' he said.

'Which one?' Jennifer wanted to know. They were seven sisters.

'That very black one.'

'You mean Kaitare Goreth?'

'Yes, that one. I like her.'

'She's still in school! She's a baby!'

'It doesn't matter, I'll wait for her. Anyway, I first have to finish my articles and become an attorney so that I can look after her.'

'Do you think she likes you?'

'I think there's a chance. That's what I want you to find out for me.'

'I will have to speak to my parents and then to Goreth.'

'Yes, do that. And please bring me good news.'

* * *

A day after Kennedy asked Jennifer to conduct negotiations for Goreth's hand on his behalf, she sat down with her parents. Her father Gerard, by now retired, at first rejected the idea. 'And how old is this guy?' he wanted to know.

'I don't know, but he's old,' answered Jennifer.

'And who is his family?'

'His parents are dead. His grandparents brought him up but they are also dead. He's an orphan. He grew up in Uganda like us.'

'So he is a Tutsi?'

'Yes, he is.'

'And would he be able to look after Goreth?'

'Yes, I think he would. I've known him for a year now and he's a very hard worker and has completed his law degree. He's a good man.'

Goreth's father pondered the matter and concluded: 'Well, maybe this is God's will. There's one condition. She must finish her schooling and this man must help her to study. But go speak to Goreth.'

Several siblings gathered around Goreth and informed her of Kennedy's proposal. She was stunned and almost speechless. 'But he's going back to South Africa in a few days?' she ventured.

'He says he'll come back in a few years' time to marry you,' explained Jennifer. 'By then you will have completed your schooling. You must think about it. He'll look after you well.'

'But I will have to go and live in South Africa!'

'Yes, but you can come and visit,' Jennifer said. 'But tell us, do you like him?'

'Yes, he's nice, but I don't know him.'

The next day, Jennifer told Kennedy that he had to propose to Goreth in person. She hadn't made up her mind yet, but didn't seem averse to the idea of him being her future husband.

On the third day of 2007, Kennedy again visited the family on their ten-hectare farm in the Mutara district of north-eastern Rwanda. It was late afternoon and Kennedy took Goreth for a prearranged walk on one of the *panya* roads that meandered to the nearby village. It was midsummer and the pastures were bursting with yellow and purple patchworks of wild flowers, while the distant mountains basked in the afternoon dusk.

He stopped and turned towards her. He had rehearsed the lines over and over the night before. Words poured out. 'I love you and I want to marry you. I have already spoken to Jennifer, who informed your parents. They are not against the idea. So will you please become my wife and the mother of my children? I promise to love you and look after you,' he vowed.

'I will think about this, Kennedy,' she murmured, casting her eyes downwards. 'This is all too sudden. I'm not sure.'

'I am aware of that. We will marry here in Rwanda and then you will come back with me to South Africa. By then I will be an attorney and I will be able to give you a good life.'

'I will have to think about it.'

'I'm afraid there is no time to think. I'm flying back to South Africa the day after tomorrow. I need an answer now.'

'So when will we get married?'

'In two or three years' time. We will have a traditional wedding here in Mutara. I promise I will help you to study and get a qualification.'

Goreth pondered probably the biggest decision of her young life before she said, 'I think it will be possible. It is good.'

'So the answer is yes?'

'I will wait for you to come back and marry me.'

* * *

It took me months to draw the story of Kennedy's courtship of Goreth out of him and it was only when I interviewed Jennifer that the full picture emerged.

'So did you at least kiss your future bride before you came back to South Africa?' I wanted to know.

If Kennedy's skin was white it would have been rosy red. 'Why do you always ask questions like that? The time wasn't right for those things.'

'But you didn't even know her!'

'That's how it works in Tutsi culture. It's not like in America or Europe, where the boy and girl know each other for years and then maybe get married. I had found myself a good girl from a good family. She was marriage material.'

It isn't unusual in Tutsi culture for a family or a man to book a girl in advance for wedlock. It's called *gufata irembo* – securing the bride. Once the future wife has been identified, a male delegation representing the prospective groom – usually the father and brothers – will, taking a crate of beer, visit the family of the girl and inform them of his desire to marry her. If the girl's father and older brothers are amenable to the suggestion, they will discuss a price – *ikwano* – for the bride, similar to *lobola* in South African culture. The bride's family will discuss the proposal with other household members and then invite the groom's folks over for a second visit. This time a cow will accompany them – or cash equal to the value of a cow – as a deposit. The wedding date, which can be several years in the future, will be set and the deal sealed.

'I was in big shit here,' Kennedy says when we discuss his then bride-to-be.

'Why?'

'I still had to negotiate *ikwano* with my father-in-law. A nice girl like Goreth with some education and from a good family can easily fetch ten cows or more. I had to do my own negotiations because I didn't have a family. You were talking about thousands here. Thousands! Where was I going to get all of that?'

* * *

With Kennedy's future wife booked, he now had to concentrate his energy on not just finishing his articles and passing his Law Society of the Northern Provinces exams, but addressing a dire constraint on his future plans: he couldn't, under South African law, become an attorney.

As a refugee, Kennedy was afforded almost full citizen rights. However, the Attorney's Act states that only citizens of the Republic and immigrants or foreigners with permanent residence can be admitted as attorneys. Kennedy only had refugee status and didn't yet qualify to get permanent residence. Refugees have to wait for at least five years before they can apply to Home Affairs to declare them 'indefinite refugees'. Only once a refugee is 'indefinite' can he or she apply for permanent residence. This step can then take several additional years.

Kennedy came to South Africa in 1998 and applied for refugee status a few months later. Home Affairs should have determined his fate within ninety days, but as a result of bureaucratic incompetence he only received his refugee status towards the end of 2003. That meant he would only be able to apply for indefinite status in 2008. Once that was granted, he would have to submit an application for permanent residence and heaven knows how long that process would take.

'I was screwed. I didn't qualify to be an attorney,' says Kennedy. 'I asked Home Affairs if I could apply to become an indefinite refugee but they said I would have to wait. I consulted immigration lawyers but they said I couldn't become an attorney. I said in that case I would take my case to the Constitutional Court because the Attorney's Act was in conflict with the Constitution. How can one Act afford a refugee the right to work, education, medical care and all of that, but then another Act discriminate against him?'

* * *

Towards the end of 2007, Kennedy passed his attorney admission exam and completed his articles. He applied to the Law Society of the Northern Provinces to be admitted as an attorney, but they rejected his application. He appointed a legal team that was prepared to act *pro bono* for him and filed an application in the High Court. The society appointed senior counsel to oppose his application and submitted a counter-affidavit. It was a battle that, if taken to the Constitutional Court, could take years and cost millions. In the meantime, Kennedy continued to get just more than R3 000 a month as an articled clerk because he hadn't yet been admitted as an attorney. A court date was eventually set for August 2008.

In March of that year, Kennedy again wrote to Home Affairs explaining his predicament and applying to be classified as an indefinite refugee. 'In July, I received a phone call from Home Affairs. They said I'd been declared an indefinite refugee. *Jissus*, I can't tell you how high I jumped! I hugged everyone around me. But my problem wasn't over. Now I had to get permanent residence. And that could take years.'

Kennedy went to Home Affairs to get a date for an interview. All indefinite refugees have to be interrogated as part of their application for permanent residence. A clerk told him the first available appointment they had was in two months' time.

'But then I'm in court already,' Kennedy lamented.

'Sorry, sir, that's the best we can do,' came the reply.

Kennedy asked to see the supervisor of the department's permanent residence section. 'This is my life. I have suffered enough. Please help me,' he begged the official. 'Once we're in court, it will drag on for years and there's no way you'll then give me permanent residence.'

The supervisor conducted the interview there and then. The next day, Kennedy submitted all the affidavits and documentation the department required. He heard nothing for several days. On 14 August, twelve days before he was due in court, the supervisor phoned.

'Mr Gihana,' she said, 'your application for permanent residence has been approved. Come in and get it. It's ready.'

Kennedy shakes his head. 'I nearly collapsed. I screamed as loudly as I could. I still have to buy that woman a bunch of flowers.'

The next day, Kennedy informed the Law Society of the Northern Provinces of his new status. They in turn responded that he now fulfilled all the requirements to be admitted as an attorney. He withdrew his High Court application.

* * *

On 26 August 2008, ten years after arriving in South Africa, Kennedy appeared before two judges in the North Gauteng High Court in Pretoria, lifted his right hand and swore allegiance to the Constitution of the Republic of South Africa. In the audience were Esperance, Jennifer, friends, colleagues from the law firm and the new Rwandan ambassador to South Africa. The day before, Kennedy had gone shopping for a black suit, a red tie and pointy black shoes – the same outfit he would wear three years later in the searing heat of Uganda when we went in search of his family.

Nobody had any objection to the applicant joining the legal profession and, minutes later, Kennedy was accepted as an attorney in the High Court. The ambassador promptly held a press conference on the steps of the court, praising Kennedy for his perseverance and for upholding the good name of the Rwandan community in the country. His achievement was splashed on the inside pages of the *Pretoria News*.

45

'My father's bones'

When the volcanoes straddling Africa's Great Lakes erupted and emptied their bowels into the air, the seething lava left a multitude of holes, caves and cavities once it had cooled down. Children growing up at the foot of the Virungas in Rwanda and the Congo play hide-and-seek in these mini *adaches*. In times of civil war and uprising, soldiers and rebels find shelter in them. During the 1994 genocide, they attained an added function: as tombs.

It is 16 December 2009 and Xavier Ngabo stands at an *adache* a stone's throw from the village of Mukamira in north-western Rwanda where he grew up. He can't see into the hole because the killers sealed it by packing stones against the opening, which were then covered with soil. Grass and weeds have grown over it since the body was dumped into the hole more than fifteen years ago. Two men with shovels scoop the weeds and soil away until they reach the rocks.

'That's fine,' says Xavier and kneels down. 'I want to do this myself.'

Almost leisurely, he removes one stone at a time. He feels it before he sees it. He extracts a brownish bone from the hole. In the next hour or so, the men exhume a whole skeleton. The skull is still intact. They sift through the soil and find pieces of rags and a necklace. One of the men holds what appears to be a bracelet in the air and passes it to Xavier.

'This is a rosary,' says Xavier, scratching the soil and dirt away. 'This is the one I bought in Goma in 1989 and gave to her as a present.' He pauses for a few second. 'This is Mama. This is her.'

Beatrice Ndebereho must have been clutching her rosary when the killers dragged her from her friend's home on the third or fourth day of the genocide and executed her.

She was then entombed with it in the *adache*.

* * *

After Xavier arrived in South Africa in 2005, he set up a small trading business. He bought clothes from Chinese importers and travelled throughout Mpumalanga, Limpopo and the North West provinces selling his goods.

He made enough money to live and even saved some to pay *ikwano* for his fiancée, Josephine Uwajeneza, whom he had promised to marry in a traditional wedding in Rwanda.

In 2009, he got a phone call from a relative in Rwanda.

'Ngabo Xavier!' the elated voice said at the other end. 'You must come home! Bandora is speaking! He's confessing!'

Xavier almost dropped the phone. Bandora was one of the neighbours who had participated in butchering his father at the roadblock near Mukamira in January 1991. The killers had since been convicted and were in prison, but none had been willing to assist Xavier in finding Edward Mushatsi's bones in order to afford him a decent burial. Until now.

Xavier's search for his father's remains was his single biggest obsession. He had virtually no information about Beatrice's demise, except for what her neighbour, Marciano, had told him. She, however, later denied that she had said anything to Xavier.

'What does he say?' Xavier wanted to know.

'He says he'll only speak to you so you must come and see him. He says he'll help you to find the bones.'

'I'm coming,' said Xavier. 'I'll be there as quickly as I can.'

Xavier flew back to Kigali in October 2009. Once there, he told Josephine that they would get married as soon as he had properly buried his father. Josephine had in the meantime finished her degree and was a social worker.

The next day, he visited Bandora at Gisenyi's central prison.

'Yes, I helped to kill your father,' he admitted. 'I didn't bury him, but I know in which direction they took his body. I will cooperate and help you to find the bones in return for leniency from the *gacaca* courts. I have been in prison for fifteen years and I need to be with my family before I die. And I also need you to forgive me for what I've done.'

'I forgive you, Bandora, but please help me to find my papa's bones. Only then will there be peace for all of us,' Xavier replied.

* * *

Gacaca – the traditional Rwandan courts – arranged for Bandora to be transported back to Mukamira. He took Xavier and the investigators back to the spot where they attacked Edward. He pointed out where they had left the wounded man to die in agony until another neighbour performed a mercy killing. Bandora said that after Edward was dead, some of the killers – among them Fati and Boniface – returned to bury him. They told Bandora afterwards in which direction they had taken the body.

He indicated several spots, and they began to dig in the black soil. Their efforts, however, turned out to be fruitless and, after a few days, the forage was called off. Bandora didn't know where the body was.

'I now came up with Plan B,' says Xavier. 'I made a list of all the people who knew Papa and drank beer with him and went to church with him. I also made a list of all the people who could have seen what happened to his body. Someone must have seen or heard something. I gave this list of about twenty-five names to *gacaca* and asked them to call a hearing in Mukamira. They ordered all of them to be present.'

The whole village gathered for *gacaca*, in this case symbolically held on an open patch of field where Edward's eucalyptus grove, which the killers had cut down after his death, once stood. Xavier addressed the villagers who had been summoned to appear in front of the community elders. 'You didn't kill my father, so that is not why you are here. But one of you must know. My father was your friend. Help me. Tell me where he is. Please, I beg you for your mercy today. Stand up and talk.'

Boniface's father was one of those summoned. Xavier told him: 'I know you didn't kill my father. Your son did. That's why he's in prison. But I beg you today, please tell me if you know what happened to Papa's body. Maybe Boniface told you something. Did he?'

The old man shook his head. Fati's brother had also been hauled before the elders, but said he didn't know either. Xavier addressed each and every villager that he had listed. Nobody knew anything. Despondent and exhausted, he was convinced that someone knew something, but that there was a conspiracy of silence to withhold the truth.

The proceeding was about to come to an end when a man in the gallery by the name of Jean-Paul put his hand in the air and got to his feet. 'I have listened to everything that was said here today and I cannot allow this man to leave us with his heart so filled with pain,' he said. 'That's why I have decided to talk. I want to start by saying that when this man was killed, I was only eleven years old. I therefore had nothing to do with his death. But I know where that body is.'

Jean-Paul said he was grazing his goats when he stumbled upon the body of a man. He knew of Edward's killing because everybody in the village spoke about it. He ran away and returned a while later. Boniface, Fati and others had dug a hole and were lifting the body into it. He ran home and told his father, who swore him to secrecy.

'Every time I took the goats to that area I looked at the place where the body is. But what is strange is that sometime after the burial, someone built a house right on top of that grave. So the bones are under the floor. I will go and show you where that house stands,' Jean-Paul concluded.

The next morning, Jean-Paul took *gacaca* and Xavier to the house, a typical three-roomed dwelling with a tiled roof found throughout Rwanda. A Tutsi lived in the house, which he rented from a Hutu widow. Neither had any idea of the gruesome secret said to be concealed under the concrete floor. The owner was not amenable to having her floor dug up. *Gacaca* would have to arrange for the excavation and that would take time.

* * *

In the meantime, Mukamira was abuzz with talk about Xavier's return and the villagers were beset by a mixture of fear and apprehension over what he might find next. He was clearly a man on a mission. He got another call, this time from a distant relative who lived in the village. He told Xavier that a villager he knew had come to see him. He claimed to know what had happened to Beatrice's body after the soldiers shot her.

'But this guy is very scared of you, Xavier,' the relative said. 'He's not willing to meet with you and he doesn't want you to know who he is. He's scared that you will say that he killed her and that you will take him to *gacaca*. But he says he will guide you to her bones.'

Xavier thought for a moment and said: 'Tell this guy that soldiers killed Mama. I therefore know it's not him. I am only interested in finding her bones. I will protect him and I promise not to involve *gacaca*.'

The relative phoned Xavier again a few days later and told him to be in Mukamira on Monday morning. Xavier had to go to a certain place in the village where he would see a broken-off eucalyptus branch. From there, a trail of branches would lead him to Beatrice's grave.

When Xavier arrived in the village on Monday morning, there was indeed a eucalyptus branch lying at the agreed place. There was another a few metres away. The branches led all the way through banana plantations and up the slopes towards Karisimbi. It ended at the *adache* that hours later revealed his mama's bones.

* * *

It took *gacaca* until April 2010 to get permission to dig up the floor. Accompanying them once more, Jean-Paul walked through the house and stopped in the bedroom. 'This is where the bones are,' he said. 'You must dig just here.'

They broke open the floor and started digging. Within half an hour, they had exhumed the first bone. An hour later, the remains of Edward Mushatsi lay in a heap at Xavier's feet.

'I washed the bones and I washed the clothes,' says Xavier. 'That was the last respect I could give him. You cannot imagine how I felt. Extraordinary! Finding Papa's bones has been the most important thing I have ever done. It was a triumph over the devil. I suffered for a long time, but in the end I'm the winner.'

The remains of both Edward and Beatrice were kept at the offices of the district authority. On 9 May 2010, the Rwandan government inaugurated a new genocide memorial and burial site in Mukamira to honour those who had perished in the genocide. More than 20 000 people attended the mass burial of 6 000 victims, among them Edward and Beatrice.

'We prayed the whole night around the bones,' recalls Xavier. 'When I buried my father and mother, I said goodbye and I saluted them. And then I sat down and I cried. For the first time, I cried for my father and my mother. When I found the bones, I tried to control my emotions because there were still processes I had to follow. But once I had buried them, I couldn't control myself. And now I am crying for the second time here with you.'

* * *

Xavier married Josephine and stayed with her for a few months before returning to South Africa in October 2010. Back in South Africa, he discovered that his business partners had either moved on or were now buying directly from the Chinese. He survived on piecemeal jobs and handouts, and the man I met in Brakpan in July 2011 was in dire financial straits. When he left Rwanda, Josephine was pregnant and a few months later gave birth to a baby girl. He named her Ilan, which means 'tree'. She symbolises the new branch growing out of his family tree that was stripped bare by the hatred and madness that engulfed Rwanda in the nineties.

I've pleaded with Xavier to get onto an aeroplane and go back to his family in Rwanda. I have offered to help him with his airfare. Why suffer alone in South Africa when you can be with your wife and child – whom you've never seen – in Rwanda? He can't be worse off there than here. He, however, maintains that he can't return empty-handed and has to take 'something' back.

Despite the hardships, Xavier has enrolled for a degree in education at UNISA and has already completed twelve modules. He says he has been greatly inspired by Kennedy, although he hasn't seen or spoken to his buddy for some time.

'I'm not sure that it's safe for me to go near Kennedy. It might be too dangerous. Do you know that he is involved in politics? He's still going to cause big problems for himself. He has to be careful.'

46

The groom and the general

Kennedy promised Goreth a traditional Tutsi wedding with all the pomp and circumstance she deserved. It would start in the early hours with herdsmen and hunters in traditional attire ushering the groom into the hall and end late at night with the couple sealing their union with a glass of fresh Ankole milk. Kennedy, Goreth and their respective best men and bridesmaids would need three outfits each for the different stages of the wedding. Three different venues had to be organised and guests would indulge in traditional fare at both lunch and dinner. Needless to say, beer flows at such events and that too would have to be in ample supply. The wedding date was set for Christmas day, 2010.

In the meantime, Kennedy had become a full-time attorney and head of debt-collecting at the law firm where he had done his articles. He got a sizeable increase, but it was still negligible when compared to what other attorneys were earning. He believes he was paid less because he was black and a foreigner. He decided to leave whenever another opportunity arose.

That happened at the end of 2008, when a company advertised a bursary for a master's degree in international law. Kennedy applied alongside tens of LLB graduates. He was interviewed by, among others, the president of the Law Society, two professors and the president of the Black Lawyers' Association. His application was successful and he was eager to start studying right away. Some of his lectures overlapped with his office hours, and his firm wouldn't allow him to take the time off. So he promptly resigned – just as Goreth arrived in South Africa to live with Jennifer and to get to know her groom better. Although she had passed matric in Rwanda, she had to repeat Grades 11 and 12 in South Africa. Having been educated in French, she spoke little English.

'This bursary was covering study fees and study material, but how was I going to live?' says Kennedy. 'I was going to survive like before. I said to Goreth that I'd do little jobs and she would eat what I ate. She said she'd support me in whatever I did.'

Kennedy entered into negotiations with Goreth's father for *ikwano* for her hand. He told Kennedy that he wasn't selling his daughter and that he realised the groom was still qualifying himself in order to look after her. They settled on two cows, or in monetary terms, a thousand dollars.

'I came off very lightly, but it was still a lot of money. Where was I ever going to get that? I also had to pay for the whole wedding and I had to fly us back to Rwanda to get married.'

'Where did you get the money to pay for Goreth's hand?' I ask.

'I have to admit I haven't paid yet. It bothers me a lot.'

The preparations for the wedding lasted throughout 2010. Kennedy wanted to afford Goreth the best day of her life, and to prove to her family and the community that despite his meagre upbringing, he was a man on the move.

'I used all my savings to live while studying,' Kennedy explains. 'I borrowed from everyone. I borrowed from my sister-in-law's husband. Nobody knows. There's one old man here, he's in Limpopo, who was my client. He lent me thousands. I sent whatever money I had to Goreth's sister to start preparing. When I got there, everything was organised, even our clothes. It stretched me to the limit. I'm still paying it off.'

* * *

I'm once again in Kennedy's flat. He pushes another DVD into the player. Goreth is sitting next to him, as always plying us with milky tea. Lisa is balanced like a puppy on her lap; her socked feet and pudgy hands fluttering in the air. Her sparkly eyes are fixated on Kennedy, begging to go to Daddy. He pushes 'play', puts down the remote and lifts the tot onto his lap. She shrieks with delight.

An image of Kennedy wrapped in cream-coloured cloth and clutching a herder's cane flickers to life. Goreth had invited around 120 family members and friends and Kennedy about thirty, mostly friends but among them his half-sister, Nyinawumuntu, and an aunt of his deceased mother.

The proceedings kick off in the early morning with a discussion between the groom and his in-laws about *ikwano* and *gukwa* – lobola and its payment. A troop of Ankole herders form a guard of honour as Kennedy and his best men stride into a hall packed with the guests, many dressed in traditional clothes for the morning's event.

This part of the ceremony is more prearranged satire and teasing than anything else, but nonetheless it lasts for hours. Goreth's family want to know why the groom isn't paying at least ten cows for his esteemed, well-mannered and amply fed bride. Kennedy counters that if he pays that many cows, she will have nothing to eat and there won't be milk on the table.

Kennedy fast-forwards. Two of Goreth's cousins leave the hall to inspect the two cows that Kennedy has presumably brought with him. They come back, nod their heads and report that *gukwa* has been executed. Two cows grazing happily on pastureland roll into the picture.

'Stop the video!' I order Kennedy. 'You haven't even paid! What are those two cows?'

'Nobody was supposed to know,' he admits. 'So they just put any two cows into the video.'

The negotiations last most of the morning and Kennedy finally lays his eyes on Goreth for the first time around noon, when she emerges with her bridesmaids. Her traditional dress resembles the hide of a white Ankole cow with small black spots. The couple join hands, smile coyly at each other and exchange gifts. A cow is slaughtered for the occasion and the guests sit down for a feast of meat, *matoke* and rice.

'It never ended,' laments Kennedy. 'After lunch I got into a suit and Goreth a white wedding dress and we went to the parish to get married. Afterwards, we dressed again and went to a hotel where guests continued eating and drinking and partying until late into the night. The two families were now one family. I had to give my father-in-law a crate of beer so that he wouldn't be thirsty on his way home. We closed the ceremony with *gutwikurura*, the uncovering of the bride. I sat down, she sat down and we drank milk. My bill was running up all the time. I'm still paying it off.'

* * *

Goreth was blissfully unaware that when she and Kennedy walked down the aisle, her groom was secretly complicit in an underground rebel movement intent on overthrowing Kagame. If any detail of his political shenanigans had leaked before or during the wedding, he would have been incarcerated in a dungeon somewhere in Rwanda – if that lucky.

Opposing Kagame is fraught with danger. His road to supremacy in the Great Lakes is littered with the skulls of his adversaries, and yet the

West continues to bestow honours and accolades on his autocracy. They will support anyone who is capable of keeping ethnicity at bay and will do anything to prevent another calamity from spilling into their living rooms, even if it means turning a blind eye to a little killing here or a tiny massacre there.

It all started in February 2010, when four of Kagame's closest allies – the former chief of staff and ambassador to Washington, Dr Theogene Rudasingwa; the former Rwandan prosecutor-general, Gerald Gahima; the former director of Rwanda's external intelligence service, Colonel Patrick Karegeya; and the former army chief of staff and ambassador to India, General Kayumba Nyamwasa – fled Rwanda after a falling-out with Kagame.

Gahima and Rudasingwa found refuge in the United States while Nyamwasa and Karegeya made it to Pretoria, where they were granted refugee status.

As they are Kagame confidants, disciples and strongmen, one would expect the latter duo's hands to be as bloodied as those of the dictator. Nyamwasa arrived in South Africa with a Spanish indictment for murder and genocide against him. Under Spain's broad human rights laws, a judge charged Nyamwasa and thirty-nine other Rwandan military officers with exterminating Hutus in the Congo and murdering nine Spanish citizens. Karegeya stands accused of masterminding the assassinations of Kagame opponents across the continent, among them Seth Sendashonga in Kenya in 1998.

Nyamwasa's absconding from Rwanda reads like a spy novel. He was attending a summit of ambassadors in Rwanda and was scheduled to have a meeting with Kagame the following morning. He was interrogated the night before by senior RPF officials about his alleged dissent and personal ambitions. He agreed to apologise to Kagame but, fearing for his life, made for the Ugandan border early the next morning, crossing it by using *panya* roads. Kagame was furious. How could the traitor have slipped his feared and revered spy network?

* * *

The arrival of Nyamwasa flushed out former intelligence soldier Emile Rutagengwa from the holes where he had been skulking for a decade. He says he hadn't done much in ten years, except for making a baby ('the mum is a Kagame sister and therefore a devil') and ducking and diving Rwandan intelligence agents he claims have tried to kidnap and assassinate him. It is impossible to verify any of what he says.

Emile was the first person Nyamwasa called when he arrived in South Africa. The relationship between the two goes back almost two decades, to when Emile joined the RPA. Emile won't say a word about Nyamwasa's or Karegeya's complicity in atrocities, although he lets slip at one point: 'The head of intelligence [which was Nyamwasa in the early nineties and again in the 2000s] has been killing for a long, long time.'

'What's the relationship between the two of you?'

'The general is a good commander. He's friendly and everybody likes him,' Emile tells me. 'Even the colonel is a friendly guy. They both love people. They respect human beings. They live *ubuntu*.'

'But the general and the colonel must be responsible for human rights abuses?'

'The general is innocent. He was abused by Kagame. He didn't always know what was going on.'

* * *

Kagame is known to be vengeful, vindictive and unforgiving. Kigali branded Nyamwasa and the other three the 'Gang of Four' and Kagame reportedly said he'd 'crush' them.

Kagame accused Karegeya and Nyamwasa of masterminding a series of hand-grenade attacks in Kigali and requested their extradition. When South Africa refused, he dispatched assassins to silence Nyamwasa in case his former crony had any intention of blabbing the regime's bloodiest secrets.

Three months after arriving in South Africa, Nyamwasa was shot in the stomach outside his home in Johannesburg's northern suburbs. In the days to follow, South African intelligence and police arrested ten suspects, including Rwandan agents. They also uncovered a second plot by Rwandan intelligence to strangle Nyamwasa while he was recuperating in hospital. Once behind bars, the assassins offered a police officer a million dollars to make the case disappear. They have been charged with attempted murder and conspiracy to commit murder.

In the months to come, South African intelligence thwarted several more attempts to kill Nyamwasa, who by then was in witness protection and a key witness against the accused.

Predictably, Rwanda professed it was preposterous to suggest that the regime would kill opponents in foreign countries. Yet, at the same time, British police warned Rwandan exiles in that country that the Rwandan government was hunting them down. In Sweden, a Rwandan diplomat was expelled because he engaged in 'refugee espionage'. A Rwandan journalist and frequent critic of Kagame was shot and killed in Uganda.

South Africa recalled its ambassador to Kigali, which in diplomatic terms is a country's strongest protest at the actions of another. The South African foreign intelligence chief, Moe Shaik, was dispatched to Kigali to dissuade his Rwandan counterparts from sending their killer squads to his country.

In a farcical display of justice, the Gang of Four was charged with forming a terrorist group, threatening state security, undermining public order, promoting ethnic division and insulting the president. A military court tried them in absentia and sentenced them to between twenty and twenty-five years imprisonment.

The court found, for example, that the gang were stirring up hatred because they warned in a discussion document that 'the Tutsi minority cannot hope to impose their will on the Hutu majority forever'. They insulted the president by asserting that there is 'more to Rwanda and Paul Kagame than new buildings, clean streets, and efficient government ... Rwanda is essentially a hard-line, one-party, secretive police state with a facade of democracy.'

* * *

In September 2010, Emile introduced Kennedy to Nyamwasa's brother-in-law, Frank Ntwali. He is also in exile in South Africa and, like Kennedy, is a law graduate. He told Kennedy that the Gang of Four was setting up a political movement and that they wanted him to join their ranks.

'Frank said I could play a big role as a lawyer and legal adviser,' says Kennedy. 'What really annoyed me was when Kagame tried to kill the general. That convinced me.'

'Don't you think you have been through enough to get involved in this?' I ask him.

'I went to see my priest and we started talking. I told him the whole story. He said, "You are a brave man but I want to give you advice: don't be caught in the middle of politics. Look after your family and good things will follow."'

'But you are involved so you didn't listen to him.'

'I cannot be quiet. When I see what the government is doing, I cannot sit still.'

* * *

The Rwandan National Congress (RNC) was born out of the Gang of Four – it became the Gang of Five after Rwandan extraordinaire Paul Rusesabagina joined the movement – and Kennedy was appointed as its African secretary-general. It took me months to unravel the full extent of Kennedy's involvement.

Jennifer, who was at the time living with Kennedy and Goreth, says she was aware from the beginning of his political conniving.

'I knew he was working underground,' she says. 'He came home very excited and told us things. I was worried and asked him not to bring problems into our family. Most work in government and they lead nice lives. I had no problem with the Rwanda government. At that point, I still thought Kagame was a hero. How could a Tutsi do a thing like that? He was a traitor.'

* * *

Almost all the guests at Kennedy and Goreth's Christmas wedding were Tutsis and avid supporters of the Kigali regime. Little did they know that the tall and elegant groom on the arm of their daughter, sister and friend was secretly conniving Kagame's demise, whom many regarded as a war hero and the saviour of their tribe.

In the days to come, Kennedy's revolt would not only have devastating consequences for his new in-laws, but he would not be able to return to his fatherland again for as long as Kagame remains in power. The groom would soon be branded an enemy of the state.

47

The birth of a revolution

In May 2011, Kennedy became a father. I sit down with him for lunch a day or two later. He babbles incessantly. 'I was nervous and counting the days. There were complications and Goreth complained of pain and had fever. Fortunately Jennifer is a qualified nurse. We rushed her to hospital where they put lots of tubes in her. They waited for three days for her blood pressure to come down and preformed a Caesarean. We took our rosary and prayed and then a nurse came to tell us the baby is fine. Lisa is my own blood. I have brought another human being into this world. I feel blessed. That girl is a gift from God.'

'What do you want for her?' I ask him.

'She must know a world which is different from the one I knew,' he says. 'She must see every human being as a gift from God. I want her to have a proper childhood, which I never had.'

A few days after Lisa's birth, Kennedy's mother-in-law jetted in from Rwanda with a bag of herbs for the newborn – which customs confiscated at the airport – and to help Goreth cope with the child.

When I see Kennedy again, he says there is tension in the Gihana household. His opposition to Kagame is no longer a secret and his mother-in-law refuses to speak to him. 'She turns away from me when I speak. She doesn't like politics. She's scared that when she goes back, they'll ask her at the airport about me and what I've been doing. I told her to tell them everything she knows, because she knows nothing.'

Kennedy's father-in-law also ignores him. His farm borders a town in eastern Rwanda, and one day the local *bourgmestre* arrived with policemen to inform him that 90 per cent of his farm had been appropriated for urban development. He protested, was arrested and thrown into prison where he contracted pneumonia. He is convinced that the debacle is linked to Kennedy's dissenting activities.

Jennifer rushed back to Rwanda to get her father out of prison. 'When I got there, he was released,' she says. 'He doesn't even want to mention Kennedy's name. He just said, "I'm praying for all of you." He's bitter and doesn't take Kennedy's phone calls.'

'And Goreth? What does she say?' I ask Kennedy.

'Of course she doesn't like it, but she has no choice,' he says. 'But I have no choice either. I am now an enemy of the state. I can't go back to Rwanda. They have sent people to South Africa to find out where I stay. They're looking for me, the general, the colonel, Frank and Emile. We are five boys in the movement that are active. And they know about us.'

'Aren't you scared?'

'Yes, of course. I have a family. It is sad what has happened to my country. We have achieved nothing. A million people died for nothing. We are back where we were before. There's no difference between Kagame and Habyarimana.'

* * *

Kennedy's life assumed a new dimension. He spent less time at his struggling law firm and instead poured his energy into the RNC. His weekends were taken up with endless strategy meetings when he wasn't sneaking off to places around the country and Mozambique to mobilise exiled Rwandans.

At the end of 2011, the RNC published its vision, values and a ten-point programme. It promises – much like the RPF two decades ago – a united, democratic and prosperous nation where every citizen is guaranteed human rights, democracy and the rule of law. When Kennedy proudly flaunted these principles, I remarked that they looked beautiful on paper but were only as good as the leaders who had to implement and respect them.

The founding of the RNC caused near hysteria in Kigali. The government mouthpiece *The New Times* warned the Gang of Four: 'You can run. You can hide. But you won't escape. Osama bin Laden learnt the lesson of this simple truth. In Rwanda we have our own criminals and terrorists sheltering in foreign countries. What has happened to Osama bin Laden should serve as notice to them that they cannot hide forever.'

* * *

Kennedy is on a knife's edge when he calls me and says: 'We got one.'

'Got what?'

'One of them. Come and see me.'

It turns out Kennedy and his RNC cronies have trapped a Rwandan government spy and a hired assassin. Nyamwasa and Karegeya, who have retained excellent contacts in Rwandan intelligence in Kigali, were warned by sympathisers that Kagame had sent yet another agent to infiltrate the organisation and set them up for elimination.

Shortly afterwards, Kennedy was contacted by an old Rwandan ac-quaintance by the name of Gustav Tuyishime who wanted to see him again. Kennedy immediately suspected him of being the plant. He took Gustav for a boozing session, during which the man said he wanted to join the RNC and asked far too many questions. Kennedy contacted Frank and Emile, who pounced and wrought a confession out of Gustav. He admit-ted that he had been hired by Rwandan intelligence to infiltrate the RNC and shoot whoever he got in his sights. They handed Gustav to the South African police's crime intelligence unit that was investigating attempts to kill Nyamwasa. Gustav provided them with a detailed statement. They released him in return for his full cooperation.

I track Gustav down to a bar frequented by Rwandans in Sunnyside, Pretoria. A small, fidgety man with eyes concealed under a beanie, he nervously clicks the joints of his fingers. He orders brandy and lemonade, guzzles it down and sends for another.

'Can you help me?' Gustav asks. 'They want to kill me.'

'Who?'

'All of them.'

'How do you mean?'

'The people from Kigali and Nyamwasa's people.'

Gustav says he was recruited by a Rwandan intelligence officer who came to South Africa and gave him $16 000 (R108 000). He was to buy an unlicensed pistol and hire gunmen to shoot them.

Shortly afterwards, Gustav's handler sent him an email containing Nyamwasa's photograph and the address of the safe house in a small town in North West province where he was being housed. The Rwandans had hired a private detective to follow the general from the courthouse where he was a witness to his safe house.

Gustav is nothing but a street boy and a hustler. Instead of annihilating Kagame's foe, he splashed out on a car and clothes, and got himself a new girlfriend who spent the last of his stash. As a result, Rwandan intelligence was looking for him. His Kigali handler had sent him an SMS demanding to know what was going on and ordering him to Nairobi for a meeting.

Gustav wants to be relocated to another country and bankrolled for the mess he has got himself into. I arrange for him to be interviewed by the UNHCR, but he doesn't pitch up for his meeting. A few days later, I receive an email from Gustav, who says he is at the Rwandan embassy, that they are protecting him and that everything he told me was lies.

* * *

When we sit down at our usual meeting place in Arcadia near the American embassy, Kennedy says he's buying a gun. 'Every Rwandan in this town knows where I live. But I won't die like a fly and I know how to shoot.'

Emile also wants a gun, but can't acquire one legally because he needs to be at least a permanent resident to get a licence. He doesn't sleep at night and has no doubt that he's been added to Rwandan intelligence's hit list and that his life is in imminent danger.

With the general and colonel in witness protection, Kennedy is convinced that Frank, Emile and he are next. 'We need to expose these criminalities of Kagame,' he says. 'If I can shoot him now, I will. God is my witness that I will kill him. I hate that man. I must get him before he gets me.'

* * *

In February 2012, Jennifer, who has a master's degree in nursing in cancer care, was asked to return to Rwanda to head up a cancer unit in the main state hospital. She excitedly agreed and the director of health bought her an air ticket back to Kigali.

It turned out to be nothing but a ploy to get her back to the country. When she walked into the director's office, he locked the door.

'You're in serious trouble,' he remarked and demanded to know who her brother-in-law was.

'Gihana Kennedy,' she answered.

'So why didn't you tell me he's in opposition to the Rwandan government?'

She lied, saying she didn't know anything about him.

'He is plotting against our president,' her boss said.

'I know nothing about that,' she responded.

'Well, the head of intelligence wants to see you. They're waiting downstairs in a car. I'm afraid I can't help you any further.'

Jennifer burst into tears and said, 'I'm not going there without you. They will take those electrical cables and burn me. I can even disappear.'

Nevertheless, she was taken to intelligence headquarters and interrogated for several hours. She persisted with her story that she knew nothing.

'You're lying, and you're putting the lives of your family at risk,' they countered. 'How do you feel about the government?' her interrogators wanted to know.

'I love my country, my president and this government,' she said.

'Will you then work for us? We will reward you handsomely and your family will be safe.'

'Give me a day or two to think about it,' Jennifer requested. She was allowed to go.

A few days later, Jennifer was picked up and taken to the ministry of defence. She agreed to work with Rwandan intelligence and infiltrate the RNC. Her handler gave her a new cellphone and made her memorise his telephone number.

A few hours after arriving back in South Africa, she sat down with Kennedy and told him that she had been sent back to infiltrate the RNC and set him up for possible assassination.

Kennedy and his mates are convinced that Kagame won't rest until he's had a shot at them, and won't hesitate in coercing family members and friends. In an interview with *Time* magazine in September 2012, Kagame referred to Nyamwasa's shooting in Johannesburg and said: 'This one in South Africa, Kayumba, is saying in the press [he] was trying to make a coup happen. If you have somebody out there saying "I wanted to carry out a coup", and later on he is shot, maybe he deserves it.'

* * *

'They want to kill Kennedy,' Jennifer tells me when we meet a few weeks later. 'And they wanted me to set him up. I wanted no part of it. They cannot abuse me and use me as a robot.'

'But you realise you cannot go back again?' I ask her.

'I'm in exile now. They call me every day and want to know what's happening. I say I'm talking to Kennedy and they must wait.'

'How do you feel towards Kennedy?' I am compelled to ask her.

She looks at him, smiles and says: 'He's right in what he's doing. I support him. He's very brave. It has affected my family very badly. My father is under lots of stress. They can even kill him. But things cannot go on like this. We have to bring it to an end. I'm now with Kennedy.'

48

The darling dictator

Kayumba Nyamwasa is the embodiment of an officer and a gentleman. In July 2012, he briefly emerges from his witness-protection hideout and, with three bodyguards in tow, sits down in a mini-boardroom of a Johannesburg hotel for an interview – his first since his attempted assassination more than two years ago. It is easy to understand why Kagame is manic about Nyamwasa and why he regards his erstwhile confidant as such a menace. Upright, elegant and with probing dark eyes, Nyamwasa gives the sense that he shoots straight and from the heart.

He is smartly dressed in a pinstriped grey suit. I observe that he looks like the ambassador he once was before fleeing into exile.

'This is all I have left,' he responds. 'I have lost everything.'

The state seized his two mansions and two farms, froze his pension and imprisoned his brother, a colonel in the army. Later on, they cancelled his passport and those of his whole family. Kennedy's Rwandan passport and those of the top leadership of the RNC were also all declared null and void on the same day.

Nyamwasa's relationship with Kagame dates back to Yoweri Museveni's liberation war against Milton Obote in the mid-eighties, when together they served as officers in his NRA. They were both founding members of the RPF/RPA and Nyamwasa exchanged his NRA uniform for rebel attire the night before the rebel invasion of Rwanda in October 1990. When Kagame rushed back from the United States days later to replace the fatally wounded Fred Rwigyema and assume the rebel leadership, Nyamwasa was at his side as his head of intelligence.

If there's one person who knows whether Kagame shot down the presidential plane on the night of 6 April 1994 and triggered the genocide, it is Nyamwasa.

'Did he?' I ask him.

'Yes,' he says.

'What happened?'

'Let me say that I was in a position to know, but that I did not participate.'

'So you didn't participate?'

'That's what I'm saying.'

'It seems very unlikely that Kagame shot down the plane and his intelligence chief didn't participate?' I probe further.

Nyamwasa refuses to elaborate, saying he will tell the full story when the time is right.

'And when will the time be right?' I want to know.

'When the RNC has created a platform where we will all tell what we know and what we've done.'

'And when will that be?'

'Only time will tell.'

After the RPF came to power, Nyamwasa served as commander of the paramilitary police, army chief of staff and head of the intelligence services before he was dispatched as ambassador to India in 2005. As such, he shared fifteen blood-spattered years on the frontline with Kagame, although he says that they had their first falling-out in 1998 and that he was afterwards sidelined.

'That was when I should have got out,' he says. 'I stayed too long.'

If Nyamwasa is to be believed, Kagame is behind not just the assassination of the Rwandan and Burundian presidents in 1994, but also of the Congolese head of state, Laurent-Désiré Kabila, in January 2001. During the first invasion of the Congo, Rwanda and Uganda abetted Kabila, the porky and grubby-handed rebel leader, to overthrow Mobutu Sese Seko.

Kabila was a lamentable choice, a kleptocrat like his predecessor. He reneged on agreements with Kagame, who, according to Nyamwasa, hoped to effectively control large parts of that country economically and commercially.

'At a meeting of military chiefs, Kagame said we must get rid of Kabila. I said it was madness and would be too expensive in terms of human life. He postponed the meeting there and then,' Nyamwasa tells me. 'He then ordered Kabila's killing behind my back.'

Kabila was assassinated by one of his own bodyguards in January 2001. The assassin was in turn killed as he attempted to flee the scene.

Nyamwasa refuses to accept any responsibility for Rwanda's mischief in the Congo. 'I never declared war on that country,' he says. 'I was always against our prolonged stay in the Congo. I told Kagame that we should get out, but he was greedy; he wanted everything for himself. He went ahead and ordered troops into the country.'

'You have to take responsibility,' I tell him. 'You were the chief of staff. The troops in the Congo were ultimately under your command.'

'I was forced to implement Kagame's decisions,' he says with a steely look in his eyes. 'That war and the others are regrettable. It is unfortunate that so many people died. But it is not of my making.'

How convenient it is, I think as the general tucks into his 300-gram prime rump, to sit thousands of kilometres from your killing field and blame the bloodletting on your erstwhile boss. I should have reminded him of what he said in a January 1998 interview with the BBC (I only discovered the article afterwards). When asked about Hutu infiltrators on the other side of the border, he is quoted as saying: 'We have the means. We have the will. We will kill until they lose their appetite for war.'

I ask Nyamwasa to describe Kagame. He thinks for a while before he sneers: 'Vicious, spiteful, erratic, insensitive, greedy and murderous.'

* * *

With the possible exception of Zimbabwe's Robert Mugabe, few African leaders stir as much emotion, debate and controversy as Paul Kagame. On a continent pillaged by kleptocrats, he is revered and reviled, adored and abhorred. He has brought security and progress to his nation, yet has stoked immense suffering and death in the Great Lakes. Whether you like or dislike the gangly man with the steel-rimmed spectacles and narrow moustache, you have to admire what he's built, yet be revolted by what he's sown. Many Rwandans credit him with the rebirth of their nation; others warn that he's building resentment and bottling hostility.

It is difficult not to be impressed by his achievements. Kigali is an oasis of orderliness and cleanliness. Plastic has been banned, palm trees line manicured boulevards and yellow cranes raise glam and glassy office towers. The hills teem with the new mansions of an emerging elite that is clearly benefiting from increasing foreign investment, aid money and government contracts.

Outside the capital, the endangered gorillas are well and even flourishing. The economic growth rate has averaged 8 per cent in the past few years and, if Rwanda's official figures are to be believed, a million Rwandans have been lifted out of poverty and per capita GDP has more than doubled.

While Kagame's economic achievements continue to shine, his human rights record is getting grubbier. A dictator's true colours are best observed when he attempts to illustrate his commitment to democracy by engaging in an election. Go back in history: it's always a farce and the tyrant never bags less than 90 per cent of the vote. Rwanda's constitution has forced Kagame into two presidential elections – in 2003 and 2010.

Kagame is the embodiment of a Tutsi and governs through a clique of Tutsi army officers and Tutsi officials in a country where six out of seven Rwandans are Hutu. How did he manage to persuade the Hutu populace to cast their ballots for him? He did what other autocrats do: he outlawed the main opposition parties and either incarcerated their leaders or drove them into exile. Then his security chiefs and top RPF officials met to discuss how many votes he should get.

In 2003, as then head of Kagame's intelligence services, Nyamwasa attended that meeting, three weeks before the election. 'Some felt he should get 100 per cent. I said it was madness because there is no way that so many Hutus would vote for a Tutsi. I suggested 65 per cent. Kagame was very upset when he heard about it. In the end, we settled for 95 per cent.'

Several opposition parties were barred from registering for the 2010 election, their leaders harassed and arrested. On the day of official registration, the deputy editor of a newspaper critical of the government was gunned down in Kigali. The decapitated body of the vice-president of the Democratic Green Party of Rwanda turned up on a riverbank near the southern city of Butare. In the end, only three opposition parties registered.

One of Kagame's election opponents, Victoire Ingabire Umuhoza, still languishes in prison. She returned to Rwanda after sixteen years in exile to contest the elections. In her first speeches, she asked for an investigation into Tutsi reprisal killings during and after the genocide. She was chucked into prison and charged with genocide denial.

Incarcerated with her are two female reporters sentenced respectively to seventeen and seven years for, among other things, criticising Kagame. The prosecution argued that they had stirred up hatred and fury. In his verdict, the judge referred to an article in which they had said that Rwandans were unhappy with their president's rule. Reporters Without Borders has branded Kagame a 'predator of press freedom'.

Come election day 2010, Kagame predictably got 93 per cent of the vote.

He has always argued that opening up too much political space might unleash ethnic hatred and lead to another genocide. He banned the terms 'Hutu' and 'Tutsi', and no one is allowed to discuss the origins and causes of the genocide, unless it is the official version as dictated by his government. His supporters contend that these draconian measures are designed to save Rwanda from itself and prevent the biggest crime from happening again. In reality, they are nothing but a crude attempt to keep Hutus from organising politically.

In the meantime, Kagame continues to paint the combustible eastern Congo in blood. Over the past decade and a half, organisations such as the UN have lambasted him for stirring up trouble in his neighbourhood. A recent UN Security Council report details evidence that Rwanda has supplied weapons and recruits to a Tutsi rebel movement in the Congo headed by a wanted war criminal. HRW says that some of the recruits were children. This assistance led to a new round of bloodshed in the provinces of North and South Kivu, resulting in at least 50 000 refugees entering Uganda and another 420 000 fleeing elsewhere in the Congo.

Kagame heaps scorn on his critics, saying they have no moral right to criticise him. He says that 'whoever does not like the Rwandan way of democracy should go and hang'. He has called the UN's findings on the atrocities committed by his troops 'baseless', saying they have 'always been wrong' on Rwanda. According to him, reports by human rights organisations are 'nonsense'.

However, even the West couldn't ignore that recent UN report. The American and British governments suspended or delayed aid disbursements, in many ways the lifeblood of the dictatorship. Other Western governments followed suit. The United States Ambassador-at-Large for War Crimes Issues has said that Rwandan authorities, including Kagame, could be charged for 'aiding and abetting' war crimes.

Why has the international community turned a blind eye to Kagame's excesses for so long? Is it because he's persuaded them that only he can prevent another genocide? Or does the world continue to be wracked by guilt for its apathy during the last genocide, and is therefore more blind to the actions of the victims and survivors? Why do they find Hutu Power reprehensible, but Tutsi arrogance acceptable?

When elected governments ignore human rights abuses perpetrated by an autocrat they support, it is usually in the name of national security or economic interest. But in the case of Kagame, the overwhelming rationale is guilt. Behind the world's glib praise and flimsy chastisement lurks raw and bitter shame.

49

The sounds of war

'How do you see your future role in Rwanda?' I ask Kennedy.

'I think I can be minister either of justice or foreign affairs,' he says. 'I want to charge Kagame with the crimes he has committed. I want to prosecute him. I want to see him stand in front of me. I want to see him go down.'

'Are you prepared to go to war to get rid of him?'

Kennedy glances sideways and contemplates the question for some time before looking up. His glasses are balanced on his nose. He nods his head. 'Yes,' he says, 'but only as a very last option.'

It is a frightening thought: the RNC acquiring arms from a war merchant, recruiting exiled Rwandans into an army, setting up bases in the Kivus in eastern Congo and launching attacks across the Virungas into Rwanda. We have learnt from past experience how Kagame reacts to military threats across the border. He orders his fighting machine into the Congo's verdant forests and targets anything and anyone that vaguely resembles an adversary. 'Do you *want* to be in a war again?' I want to know from Kennedy.

'I won't be on the frontline because I will be a policy maker,' he confidently concludes. 'I will be behind the lines. War is a terrible thing and it is not our first priority. It is our last resort.'

I tell him it's easy to muse about revolt if you can dictate the bloodshed from your snug hideout in Pretoria and usher peasants into combat to do your dirty work.

'We will do everything in our power to resolve the mess in our country peacefully. We don't want war, but it's up to him. He has to negotiate with us.'

I tell Kennedy that he and his party live in cuckooland if they think Kagame will negotiate with them. In any case, why should he?

'We know he won't negotiate,' he says.

'You realise there will be bloodshed?'

'But for a good cause. The problem in Rwanda is one person: Kagame. We cannot allow him to dictate the lives of many. We have to get rid of him.'

* * *

Emile is more forthcoming about war emanating from the Congo's anar-
chical and ungovernable eastern provinces. For once, I think, he's shooting
his mouth off.

'That's Kagame's weak point,' he says. 'The Congo. It's easy to set up
bases and attack from there.'

'And when will this happen?'

'Only when there's no other option. If he doesn't want to talk and he
doesn't want to change, we will have no other option. But we want change
through peaceful means.'

'Kagame doesn't talk to anyone. It's not his style.'

'Then it's war,' counters Emile. 'We're in contact with many army officers
in Rwanda. They still love the general. They're ready to join us when the
time is ripe.'

The RNC's ultimate strategy is to use Nyamwasa's popularity and
contacts in the armed forces to stoke a military revolt and bring about a
bloodless coup in Kigali.

* * *

'Are you plotting an uprising in Rwanda?' I ask Nyamwasa.

'We are hoping for an uprising,' he says. 'If there is one, Kagame will
be gone within three months. He's a coward; he'll run. During most of
the civil war he was in hiding. Don't be surprised if the Rwandan people
extract him from a pipe like the Libyans did with Muammar Gaddafi.'

* * *

After my interview with Nyamwasa, I wrote an article saying that he admits that he's plotting the overthrow of Kagame, albeit through peaceful
means. The story caused near hysteria in Kigali, and shortly afterwards, the
director-general of the Department of International Relations summoned
Nyamwasa to the Union Buildings in Pretoria. The director-general told
him in no uncertain terms that South Africa will not allow him to plot the
overthrow of a legitimate government from its soil. He ordered Nyamwasa
to refrain from any political activity.

'How could you have written that?' Kennedy wants to know a day or
two later. 'Now we are under attack again!'

* * *

The RNC has achieved an awful lot in a short space of time. It has set up branches across the world, recruited Rwandans in the diaspora established a radio station, protested against Kagame wherever he travels and recruited esteemed activists like Rusesabagina.

There are certain of the RNC's principles I admire, among them that everyone has to confess what he or she did. At the end of the day, the RNC says it will declare a general amnesty so that the nation can start on a clean slate.

'The general and the colonel have a lot to confess,' I tell Kennedy. 'Their hands are not clean.'

'Same as me,' he replies.

'There's a difference between a soldier and a general.'

'But he was also under another general. You execute the policy that the boss ordered. Whatever happened, it was never the general's own decision.'

'There seem to be very few clean people in Rwanda?'

'Everybody participated in one way or another. We are all guilty.'

* * *

Kennedy's premonition that the Rwandan regime had set their sights on him, Emile and RNC chairperson Frank Ntwali turned out to be prophetic. On a sunny winter's day in August 2012, Kennedy phones me. 'It's Frank!' he pants. 'He's been attacked.'

'What's happened?' I ask.

'I don't know yet, but he's in hospital,' he says. 'I'm on my way. I'll call you later.'

It turned out that earlier that afternoon, Frank and a friend were in his car driving back from Kempton Park to Pretoria when another sedan pulled up behind them, flashed its lights and the driver waved them off the road. Frank thought it was the police and told his friend, who was driving, to pull over. Three men came rushing to their car shouting: 'Police, police!'

By the time Frank had asked them for their identity cards, one of the men had got into the back of the car and pulled out a knife. He stabbed Frank nine times before the injured man managed to clamber out and stumble away. The assailants fled the scene, taking with them only Frank's car keys. They left behind two cell phones and two wallets. They were clearly not robbers. Frank was rushed to hospital where his condition was pronounced serious but stable.

The incident infuriated RNC supporters, and the next day Kennedy told me that they were threatening to take to the streets, march to the Rwandan embassy and burn it down. A few months earlier, Frank and Emile had a run-in with its *chargé d'affaires*, Didier Rutembesa, who allegedly told them at an embassy meeting that he would 'hunt them down and kill them'. Frank laid a charge of intimidation, but nothing came of it. Rutembesa in any case enjoys diplomatic immunity. The RNC have long suspected him of being instrumental in the campaign against them.

When I contact Rutembesa to discuss the attack on Frank, butter couldn't melt in his mouth. He says: 'Like we have been mentioning to you many times before, we have no interest in murdering people, moreover a young man who is trying to make a life and who doesn't represent any threat to us.' His alleged warning to Frank and Emile was nothing but 'concocted hearsay'.

'I'm trying to calm down the people,' Kennedy tells me. 'We've had enough. We want Didier to leave. If this doesn't stop, there's going to be blood on the streets of Pretoria.'

* * *

Aside from Nyamwasa, Kagame could not have saddled himself with a more formidable adversary than Kennedy Gihana. The unseating of Rwanda's president is consuming him, much the same as his decade-long obsession with obtaining an education. Nobody then gave him a chance of success, just as he's probably being dismissed in Kigali today as a former army deserter with an inflated ego. I've looked into his eyes when he's talked about Kagame and the RNC, and they are those of a revolutionary inflamed by a sense of purpose and resolve. He will stop at nothing until he's achieved his goal. Don't be surprised to see Kennedy in the not-too-distant future as a minister or some or other power-monger in Rwanda. The last chapters of his life are yet to be written and they'll be as compelling as the first.

* * *

Rwanda says the RNC has declared war on it. The formation of the organisation is reminiscent of the birth of the RPF in the latter half of the eighties. Once again, there's not enough space in pocket-sized Rwanda for the inflated head of Kagame and the political aspirations of his adversaries.

You don't have to be a visionary to know that the feud is probably going to be decided over the barrel of a gun. The path to power in Rwanda is traditionally littered with the skulls and bones of rivals, and I fear that this conflict is not going to be any different. Dialogue, decency and common sense have never been elements of the Rwandan political landscape. Much like the events of the early nineties, the feud between the RPF and the RNC has the potential to reignite the Great Lakes. The Hutu uprising of 1959 was bad and reprisals against Tutsis in 1973 were worse, but nothing in comparison with the mass killings of 1994. Heaven knows what awaits Rwandans – and Congolese – this year or the next, or the year after that.

Kennedy and I have debated for hours about the RNC and his role in the machinations of the new revolution. I've told him I don't trust politicians because I've seen far too many well-intentioned activists degenerate into corrupt fat cats the moment power is bestowed on them. Why would the RNC be any different?

I have no reason to doubt Kennedy's sincerity in joining the organisation and his genuine concern for people suffering under Kagame's repressive regime. Their revolt against Kigali is completely legitimate and should be applauded and supported. Taking up arms, however, is another matter. But then, how else do you rid nations of tyrants? The fall of illegitimate regimes in countries like Libya, Egypt and South Africa was brought about by the sacrifices of valiant men and women who stood up against the excesses of their rulers.

I hope that Kennedy doesn't let his sense of decency and humanity be blinded by a lust for power and revenge. Goddamnit Kennedy, you have suffered enough and your people have bled themselves dry. Tread carefully, and don't get more dirt on your hands.

* * *

Kennedy remains a struggling lawyer who battles to pay his bills. He specialises in immigration and civil law, and most of his clients are foreigners (Nyamwasa is his most high-profile client) who have encountered problems with Home Affairs. There's no shortage of clients, but they often can't pay and cases take months or even years to resolve. Clients phone him at all hours of the day and he dishes out his legal expertise irrespective of whether they can fork out or not.

'I have a client, a Rwandan woman, who has been a refugee since 1993!'

Kennedy says. 'She runs an orphanage with 103 HIV-positive children. This lady has to attend an international conference in Uganda. She can't go because as a refugee she needs a signature from the chairperson of the standing committee. There's no chairperson at the moment; she can't get it! I know someone who has been an asylum seeker for ten years and still hasn't heard about his refugee status.'

Kennedy has paid a heavy price for years of living unhealthily and under unusual stress. 'I have been diagnosed with a chronic ulcer and I drink lots of medicine,' he tells me. 'My doctor is called Max and he is from the Ivory Coast. I told him my background. He told me to get a psychologist. When the smallest thing happens, everything comes back. I've told my wife a little bit, but not everything. I have this thing that follows me and I cannot forget. I don't sleep well. I go to bed at eleven, I wake up at five. I want to buy things for my wife but I cannot. I want to buy a suit but I cannot. My biggest desire is to have my own house, and to see Rwandans live in peace. Will it ever happen?'

* * *

When Kennedy received his master's degree in international law, he was again presented at the graduation ceremony with an empty envelope. Although he had a bursary for his LLM and his class fees had been paid up, he still owed the university money for his LLB degree and would therefore not get any degree certificate until he had fully settled his account. He also faced the threat of legal action.

'I thought I would get my master's degree certificate,' he lamented the night after the ceremony when I took him for dinner. 'My clients don't believe me when I say I've qualified at that white university. Lawyers put their certificates against their walls but I've got nothing to show. It's as though I've never studied. I'm like a farmer who has sown seeds but has no harvest to show for it.'

Kennedy had asked me several times if I could think of any solution to his predicament. Don't I perhaps know of a sponsor or aid organisation that can help him settle his debt before the university embarks on legal action against him?

I told him to access his account. He phoned a few days later, out of breath and exasperated. With accumulated interest, his university debt had swollen to R80 257.91.

I spoke to a debt collector at the university, told her about the adverse conditions under which Kennedy had studied and requested that his debt be scrapped. She refused and said that legal action was imminent.

I wrote an email to Radio 702's John Robbie. I had met him a few times and had played 'gentleman's' cricket against him – he caught me out. I reminded him of his interview with Kennedy a few years earlier when he received his LLB degree. The man was now a master of law but with nothing to show for it. Was there any chance John could appeal to his listeners to contribute towards paying Kennedy's debt?

It was a long shot. The station receives hundreds of requests for financial assistance and there were probably worthier causes than Kennedy's. A few days later, John responded. 'Come onto my show,' he said, 'and let's see what happens.'

On a Friday morning just before eight, I hastily chronicled Kennedy's story on radio and appealed to listeners for help. Half an hour later, John's producer, Jonathan Fairbanks, phoned.

'Guess what?' he said.

'What?'

'We've got the money!'

'No way!'

'The calls are streaming in. We've got enough, everything we need. I'll send you the names and numbers of everyone who pledged.'

A businessman from East Rand pledged R20 000 on condition that Kennedy spoke to his delinquent sons. An Indian woman from Johannesburg gave the same amount but wanted to remain anonymous. A host of people pledged R1 000 or R2 000. The pharmaceutical company Dis-Chem promised to pay the balance.

Kennedy was at home when I phoned to tell him the good news. He went silent, but a few seconds later I could hear him babbling in Kinyarwanda to Goreth and Jennifer. The next moment they all squawked and shrieked at the same time. Kennedy said they were jumping up and down.

50

My brave friend

Throughout the writing of this book, Kennedy and I had a protracted debate about how I should portray his life. I was steadfast in my belief that I should depict him with undiluted candour and sincerity.

'I don't want all these things in a book, because people are going to read this and remember me as a killer,' he said.

'You are one,' I countered.

'But how are you going to write it so that people don't remember me only as a killer?'

'Exactly how and why it happened. I'm sure they'll understand.'

On another occasion, he remarked: 'You cannot write that, because it is a secret.'

'Why then did you tell me?'

'But why don't you write about my suffering?'

'I am.'

'Or about my achievements?'

'Of course I am.'

'We were all victims, from all sides. I wish it could have been different, but how? I had no option. I had to do it. I think about it every day. It's a terrible thing to live with.'

* * *

In June 2012, I gave the first two-thirds of the manuscript to Kennedy to read. It is a daunting task for any writer to afford your subject a glimpse into how you have construed his life. I've learnt from experience that people seldom like what you write about them.

Kennedy has told me very private and deeply hidden secrets that he probably never intended to be aired in public. They poured out over months of conversation and probing, and I knew he was going to regret having said some things when he saw them in print. I wasn't just a writer, but also a friend and confessor to whom he unbolted the darkest cavity of his heart.

Other authors have experienced similar difficulties. In *Little Liberia*, a chronicle that centres on the lives of a Liberian community in New York City, author Jonny Steinberg describes what happened when he gave the manuscript to his two main protagonists, Rufus and Jacob. When he met the latter a week later, the manuscript was covered in green, pink and yellow highlighter. Jacob had serious problems with the book. There were errors of fact, facts that were true but not intended for publication, and facts that the author had used inadmissibly. Jacob described Jonny as both a gentleman and a cunning bastard.

'Reading a book-length description of yourself for the first time is shocking,' says Jonny. 'You have sat and spoken into a voice recorder for months, years. As you talked, you censored here and embellished there; you felt increasingly comfortable and in control; you were in fact writing a persona into the pages of the book that was still to be written. When you finally open the manuscript, you discover that you never were the one with the pen. The writer has cheated. He has written a you that is not you; certainly not a you that you would care to present.'

I'm not always sure that Kennedy fully grasped what this book was. At the outset of the exercise, he would point at me and tell people, 'He is writing my book', as though I was merely his ghostwriter. He asked me if his name was also going to be on the cover. He was visibly disappointed when I explained that I had the ultimate say in what goes in and what not.

Kennedy and I had an agreement that he could see the manuscript before publication in order to check facts. He had no right to change or remove anything unless it was factually incorrect. I was not going to let our friendship and closeness come between us and a brutally honest depiction of his life. And yet, I knew I was dealing with a human being who had been ravaged by circumstances and events in his country and in his life and who deserved all the empathy and compassion I could afford him.

I didn't hear from Kennedy for two weeks after giving him the manuscript. When I eventually phoned him, he said he hadn't had time to read it. Another week on, I phoned again. He said he had gone through it and added: 'You have left nothing out, have you?'

We met for dinner and spoke for two hours about everything but the book. We were like a couple on the verge of a break-up but no one had the guts to tell the other. The red folder with the manuscript lazed like a coiled serpent between us.

'Kennedy,' I said finally, 'we have to talk about the book.'

He slid the folder across to me. I opened it and glanced through the manuscript. There were remarkably few changes. I paged to the shooting of the mother and child. There was a red question mark next to it. When I looked up, he had tears in his eyes.

'It is not easy to read those things and see what you have done.' He cleared his throat. 'In general the book is good. What I have a problem with is the killing of the mother and her child. Why do you have to put it in? People are going to see me as a genocider.'

'We have to put it in,' I countered. 'This is who you are. It is events like this that have shaped you into the human being you are.'

'I don't want to lie to you, but I'm scared,' he said. 'I don't want to find myself tomorrow in a court of law.'

Although the RPF soldiers committed war crimes, they were cannon fodder carrying out orders. The ICTR is not taking any new cases and has a mandate to only prosecute the planners and worst perpetrators of genocide. The International Criminal Court was set up in 1998 to deal with the most serious international crimes. Only sixteen cases have been brought before the court and it doesn't deal with ordinary foot soldiers who were just obeying orders.

'I'm very happy with the way you've explained why such actions happened,' he said. 'I appreciate that you said that had you been in the same position you might also have done it. That's why I have left it like that. But what are people going to think of me?'

I told Kennedy that everyone who had read the manuscript had expressed enormous empathy. Author Mike Nicol said: 'As I read I kept thinking of that old adage: there but for the grace of God ... Those readers with an ounce of compassion will understand what he did. The whole awful account is Shakespearian in its tragedy.'

* * *

The last time I saw Kennedy before submitting the final manuscript was when we met his university friend, Sabelo Khumalo, in a country hotel outside Mbabane.

We were sitting in the pub and Sabelo was telling me how Kennedy had lied to him and other friends about being a diplomat at the Rwandan embassy. He had never told anyone that he was a soldier or even that he had walked to South Africa.

Kennedy cleared his throat. 'It is true, Sabelo. I have not told you every-thing. The time was not right then. Now I have accepted who I am. There is now nothing to hide any longer.'

'Does that mean you are ready to let the world know who you are?' I asked Kennedy. 'Are you ready to tell everything?'

'Yes, I am,' he said. 'This is anyway part of our programme in the RNC. We have to confess.'

When I left the two a while later, their heads were huddled together and Kennedy was telling his friend about the genocide.

He was talking about bodies, some of his own making.

I then realised how far Kennedy has advanced since we embarked on this extraordinary journey. I felt incredibly proud of my brave friend.

References

BOOKS

Des Forges, Allison. *'Leave None to Tell the Story': Genocide in Rwanda.*
New York: Human Rights Watch, 1999

Gourevitch, Philip. *We Wish to Inform You that Tomorrow We Will Be Killed with Our Families: Stories from Rwanda.* New York: Picador, 1999

Hatzfield, Jean. *Machete Season: The Killers in Rwanda Speak.* New York: Picador, 2003

Kapuściński, Ryszard. *The Shadow of the Sun: My African Life.* London: Penguin Books, 2003

Kehrer, Brigitte. *Rwanda: Work of God, Work of Evil.* Destinée Media, 2004

Kinzer, Stephen. *A Thousand Hills: Rwanda's Rebirth and the Man Who Dreamed It.* Hoboken, NJ: John Wiley & Sons, 2008

Malvern, Linda. *A People Betrayed: The role of the West in Rwanda's Genocide.* London: Zed Books, 2000

Rice, Andrew. *The Teeth May Smile but the Heart Does Not Forget: Murder and Memory in Uganda.* New York: Henry Holt and Company, 2009

Rusagara, Frank K. *Resilience of a Nation: A History of the Military in Rwanda.* Kampala: Fountain Publishers, 2009

Rusesabagina, Paul. *An Ordinary Man: The True Story Behind Hotel Rwanda.* London: Bloomsbury, 2006

Ruzirabwoba, Pierre. *History and Conflicts in Rwanda.* Kigali: Institute of Research and Dialogue for Peace, 2006

Steinberg, Jonny. *Little Liberia: An African Odyssey in New York City.* London: Jonathan Cape, 2011

Waugh, Colin M. *Paul Kagame and Rwanda: Power, Genocide and the Rwandan Patriotic Front.* Jefferson, NC: McFarland, 2004

Zimbardo, Philip G. 'A situationist perspective on the psychology of evil: Understanding how good people are transformed into perpetrators'. In A. G. Miller (ed.), *The Social Psychology of Good and Evil.* New York: Guilford Press, 2004

ARTICLES

'A dying breed', *New York Times*, 27 January 2008

'Africa's last frontier', *National Geographic*, March 2010

'Aleksandr Solzhenitsyn: Spitting in the face of evil', www.scragged.com,
    6 August 2008

'Arming Rwanda: The arms trade and human rights abuses in the Rwandan
    war', Human Rights Watch, January 1994

'Beyond the rhetoric: Continuing human rights abuses in Rwanda', Amnesty
    International, June 1993

'British police warn Rwandan dissidents of threat', *New York Times*, 19 May 2011

'Congo examines mass graves to find proof of revenge genocide on Hutus',
    Guardian, 12 September 2010

Davenport, Christian, and Allan C. Stam. 'What really happened in Rwanda?'
    www.miller-mccune.com, 6 October 2009

'Delayed UN report links Rwanda to Congo genocide', *Guardian*,
    1 October 2010

'DR Congo: Rwanda should stop aiding war crime suspects', Human Rights
    Watch, 4 June 2012

'Eastern Congo ravaged: Killing civilians and silencing protest', Human Rights
    Watch, 16 May 2000

'General saga: Accused tried to bribe cops', *Independent Online*, 7 October 2010

'Gentle gorillas, turbulent times', *National Geographic*, October 1995

'Hannah Arendt's challenge to Adolf Hitler', *Guardian*, 29 August 2011

'Heartbreak on the Serengeti', *National Geographic*, February 2006

'ICTR: Address crimes committed by the RPF', Human Rights Watch,
    11 December 2008

'Identify the Congo killers and bring them to justice', Human Rights Watch,
    1 October 2010

'Idi Amin: Ruthless dictator whose rise to power was facilitated by the
    British colonial authorities, he went on to devastate Uganda', *Guardian*,
    18 August 2003

'If Tutsis died it was because the people were angry with them', *Guardian*,
    19 December 2008

'Ituri: Covered in blood: Ethnically targeted violence in north-eastern
    DR Congo', Human Rights Watch, July 2003

'Justice dept mulls Rwanda general's extradition', *Mail & Guardian*, 23 June 2010

'Kagame vs Kayumba', *Independent*, 13 June 2010

'Kagame's authoritarian turn risks Rwanda's future', *Guardian*, 27 January 2011

'Killing human decency', Amnesty International, 31 May 2000

'Leaked UN report accuses Rwanda of possible genocide in Congo', *Guardian*, 26 August 2010

'Legal battle begins to strip Rwandan general and suspected war criminal of refugee status', Southern Africa Litigation Centre, 14 June 2011

'Life before genocide', www.survivors-fund.org.uk, February 2007

'Nairobi, inventing a city', *National Geographic*, September 2005

'On Africa's largest lake, fishers suffer falling stocks, rising demand', *National Geographic*, March 2007

'Paul Kagame: A tarnished African hero', *Guardian*, 18 July 2010

'Paul Kagame: Rwanda's redeemer or ruthless dictator', *Telegraph*, 22 July 2010

'Predators of press freedom: Africa', Reporters Without Borders, 2010

'Return Nyamwasa, SA told', *Independent Online*, 23 September 2010

'Revealed: How even German civilians took part in killing concentration camp survivors', *Daily Mail*, 21 January 2011

'Rift in paradise', *National Geographic*, November 2011

'Rwanda in six scenes', *London Review of Books*, May 2011

'Rwanda president faces arrest', *Financial Times*, 22 November 2006

'Rwanda pursues dissenters and the homeless', *New York Times*, 30 April 2010

'Rwanda puts pressure on exiled dissidents', *Independent Online*, 21 January 2011

'Rwanda sorrow', *Time*, 17 April 2000

'Rwanda: A president in crisis', Human Rights Watch, 19 September 2010

'Rwanda: Exiled General Kayumba', www.allAfrica.com, 19 June 2010

'Rwanda: General's status as refugee called into question', *Business Day*, 28 June 2010

'Rwanda: Govt denies any role in attempt to kill Nyamwasa', www.allAfrica.com, 20 June 2010

'Rwanda: Hundreds of killings by Rwandese soldiers confirmed', Amnesty International, 20 October 1994

'Rwanda: Observing the rules of war?' Human Rights Watch, December 2001

'Rwanda: The dead can no longer be counted', Amnesty International, December 1997

'Rwanda's ghosts refuse to be buried', *BBC News*, 8 April 2009

'Rwanda's Paul Kagame: Visionary or tyrant?' *Washington Diplomat*, August 2010

'Rwanda's rebel reformer: Paul Kagame', *Time*, 9 August 2010

'Rwandan assassin "sent to kill dissidents in UK"', *Independent*, 20 May 2011

'Rwandan opposition leader found dead', *Guardian*, 14 July 2010

'Rwandans led revolt in Congo', *Washington Post*, 9 July 1997

'Rwandans say the victors kill many who go back', *New York Times*, 5 August 1994

'SA's "warning message" after general shot', *Independent Online*, 6 August 2010

'Spain seeks extradition of Rwandan general', *Radio Netherlands Worldwide*,
    24 September 2010

'Taking sides on genocide', *Guardian*, 15 September 2010

'The enduring legacy of the genocide', Amnesty International, August 2004

'The evil that men do', *American Scientist*, 2007

'The power of horror in Rwanda', Human Rights Watch, 11 April 2009

'The real meaning of evil', *Time*, 24 February 2003

'The Rwandan genocide: Why early warning failed', *Journal of African Conflicts
    and Peace Studies*, September 2009

'The Rwandan Patriotic Front's record and the history of UN cover-ups',
    San Francisco Bay View, 15 September 2010

'The volcano next door', *National Geographic*, April 2011

'Two sides to every story: Congo and the Rwandan genocide', *Crimes of War*,
    30 September 2010

'What Kagame has cost us', *Guardian*, 18 August 2010

'Who is Paul Kagame?' *African Dictator*, 26 April 2011

'Who murdered the Virunga gorillas?' *National Geographic*, July 2008

'Why do ordinary people commit evil deeds', *BBC News*, 18 April 2007

'Why not everyone is a torturer', *BBC News*, 10 May 2004

'Why? The killing fields of Rwanda', *Time*, 16 May 1994

'Will we ever learn the truth about this genocide', *Independent*, 22 November 2006

REPORTS

Amisi, Baruti, and Richard Ballard. 'In the absence of citizenship: Congolese
    refugee struggle and organisation in South Africa', www.refugeeresearch.net,
    April 2005

Bidandi, Fred, and Alice Wamundiya. 'Evaluating refugee access to institutions
    of higher learning in South Africa', University of the Western Cape

'Democratic Republic of Congo. Rwandese-controlled east: Devastating human
    toll', Amnesty International, 19 June 2001

Nyamwasa, Kayumba, and Patrick Karegeya. 'Rwanda briefing', August 2010

Rusesabagina, Paul. 'Compendium of RPF crimes: October 1990 to present.
    The case for overdue prosecution', November 2006

'Rwanda: Briefing to the UN Committee Against Torture', Amnesty International, May 2012

'Rwanda: Reports of killings and abductions by the Rwandese Patriotic Army', Amnesty International, April–August 1994, October 1994

'Rwanda: The Preventable Genocide', Organisation of African Unity, 2000

'The documented experience of refugees, deportees and asylum seekers in South Africa: A Zimbabwean case study', Civil Society Workers Working on the Refugee and Asylum Seekers' Human Rights Issues in South Africa, April 2006

'The Gersony Report', UNHCR Emergency Repatriation Team, 11 October 1994

'The Rwandan Patriotic Front, HRW word report', Human Rights Watch, 1999

'The unity of Rwandans', Office of the President of the Republic of Rwanda, August 1999

WEBSITES

Rwandan Stories, www.rwandanstories.org

Acronyms and abbreviations

ALiR: Armée pour la Libération du Rwanda
ANC: African National Congress
DRC: Democratic Republic of Congo
EPC: Eritrean People's Congress
FAR: Forces Armées Rwandaises
FRELIMO: Liberation Front of Mozambique
HRW: Human Rights Watch
ICTR: International Criminal Tribunal for Rwanda
IS: intelligence staff (RPA)
LMG: light machine gun
MPLA: People's Movement for the Liberation of Angola
MRND: Mouvement Révolutionnaire National pour le Développement
NRA: National Resistance Army
RNC: Rwandan National Congress
RPA: Rwandan Patriotic Army
RPF: Rwandan Patriotic Front
RPG: rocket-propelled grenade
RTLM: Radio-Télévision Libre des Mille Collines
SPLA: Sudan People's Liberation Army
SWAPO: South West Africa People's Organisation
UN: United Nations
UNAMIR: UN Assistance Mission for Rwanda
UNHCR: UN High Commissioner for Refugees
UNISA: University of South Africa
ZANU: Zimbabwe African National Union
ZAPU: Zimbabwe African People's Union

Glossary

adache: hole or cave
Akazu: Hutu ideologues; literally 'little hut'
bayaye: homeless, street people
bosveld: bushveld
bourgmestre: mayor
brudders: brothers; slang for West African immigrants
collines: cells within communes
gacaca: traditional Rwandan court; literally 'on the grass'
gukwa: payment
guterura: bride-kidnapping
ikwano: bride price, similar to *lobola*
inka: cow
Inkotanyi: RPF soldiers; fierce warrior
interahamwe: Hutu militia; those who stand/fight/attack together
intore: traditional Rwandan 'ballet'
inyenzi: cockroach; hateful term for Tutsis
mama: mother
matoke: steamed bananas
muzungu: white person
mwami: king
panya: rat
pap: maize porridge
papa: father
poppie: doll
samp: maize porridge
ubuhiri: stick studded with nails
ubuntu: human generosity
Uhuru: independence movement; literally 'freedom'
urwagwa: beer

Index

101st Battalion 170–171

Abanyiginya clan 17–18
Abel (diplomat) 222–224
Aceper Secondary School 209
adaches 97–98, 104, 107, 176, 246
 see also trenches
Afewerki, Isaias 208
African airlines 5
African National Congress *see* ANC
Afrikaner Weerstandsbeweging (Afrikaner
 Resistance Movement) 212
AIDS 51–52
airlines, African 5
Akazu (Hutu ideologues) 85, 87–88, 116, 120
Alcatraz of Rwanda *see* Iwawa island
ALiR 204–205
America *see* United States of America
American Holsteins 51, 61
Amin Dada, Idi 8, 30, 33–35, 54
Amnesty International 111, 173
ANC 110, 190–191
Ankole cows *see* cows
Annan, Kofi 126
Arendt, Hannah 167–168
Army for the Liberation of Rwanda
 (Armée pour la Libération du Rwanda)
 see ALiR
Arusha Accords 115–117, 121, 124
Attorney's Act 243–244
Augustine, Raturamaruga 139–143

Baganda people 30–32, 43, 47–48, 50, 64
Bagogwe (Tutsi subgroup) 88
Bagosora, Col. Théoneste 120, 123
Bahima ethnic group 53, 59
banana beer (*urwagwa*) 18, 33
Banda, Hastings 217
Bandora (neighbour of Xavier) 88, 90, 163,
 247–248

Batwa people 18–19, 21–22
bayaye 8
Bayingana, Alex 6, 29–30
BBC 154, 267
BBC's Swahili service 54
BBC World Service 29, 33, 67
Beitbridge 193
Belgium 21–27, 124
Bigada Primary School 1, 49–52
Bin Laden, Osama 260
birth control 42, 62
Bisangwa (friend of Emile) 102
Bizimungu, Dick 45
Black Lawyers' Association 252
Blatman, Daniel 171
blitzkrieg on Ruhengeri 87
Boniface (neighbour of Xavier) 88–93, 161,
 164, 211, 248–249
border posts 186, 193
Boutros-Ghali, Boutros 135, 155
Brakpan 76
bride-kidnapping (*guterura*) 59–60
Britain 27, 34, 257, 269
Browning, Christopher 170
Burundi 11–12, 25, 27–28, 30, 68, 119–120, 141

Canada 42, 81, 204
Carnival City 76–77, 86
Catholic Church 23–24, 29, 50–51
 see also Nyarubuye
caves *see adaches*
cellphones *see* mobile-phone companies
Chantelle (friend of KG) 204–205
child soldiers 53–54
China 117
cholera 98, 127, 155, 159
Churchill, Winston 27
civilians 108, 111–113, 129–138
classification according to race 22–23
Clinton, Bill 153, 155, 206

cobra attacks KG 48
colonialism 20–24, 27
coltan (columbite-tantalite) 206–207
Congo 11–12, 27, 180, 183, 206–208, 266–267,
    269, 271–272
    see also Zaire
Constitutional Court 244
cows 9–10, 12, 17, 20, 22–23, 32, 47–48, 51, 53,
    61, 253–254
crime
    in Hillbrow 195–196, 198–199
    KG on 228

Dallaire, Lt Gen. Roméo 119, 126, 153–154,
    156, 165
dancers in royal palace, Rwanda 19
Dar es Salaam, Tanzania 2, 190–191
death marches (World War II) 171
Death Marches, The 171
Democratic Green Party of Rwanda 268
Democratic Republic of Congo *see*
    Congo
Department of Home Affairs *see* Home
    Affairs
Dis-Chem 277
DRC *see* Congo
drums 19

education *see* schools
Eichmann, Adolf 167–168
elections in Rwanda 268–269
Elizaphan (son of Enose) 141–143, 150
England *see* Britain
evildoing 15, 170–173

Fairbanks, Jonathan 277
family planning 42, 62
FAR 55, 67, 86, 116–117, 122, 124, 146–148,
    156–157, 165–166, 188, 204
Fati (neighbour of Xavier) 88, 90, 92, 161, 163,
    211, 248–249
Feisal (son of Nyinawumuntu) 62
Felix, Fundi 204–205, 213, 216, 220, 222
Festus (diplomat) 223–224
First World War 21
food 33, 98, 187, 197, 220–221, 226

Forces Armées Rwandaises *see* FAR
France 67, 81, 87, 145, 165

gacaca system 18, 210–211, 247–250
Gacumbitsi, Sylvestre 149–150, 154
Gaddafi, Muammar 272
Gahima, Gerald 255
Gakunzi, Gasigwa 179
Gang of Four 256–260
Gatarayiha, Gratien 204–205
Genocide Convention of 1946 155
genocide in Rwanda 1–2, 13–15, 25, 28, 75,
    93–94, 113, 119–121, 123–138
Geoffrey (son of Dominique) 39–40, 42
Gerard (father-in-law of KG) 241, 259
Germany 21, 163
    see also Holocaust
Gersony, Robert 135
Gersony Report 135, 172
Ghana 27, 124
Gihana (warrior prince) 29
Gihana, Goreth (wife of KG) 5–7, 46, 236–237,
    240–243, 252–254, 258–260, 277
    mother of 6–7, 259
Gihana, Kennedy Alfred Nurudin
    names of 29–30, 199–200
    nicknames of 1, 48, 50, 217
    youth of 12–13, 15–20, 28–37, 47–48, 64
    school education 1, 35, 37, 49–51, 55–59
    on girlfriends 56, 64, 181–182, 239
    as soldier 1–2, 7, 16, 65, 67–69, 95–100,
        104–109, 118, 121–123, 129–138, 144–148,
        156–157, 165–169, 173–178, 180–183
    journey to SA 2, 16, 183–194
    in Hillbrow 16, 196–202, 204–205, 209
    employment 202–203, 220, 222–227,
        238–239, 275–276
    university studies 2–3, 16, 203–204,
        212–222, 228–237, 243–245, 252,
        276–277
    in Magnolia Park 226–229
    meets author of book 13–15
    meets and marries Goreth 239–243,
        252–254, 258
    mother-in-law of 6–7, 259
    birth of daughter 5–7, 259

visits family and friends 5, 7–10, 38–48,
  51–52, 60–62, 70–73, 175–178,
  180–181
  Gang of Four 251, 254–255, 257–265,
    271–275
  health of 131, 199, 276
  remarkability of achievements 72–73,
    278–281
Gihana, Lisa (daughter of KG) 5–6, 15, 46,
  253, 259
Gihanga (ancestor of Rwanda) 19
Gishuro camp 97–98, 104
glue-sniffing 198
Goma, Zaire 82–83
gorillas *see* mountain gorillas
Great Lakes 12, 180
gufata irembo (securing the bride) 243
Gulag Archipelago, The 170
guterura (bride-kidnapping) 59–60

Habimana, Paul 204–205
Habyarimana, Agathe 80, 84–85
Habyarimana, Juvénal 36, 55, 66–68, 80–81,
  84, 115–116, 119–120, 260
Hamitic hypothesis 22, 53
Hartley, Aidan 153
Hassan (KG's friend in Hillbrow) 203
Hassan (KG's friend in Lilongwe) 192, 196,
  199–200
hate radio *see* RTLM
Hatzfeld, Jean 125
Hewa Bora Airways 5
Hillbrow 194–199
hit squads 169
HIV/AIDS 51–52
Holocaust 167–168, 170–171
Home Affairs 200, 223, 243–245, 275
Hôtel des Mille Collines 112
Hotel Rwanda 111–112
HRW (Human Rights Watch) 111, 135, 155,
  172, 269
Hutu Manifesto 24
Hutu Power 27, 113, 115–117, 154, 165, 183, 204,
  239, 269
Hutus 18–28, 43–44, 78–82, 84–85, 87–88, 102,
  111, 126–127, 136–137, 165–167, 269

ICTR 87–88, 113, 120, 154, 280
iguse (street food) 197
ikwano (similar to *lobola*) 243, 247,
  252–254
Ilan (daughter of Xavier) 251
India 182
Inkotanyi 65
  see also RPF
intelligence units 100
interahamwe (Hutu militia) 87, 116–119,
  123–127, 131–134, 141–143, 149–151, 154,
  160–162, 165–166, 188–189
international community, reaction to
  genocide 81, 112, 134, 155, 269–270
International Criminal Court 280
International Criminal Tribunal for Rwanda
  see ICTR
inyenzis (label for Tutsis) 28, 53, 67, 116
Isha (girlfriend of KG) 181–182, 184
Iwawa island 176–179
Izibagiza, Valentina 149–151, 154

Jacques (flatmate of KG) 203
Jean de Dieu (brother of Xavier) 91
Jean-Paul (neighbour of Xavier) 88, 90,
  163, 211
Jean-Paul (witness to Edward's burial)
  248–250
Juru Camp 67, 95–97

Kabale Senior Secondary School 58, 64
Kabila, Laurent-Désiré 183, 266
kadogos (child soldiers) 53–54
Kagame, Paul
  background of 23, 54
  Iwawa island 176, 178–179
  as leader 113–114, 158, 165, 172, 180, 183,
    188–189, 206–208, 254–257, 258, 265–271
  war in Rwanda 67, 87, 112, 115, 120–121, 134,
    145, 174
Kagubare, Esperance 220–226, 229–230, 232,
  236, 239, 245
Kahira, Rwabuduri 50–51
Kaitare, Steven 118, 146–147
Kajelijeli, Juvénal 87–88
Kaku (friend of KG) 146

Kamabera (grandmother of KG)
life of 1, 3, 7, 19, 25, 29, 31–32, 34, 59–60,
    68–69, 220
death of 40–41, 63, 71, 181
Kambanda, Jean 127, 136–137
Kangura newspaper 141
Kanombe Military Hospital, Rwanda 240
Kapuściński, Ryszard 119
Karahamuheto, William 88–89, 92, 96–97
Karegeya, Col. Patrick 255–256, 260–261
Karemera, Col. Joseph 213–214, 224–226, 228
Karusigarira (district education officer)
    57–58
Kashugi, Dominique 9, 35–43, 45, 48, 57,
    63, 72
Kayibanda, Grégoire 24, 27, 80
Kayinga (friend of Emile) 102
Kazungu (friend of Emile) 102
Keane, Fergal 154
Kennedy, John Fitzgerald 29
Kenya 185, 188, 211
Khumalo, Sabelo 216–219, 230, 235, 280–281
Kidigi, Roger 201–203
kidnapping *see* bride-kidnapping
Kigeli IV 65
Kigeli V 25–26
killing, terms used for 169
Kingdom of Banyarwanda 12, 29, 119
king of Rwanda *see mwami*
Kirabo, Veronica 39–40, 42
Kleyn, Prof. Duard 234–235, 237
Kuwait (FAR base) 156–157

Law Society of the Northern Provinces
    244–245, 252
laws on genocide in Rwanda 113, 137
Liberal Party (Rwanda) 116
Libération 189
light machine guns 121, 129–130
Lincoln, Abraham 206
lions 187, 190
Little Liberia 278–279
living dead 139–143
LMG *see* light machine guns
lobola see ikwano
locals *see* civilians

machetes 117, 118, 125, 138
Machete Season 125
Magnolia Park 226–229
makwerekwere 197
Malawi 185, 187, 192
Malik, Jamal 233
Mandela, Nelson 191, 206
Manzi (uncle of Xavier) 86
Marciano (neighbour of Xavier) 162,
    211, 247
marriage in Tutsi culture 243
    see also ikwano
Matsiko, Feisal 62
Matsiko, Nyinawumuntu (half-sister of KG)
    31–32, 59–63, 72, 253
Matsiko, Yassim 60–63
Mbayire, Alphonse 189
meals 33, 98, 187, 197, 220–221, 226
mental health of soldiers 167
Merensky Library 229–230
military intelligence units 100
Mitari (friend of Emile) 102
Mitterrand, François 67
mobile-phone companies in Uganda 9
Mobutu Sese Seko 67, 83–84, 183, 266
Mofokeng (street child) 198
monarchy of Rwanda *see mwami*
Mont Jari, battle for 144–148
mother-in-law of KG 6–7, 259
mountain gorillas 13, 74–75, 77–78, 267
Mount Karisimbi 75
Mount Nyiragongo 83
Mouvement Révolutionnaire National pour le
    Développement *see* MRND
Mozambique 110, 185, 190, 192–193, 260
MRND 80, 115
Mugabe, Robert 267
Mugenyi, Peter 45
Mugesera, Léon 115–116
Muhire (friend of Edward) 93
Mukakabanda, Ephiphanie 142
Mukayuhi, Getruida 69–71
Murambi hill 209
Museveni, Yoweri 8, 51–55, 57, 61–62, 65–66,
    265
Mushabe, Joffrey 45

Mushatsi, Edward (father of Xavier) 75, 78, 82, 86, 88–93, 96–97, 211, 247–250
Mushiha refugee camp 25, 28–29, 68
Muyambi, Mugara 45
mwami (king of Rwanda) 17–20, 24–26, 34, 65
Mwinyi, Ali Hassan 120

National Resistance Army *see* NRA
National Revolutionary Movement for Development *see* MRND
Ndebereho, Beatrice (mother of Xavier) 75, 91–94, 162, 211, 246–247, 249–250
New Times, The 260
New York Times 178–179
Ngabo, Xavier Mushatsi Niyonzima
    youth of 75–85
    family of 86–91, 93–94, 96–97, 160–164, 210–211, 246–251
    as soldier 94, 96–99, 115, 117, 122–123, 137–138, 145–146, 174, 182
    returns to school 209–210
    in South Africa 246–247, 250–251
Nicol, Mike 280
Nindaga, Masasu 118
Nkunda, Laurent 111
NRA 53–54, 66, 265
Nsabimana, Enose 139–143, 149–151
Ntaryamira, Cyprien 119–120
Ntwali, Frank 257, 261–262, 273–274
Nurudin (brother of Hassan) 199–200
Nyamwasa, Gen. Kayumba 255–256, 260–261, 265–268, 272, 274, 275
Nyarubuye 100–101, 149–154, 184
Nyerere, Julius 34
Nyilinkwaya, Frederic 142
Nyirashene, Charlotte 87, 90–91, 94, 163

Obote, Milton 8, 35–37, 50, 53–54
Ordinary Men 170

panya roads 15–16, 91, 108, 122, 185
Pauw, Jacques (author of book) 13–15, 46, 77–78, 152–154, 215
peasants *see* civilians
Pienaar, Laura 233–234
Poland 153, 170–171

population growth in Rwanda 36, 75
Pretoria News 245
Prisca, Sister Alirwa 51–52
prison caves *see adaches*
prisons in Rwanda 139–140, 163–164

race, classification according to 22–23
race science 21–22
Radio 702 13, 277
Radio Rwanda 123
Radio-Télévision Libre des Mille Collines (RTLM) 116, 119, 125–126, 133, 136–137, 142
Ramadan 199–200
rape 25, 59, 106–107, 128, 154
rat roads *see panya* roads
rebel armies in Africa 110–111
refugee camps 25, 28–29, 68, 159, 165–166
Reporters Without Borders 268
Reserve Police Battalion 101 170–171
Rift Valley 11–12
RNC 258, 260–261, 263, 265–266, 271–275, 281
Robbie, John 13, 277
Roman Catholic church *see* Catholic Church
Rose (wife of Augustine) 141
RPA 7, 64–68, 84, 87, 91, 95–100, 107–109, 111–114, 117–118, 121–123, 133–137, 155, 167, 172, 174
RPF 54–55, 64–68, 99, 112, 115, 117, 137, 142, 144–145, 158, 177
RTLM *see* Radio-Télévision Libre des Mille Collines
Rubarasi the bull 47–48
Rudahigwa, Mutara 24
Rudasingwa, Dr Theogene 255
Rukabo (businessman in Mukamira) 96–97
Rukumba, John 45, 47
Rusesabagina, Paul 111–113, 117, 136, 258, 273
Russell, Bertrand 28
Rutagengwa, Emile
    Gang of Four 257, 261–262, 272, 274
    in Rwanda 100–103, 112–113, 117, 137, 148, 152, 162–163, 206, 208
    in South Africa 101, 208–209, 255–256
Rutagengwa, Kalisa Boniface 102, 162
Rutembesa, Didier 274
Ruyenzi, Lt Aloys 113–114

Rwagitare, Teddy 45
Rwamugire, Jennifer 239–242, 245, 252,
    258–259, 262–264, 277
Rwanda, description of 11–12, 17, 74–75
Rwandan Armed Forces *see* FAR
Rwandan National Congress *see* RNC
Rwandan Patriotic Army *see* RPA
Rwandan Patriotic Front *see* RPF
Rwandans in South Africa 196
Rwigyema, Gen. Fred 54–55, 66, 265

Sankoh, Foday 111, 208
Sarah (cousin of KG) 43
Saudi Arabia 35
Savimbi, Jonas 111
schools 35, 40, 42, 49–52, 57–58, 62,
    82, 209
Second World War 167–168, 170–171
Semandwa, Francis (grandfather of KG)
    life of 1, 3, 6–7, 17–20, 25, 28–37, 40, 43,
        49–50, 55, 64, 68–69
    death of 41, 63, 71, 181
Sendashonga, Seth 188–189, 255
Serengeti 11, 190
Serunjogi, James 8, 39, 43–44, 61
Sezibera, Maj. Dr Richard 181
Shaik, Moe 257
Shaka, Colonel 121
Shake Hands with the Devil 154
silverback *see* mountain gorillas
Sindikubwabo, Théodore 127
Slumdog Millionaire 233
snake attacks KG 48
Solzhenitsyn, Aleksandr 15, 170
songs 81, 97, 177, 209–210
South Africa 34, 116, 191, 193–194, 257
Soyinka, Wole 128
Spain 255
Speke, John Hanning 22
Stanford Prison Experiment 171–172
Stanley, Henry Morton 21
Steinberg, Jonny 279
stick-fighting 48
street children 197–199
Sudan 27, 110
surnames in Rwandan culture 6

Sweden 257
Switzerland 81
Syria 131

Tanzania 2, 34–35, 188, 190–191
Taylor, Charles 111
trenches 144, 146–147
    see also adaches
Tuksdorp 234–235
Tutsis 12–13, 18–19, 21–28, 43–44, 67, 78–79,
    81–82, 84–85, 87, 102, 127, 136–137, 269
Tutu, Archbishop Desmond 153–154
Tuyishime, Gustav 261–262
Twagiramungu, Faustin 178
Twa people *see* Batwa people

ubuntu 37, 187
Uganda 7–9, 11–12, 30, 33–34, 36–37, 53–54,
    206
Umuhoza, Victoire Ingabire 268
UN 37, 66, 111, 115, 117, 124, 126–127, 134–135,
    153, 155–156, 165, 183, 207, 269
UNAMIR (UN Assistance Mission for
    Rwanda) 119, 126, 155
UNHCR 25, 135, 262
UNISA 203, 213, 251
United Nations *see* UN
United Nations High Commissioner for
    Refugees *see* UNHCR
United States of America 126, 155–156,
    165, 269
universities, requirements for immigrants 213
University of Pretoria 212–216
University of South Africa *see* UNISA
UNSC (UN Security Council) 124, 127, 269
urwagwa (banana beer) 18, 33
USA *see* United States of America
Uwajeneza, Josephine 210, 247, 250–251
Uwamaria, Teddy (mother of KG) 6, 29–31,
    57, 180
Uwilingiyimana, Agathe 124

Virunga mountain range 74–75, 107, 180, 246
Von Beringe, Captain Robert 74
Von Götzen, Count Gustav Adolf 21
Vorster, John 212

wedding of KG 6, 252–254
World War I 21
World War II 167–168, 170–171

xenophobia in Hillbrow 197

Zaire 82–84, 127, 158–159, 165–166, 182–183, 221
  see also Congo
Zanzibar Chest, The 153
Zimbabwe 110, 187, 190, 192–193, 207
Zimbardo, Philip 171–172

Do you have any comments, suggestions or
feedback about this book or any other Zebra Press titles?
Contact us at **talkback@zebrapress.co.za**

*

Visit **www.randomstruik.co.za** and subscribe
to our newsletter for monthly updates and news